The Post-Racial Church

A Biblical Framework for Multiethnic Reconciliation

The Post-Racial Church

A Biblical Framework for Multiethnic Reconciliation

Kenneth A. Mathews *&*
M. Sydney Park

Kregel
Academic & Professional

Library of Congress Cataloging-in-Publication Data

Mathews, K. A.
    The post-racial church : a biblical framework for multiethnic reconciliation / Kenneth A. Mathews and M. Sydney Park.
        p. cm.
    1. Church and minorities—United States. 2. Reconciliation—Religious aspects—Christianity. 3. Race relations—Religious aspects—Christianity. 4. Ethnic relations—Religious aspects—Christianity. I. Park, M. Sydney. II. Title.
    BV639.M56M38 2011
    277.3'083089—dc22

                                                                    2010027938

ISBN 978-0-8254-3586-7

To Robert Smith Jr.,
our colleague and friend,
whose life and ministry
reflect the love of God for all peoples

Contents

Acknowledgments / 9

Abbreviations / 11

Introduction: The Wonder of God's Human
   Kaleidoscope (Mathews) / 15

1 God's Design for Creation (Mathews) / 37

2 God's Blessing for *All* Nations (Mathews) / 67

3 "God's People" and the "Also Peoples"
   (Mathews) / 95

4 God's Welcome to All (Mathews) / 125

5 Jesus' Stories of Reconciliation (Park) / 145

6 Stories of Peace and Worship (Park) / 173

7 The Proclamation of the Church (Park) / 201

8 One Salvation, One Fellowship (Park) / 229

Conclusion: From Here to Eternity (Park) / 257

Person and Subject Index / 273

Acknowledgments

AS FREQUENTLY OBSERVED, BOOKS are written and produced not in isolation, but in community. Our book is no exception to this. We give thanks to Daniel Williams and Dustin Curtis and Devon Bagwell and Dea Mathews for their careful attention to detail in their reading of the manuscript. We are also grateful to Julie Beckwith for her speedy yet meticulous work with indexes. Paul Hillman and the editorial team at Kregel have been persistent in their efforts to bring this to publication. And finally, we thank our respective families and colleagues at Beeson Divinity School for their support and prayer.

Abbreviations

GENERAL ABBREVIATIONS

cf.	*confer*, compare
cp.	compare
ed.	edition
e.g.	*exempli gratia*, for example
esp.	especially
f., ff.	following [verse(s); page(s)]
ibid.	*ibidem*, in the same place as previous citation
i.e.	*id est*, that is
lit.	literally
par.	parallel (to)
pars.	paragraphs
p., pp.	page, pages
rev.	revised
v., vv.	verse(s)
vol.	volume

VERSIONS AND TRANSLATIONS OF THE BIBLE

ESV	English Standard Version (2001)
HCSB	Holman Christian Standard Bible (2004)
NIV	New International Version (1983)
NLT	New Living Translation (1996)
NRSV	New Revised Standard Version (1990)

PERIODICALS, REFERENCE WORKS, AND SERIALS

AAR	American Academy of Religion
AB	Anchor Bible Commentary
ANTC	Abingdon New Testament Commentary
BECNT	Baker Exegetical Commentary on the New Testament
ICC	International Critical Commentary
JBL	*Journal of Biblical Literature*
JSOT	*Journal for the Study of the Old Testament*
JSOTSup	JSOT Supplements
NAC	New American Commentary
NICNT	New International Commentary on the New Testament
NICOT	New International Commentary on the Old Testament
NIGTC	New International Greek Testament Commentary
PNTC	Pillar New Testament Commentary
Ta.	*Tarbits*
TDNT	*Theological Dictionary of the New Testament*, ed., G. Kittel and G. Friedrich
TNTC	Tyndale New Testament Commentary
WBC	Word Biblical Commentary

PUBLISHERS

B&H	Broadman and Holman
JPS	Jewish Publication Society
SPCK	Society for Promoting Christian Knowledge

BOOKS OF THE BIBLE AND OTHER WORKS

Old Testament

Gen.	Genesis
Exod.	Exodus

Lev.	Leviticus
Num.	Numbers
Deut.	Deuteronomy
Josh.	Joshua
Judg.	Judges
1 Sam.	1 Samuel
2 Sam.	2 Samuel
1 Chron.	1 Chronicles
2 Chron.	2 Chronicles
Neh.	Nehemiah
Eccl.	Ecclesiastes
Ps(s).	Psalm(s)
Prov.	Proverbs
Isa.	Isaiah
Jer.	Jeremiah
Ezek.	Ezekiel
Dan.	Daniel
Hos.	Hosea
Zech.	Zechariah

New Testament

Matt.	Matthew
Rom.	Romans
1 Cor.	1 Corinthians
2 Cor.	2 Corinthians
Gal.	Galatians
Eph.	Ephesians
Phil.	Philippians
Col.	Colossians
1 Tim.	1 Timothy
2 Tim.	2 Timothy
Heb.	Hebrews
Rev.	Revelation

Jewish Writings

Ant.	Josephus's *Antiquities*

The Wonder of God's Human Kaleidoscope

KALEIDOSCOPES ARE OPTICAL DEVICES that never fail to entertain. These fragile instruments elicit the wonder of colorful images and mesmerizing geometric patterns. The simplest kaleidoscopes are enclosed, tube-like devices that have an eyepiece, bits of colored glass, and two or three mirrors that are directed toward each other. The arrangement of the mirrors determines the number of multiple reflections and thus the diversity of the changing patterns. Despite the irregularity of the shapes, the mirrors transform them into proportioned images that are esthetically pleasing and intellectually interesting.

Removed from the tube, the bits of colored glass become piles of rubble. They work *together in tandem* or they don't work at all. Also, the mirrors must be *directed toward each other* to have the visual effect. We have chosen a kaleidoscope as a metaphor for understanding God's creation of the human family because diversity and unity are its hallmarks.

The beauty and wonder of God's human kaleidoscope involve the same principles of *cooperation* and *integration*. The church has shown some advancement in cooperation across racial lines. Joint worship services and various projects provide opportunities for collaboration. Parachurch groups such as Promise Keepers have reached beyond racial lines. Yet the second principle—integration of racial groups—remains dormant. But like a sleeping giant, the church, once awakened, can be a powerful force for integration.

This is not a pipe dream. The church began in just this way. The first worship service was at Pentecost in Jerusalem. People from across the Roman Empire who had gathered for the Feast were among those who came to faith at the preaching of the apostle Peter. This new worshipping community shared their lives and possessions (Acts 2:42–46). We sometimes forget the integration principle that characterized the formative days of the church. Young Timothy, a second generation believer who was of mixed racial heritage—a mother who was a Jewish believer and a father who was a Greek (Acts 16:1)—exemplified the cross-cultural adaptations of the church.

Sometimes God must use social upheaval as a means of propelling the church to accomplish his purpose. Persecution drove the church to migrate from the comfortable confines of Jerusalem to Judea and Samaria (Acts 8). Out of this dispersal was Philip's witness to the Ethiopian officer of the queen of Ethiopia. Today's globalization is perhaps a tool in the hands of the Spirit for creating a social and economic environment that will foster greater cooperation among racially different individuals and groups. Will authentic *integration*, not just toleration, be the next step for the church?

HOW DID WE GET HERE?

Few today would object to a white, fair-skinned, flaming red-head marrying a Cuban-born, Latin immigrant. "No problem," we say. It happens every day. But not so in 1951 when the creators of the "I Love Lucy" television show faced the hurdle of presenting a new sitcom whose leading characters, Lucy and Ricky Ricardo (Lucille Ball and Desi Arnaz), were an interracial couple both on and off the set. CBS did not initially believe that the American public would accept Desi as the typical American husband. The wildly popular show whose characters have become cultural icons proved otherwise.

The year 2008 celebrated the sixtieth year of the United Nations' proclamation of the Universal Declaration of Human Rights, which was adopted by the General Assembly of Member States on December 10, 1948. Essentially, the proclamation affirmed fundamental human rights, believing in "the dignity and worth of the human person and in the equal rights of men and women."

Despite the good intentions of the United Nations, these sixty years have witnessed the same social ills and atrocities that the United

Nations hoped to curb if not cure. Genocide based on race, tribe, or religion has been pervasive. Generally we think that such murderous rampages occur in the Third World where "uncivilized" cultures remain. Yet the Western world has not avoided genocide, as the Serbian atrocities against cultural Muslims in the heart of Europe showed (1995).

In the United States, racial discrimination in public venues was prohibited in the Civil Rights Act of 1964. No longer can discrimination against racial minorities impede voting rights, integrated housing, and equal hiring opportunities. By this legislative action the power of the state was transformed from sustaining racial segregation to empowering racial integration in the public sector. The mid-twentieth-century social movement, known as the Civil Rights Movement, came to its public pinnacle with the election of President Barack Obama, the child of an interracial marriage.

President Obama's father was Kenyan-born, and his mother was white, a native Kansan. They met and married in 1961. *Time* magazine provided a pictorial history of the family of President Obama, giving the visual of white and black branches.1 The picture of his parents reveals the integration of the two branches. The photo gallery has the cutline, "With roots in Kansas, Kenya, and beyond, the candidate is a one-man melting pot."

That the American public generally accepted this racial profile for its chief governing official shows significant progress. Although some were troubled by his skin color and his Muslim-sounding name, most who opposed his candidacy were put off by his policies and inexperience, not by his race or his father's religious tradition.

A headline in *USA Today* recognized the immediate impact of Obama's election: "Nation's first lady hopes for 'Obama Effect' transformation."[2] No, the "first lady" was not Michelle Obama but France's first lady Carla Bruni-Sarkozy, who remarked that racism in France is "insidious" against blacks and Arabs. She hoped that the "Obama Effect" would improve race relations. At the time of her

1. Amanda Ripley, "The Story of Barack Obama's Mother," *Time*, April 9, 2008.
2. Associated Press, "Manifesto Takes Aim at Racism in France," *USA Today*, Monday, November 10, 2008: 4A.

comments, the lower house of Parliament numbered 555 members from France's mainland but had only one black member. Another article in the same issue of *USA Today* reported that Kenyans found in the election of Obama hope for "miracles" in resolving Africa's problems of AIDS, poverty, and genocidal wars.[3]

After his victory in the Democratic primary in South Carolina, Obama commented, "But we are here tonight to say that this [a politically and racially divisive America] is not the America we believe in. I did not travel around this state over the last year and see a white South Carolina or a black South Carolina. I saw South Carolina." Although the president's hope and the hope of many voters was to exhibit by his election a post-racial America, the issue of race in public policy and religious life seems as strong as ever.

Another icon of racial integration is professional golfer Tiger Woods. Sports enthusiasts know that there is only one "Tiger." People whose viewing habits don't include golf will tune in just to see Tiger make his bid for another major championship. Like Obama, he has transcended racial barriers. Tiger is a child of a racially mixed marriage. His mother described herself as "half Thai, one-quarter Chinese, and one-quarter white." His father described himself as "half black, one-quarter American-Indian, and one-quarter Chinese." So what is Tiger's ethnicity?

New standards in 1997 by the Office of Management and Budget for collecting data on race and ethnicity recognized multiple race identity in part because of the Tiger Woods phenomenon. The National Center for Education Statistics reflects the diverse plurality of our society by requiring institutions to report their demographic statistics according to nine categories, one of which is the vague category "Two or more races."[4]

As we have inferred from our discussion thus far, the American ethnic scene cannot be limited to the classic black-white race relations.

---

3. Zoe Alsop, "Some in Africa Expect Miracles From Obama," *USA Today*, November 10, 2008, 7A.

4. U.S. Department of Education posted to the Federal Register the "Final Guidance on Maintaining, Collecting, and Reporting Racial and Ethnic Data to the U.S. Department of Education." (See the Federal Register, Volume 72, Number 202, pp. 59266–59279: http://edocket.access.gpo.gov/2007/pdf/E7-20613.pdf).

This is easily overlooked because the change in the social fabric of our times was fueled by the black-white civil rights struggle. Moreover, this black-white tension will always be unique to the American experience due to the horrific era of black slavery and legalized racial segregation.

Yet the global village has generated increasingly stronger racial tensions among other groups as immigrant populations increase, especially against Hispanics, Muslims, and Asians. For example, in 2007 the U.S. Justice Department's "Hate Crime Statistics" differentiated between racially motivated crimes and crimes based on ethnicity.[5] In the former category the overwhelming victim group remained blacks and the second victim group was white. Yet in the ethnicity category, almost two-thirds of crimes were directed against Hispanics. Instead of race-related problems fading from the American scene, they have in some ways become more pronounced due to the increase of minority populations and the media's ongoing attention.

WHAT ABOUT THE CHURCH?

The two leading voices of the evangelical movement in North America in the past century were theologian Carl F. H. Henry (1913–2003) and evangelist Billy Graham. Each in his own way forged a consensus that retained the historic teaching of the Christian faith, emphasized personal evangelism, and revitalized the evangelical movement's voice in social reforms.

Henry's background in Long Island, New York, afforded him the experiences of mass urban life. As a newspaper reporter and editor, he witnessed the social sins and inequities that characterized the burgeoning growth of post–World War II cities. Although he is chiefly remembered for his theological response to the excesses of the German theological movement neo-orthodoxy, Henry awakened a generation of Christians to the gospel necessity of Christian engagement with modern culture. His work *The Uneasy Conscience of Modern Fundamentalism* (1947) launched a new kind of theological

---

5. Statistics available on the Web site of the Federal Bureau of Investigation, http://www.fbi.gov/news/stories/2008/october/hatecrime_102708.

orthodoxy that turned evangelicals to look outward, encountering the social issues of their day, especially race relations.[6]

Billy Graham focused on societal change through the transformation of one person at a time. He believed that lasting social change would occur only when individuals experienced personal salvation. A changed heart meant a changed view toward others.[7] Therefore, his aim was to see people come to Christ and then make a difference in the moral and social fabric of the nation and ultimately the world. In a 1997 interview, Graham answered detractors who had charged him with being "too timid in speaking out on the great social issues." Here is his response:

I don't think there is a single social issue I haven't spoken on. Especially on the race question. Because in the '50s, I wrote major articles in *Life* magazine and *Reader's Digest* saying church is the most segregated hour of the week. I took trips with Martin Luther King Jr. I became friends with so many civil rights leaders. In 1951, when there was segregating of the audience in Chattanooga, TN., they put ropes up to divide the audience, with the black people sitting behind and the whites sitting up front. I went down and personally removed the ropes.[8]

Some people argue that religious conservatives have been woefully delinquent in striving for racial justice, if not outright responsible for its inequalities. This opinion probably carries over from the historical fact that a segment of the American church once justified slavery and later advocated racial segregation. The accounts of these crimes are many and deserve to be recalled. Nevertheless, the church has also been instrumental in securing civil rights in America and around the world, wherever the gospel has penetrated a culture.

---

6. For an evaluation of the roles of Henry and Graham regarding race relations, see Ronald C. Potter, "Race, Theological Discourse, and the Continuing American Dilemma," ed. Dennis Okholm, *The Gospel in Black and White: Theological Resources for Racial Reconciliation* (Downers Grove: InterVarsity, 1997), 30–32. Potter characterized the white evangelical response to racism as the "unfinished agenda."
7. Lewis Drummond, *The Evangelist* (Nashville: Word, 2001), 77–88.
8. Larry Jordan, "A Conversation with Billy Graham," *Midwest Today* (January 1997).

It is often forgotten that the Civil Rights Movement was largely driven by Christian ministers, in particular the Southern Christian Leadership Conference, founded in 1957, which sponsored the famous march on Washington in 1963. In Martin Luther King Jr.'s "Letter from Birmingham Jail" (1963), he responded to the plea of eight prominent white clergy who had publicly called for the cessation of demonstrations, instead contending for a peaceful, law-abiding incremental desegregation.

King argued effectively from his Christian and ecclesial stance that the time to do right was never to be delayed. He commented, "I am grateful to God that, through the influence of the negro church, the way of nonviolence became an integral part of our struggle."[9] He chided the white church that had not fully supported the movement by quoting Jesus, Amos, Paul, and historic church leaders who were considered "extremists" in their day.[10] Although clearly "disappointed with the white church and its leadership," King commended some "white brothers in the South" who had stepped up.[11] Near the close of his appeal, he showed the foundational grounding of the Judeo-Christian ethic:

> One day the South will know that when these disinherited children of God [black demonstrators] sat down at lunch counters, they were in reality standing up for what is best in the American dream and for the most sacred values in our Judaeo-Christian heritage, thereby bringing our nation back to those great wells of democracy which were dug deep by the founding fathers in their formulation of the Constitution and the Declaration of Independence.[12]

Another notable example was William Wilberforce (1759–1833), the main character in the movie "Amazing Grace" (2006), whose conversion to Christianity was the seminal event that led to his life-long fight against the slave trade in the British Empire and ultimately

9. Martin Luther King Jr., "Letter from Birmingham Jail" in *Why We Can't Wait* (New York: Harper & Row, 1964), 90–91.
10. Ibid., 92.
11. Ibid., 93.
12. Ibid., 99.

to the abolition of slavery. What is not commonly known is that Wilberforce also contended for better conditions for workers and organized the first animal welfare society.

The gospel, by its very nature, calls for social engagement or it is not the full-orbed expression of the gospel of Jesus Christ. The first founding of the church in Jerusalem reflected this by its two-pronged attention to evangelization and to social concerns. The unity of the congregation ("in one heart and mind," Acts 4:32–35) was expressed in their powerful witness to the resurrection of Jesus *and* in their social conscience by helping the needy. They considered their worldly goods "not their own," freely giving their money to the apostles, and it was distributed to those who were lacking.

WHY THIS BOOK?

The apostle Peter exhorts his readers to be ready to give an answer to those who inquire why Christians have hope in the gospel (1 Peter 3:15). It has been the practice of the church from its inception to defend the Christian message. This book seeks to better equip the church in answering why Christians claim that the gospel and the Christian church are the first and last best hope for peace in a racially diverse world.

Correcting the Record

The modern conception of racial tolerance stems from the belief that human dignity and social equity are the results of evolved human thinking regarding the inherent worth of the human self. Professors Kendall Soulen and Linda Woodhead contend that the modern era has abandoned Christian theology as the proper context for interpreting the idea of human dignity, adopting the secularist view that "meaning, value, and substance are located in the self itself and, more specifically, in some aspect of subjectivity."[13] Historic Christian thought, however, saw human dignity as being bestowed by God on

---

13. R. Kendall Soulen and Linda Woodhead, eds., "Contextualizing Human Dignity," *God and Human Dignity* (Grand Rapids: Eerdmans, 2006), 9.

all humans. Human dignity is indebted to God, not to human self-awareness, human achievement, or social assignment.

According to some, those who are racist are not necessarily "bad," just unenlightened. Through education and sensitivity training, the tensions that characterize race relations will be neutralized. But how is it that secularists find comfort in the Christian doctrines of human equality without appealing to the Bible as the grounds for this moral perspective? Most people agree that racism is a horrible moral virus that has wreaked havoc upon the world and must be eradicated. Yet what is the basis for this judgment if not the Bible's view of human dignity?

The answer resides in the European philosophical movement of the seventeenth and eighteenth centuries known as the Enlightenment. This intellectual movement elevated the moral capacity of human reason and civility, contending that reason and the essential goodness of human character were universal traits that could result in universal peace and equity.

John B. Cobb Jr., Professor of Theology Emeritus at Claremont School of Theology, rightly captured the clash of the Christian and secular worldviews in his essay "Human Dignity and the Christian Tradition": "[W]e are not deriving our notions of human dignity primarily from our several [Jewish, Christian, Islam] traditions. Instead we are taking it from contemporary discourse that itself has a more universalistic ring. . . . [W]e are taking it from a consensus that is rooted in the European Enlightenment and that, to a remarkable extent, has become universal, at least among the cultural elites of the world."[14]

Cobb points to the Enlightenment dogma that "All human individuals are ends in themselves" and thus all human beings have human rights. But the assumption underlying the European Enlightenment's view toward universal common sense, universal human traits, and the belief that human dignity is self-evident was rooted in the biblical proclamation. What was for them self-evident was only so because the

---

14. John B. Cobb Jr., "Human Dignity and the Christian Tradition," August, 1990. http://www.religion-online.org/showarticle.asp?title=100.

Western world had been so thoroughly Christianized that the propo-
sition was accepted as a common human understanding.

With an alarming prediction, Cobb further observes that the program of the Enlightenment will not be adequate for maintaining the
belief in individual human dignity. Eventually, in our post-Enlighten-
ment world, the virtues espoused by the movement will no longer be
self-sustaining. Among these are four of special note. First, the basic
dependence of the Enlightenment on Christianity's teaching will not
be sufficient as Third World countries go their own way, resisting
Western values and opening the door to different understandings of
human dignity. Second, universal common sense does not satisfy the
judgments that must be made about human dignity. It is not so self-
evident, Cobb notes, what the definition of human life *is* when it
comes to the beginning or ending of life. Other moral factors must
be given a say. Third, the Enlightenment failed in its understanding
of human nature by neglecting the real cultural differences that shape
the lives of individuals. Christianity, on the other hand, acknowledges
the role of history and tradition in shaping the lives of individuals and
provides a better rationale for appreciating cultural differences. And
last, modernity's exaggeration of individual rights has had the devastating consequence of fragmenting communities. Community gives
individuals a sense of identity and belonging; the rights of individuals
do not always trump the good of communities. In their study of the
Christian proposal for human dignity, Soulen and Woodhead observe
that Christianity set human dignity in the context of the church as
community. Human beings are connected with one another in community with Christ and his church, so that human value "has an
ecclesial rather than individual horizon."[15]

Human beings belong to a shared kinship, but one that is a transcendent kinship with God and with the body of Christ. Christianity
has fared much better in balancing individual rights and community
stability. Christopher Marshall summarized what we have said when he
remarked, "So profound is the biblical story's insight into the meaning
of being human, so consistent, so uncompromising, is its insistence
on human dignity, that those who look to the Christian Scriptures for

---

15. Soulen and Woodhead, *God and Human Dignity*, 7.

guidance in this area should become both the world's greatest champions of human rights and the world's greatest critics of rights gone awry."[16]

Stoking the Fires

The late biblical scholar Brevard Childs observed that reformation movements historically have receded when taken up by the second and succeeding generations. Children of the reformation movement cannot replicate the past with the passion and vision of their fathers because of changing circumstances. "It is as if each new generation were called upon to re-win the battles once fought or to risk losing its theological legacy."[17] We have presented this book to set before the Christian reader *again* the theological basis for the battle fought in the mid-twentieth century when the American church and society underwent self-examination and change.

Do we need to stoke the fires?

Edward Gilbreath, the first African American on the editorial staff of *Christianity Today*, interviewed black evangelicals who were ministers in white evangelical church and parachurch settings. He found that they despaired at the state of race relations in their assignments, and the consequence was an exodus of ethnic minorities. The fundamental reason for despair was the superficial nature of interracial relationships that the church has settled for.[18]

The evangelical community is not faring as well toward racial reconciliation as it thinks it is, say sociologists Michael Emerson and Christian Smith in their study *Divided by Faith*.[19] Although evangelicals are well intentioned, say the authors, the worldview that white evangelicals hold and the nature of their institutional organizations produce the segregation that they hope to overcome.

---

16. Christopher D. Marshall, *Crowned with Glory and Honor: Human Rights in the Biblical Tradition* (Telford, PA: Pandora Press, 2002), 17.

17. Brevard Childs, "Interpreting the Bible amid Cultural Change," *Theology Today* 54 (1997): 208.

18. Edward Gilbreath, "Exit interviews: Why Blacks Are Leaving Evangelical Ministries," *Christianity Today* 51, no. 2 (February 2007), 101–4.

19. Michael O. Emerson and Christian Smith, *Divided by Faith: Evangelical Religion and the Problem of Race* (New York: Oxford University Press, 2000).

Although the authors identified four contributing factors, two especially are telling. First, white evangelicals "minimize and individualize the race problem" more than their black counterparts. White Christians acknowledge the race problem but do not consider it *as* significant as blacks perceive it. Also, whites tend to view it as an individual's problem, not a corporate problem, which differs from the perspective of black Christians. Second, whites typically offer simple, unidimensional solutions for dealing with a complex problem.

However, what evangelicals have going for them that the general public does not, according to Emerson and Smith, is their Christian teaching on confession and forgiveness. These strong points must be coupled with more careful thought to address structural, systemic problems.[20] The natural inclination of evangelicals is to stress personal, individualized response to their faith, the researchers concluded. White evangelicals are not as likely to see structural factors in American society as causative for continued racial inequality. Further, Emerson and Smith doubt that the church is better positioned to resolve the tension than society in general since the evangelical church—white or black—usually is highly segregated.

If you find the results of this study demoralizing, do not! The first step toward resolution is identifying the source of the problem. To that end Emerson followed up his study with a counter voice entitled *United by Faith*.[21] He and his coauthors, made up of an interracial group of researchers, proposed a potential solution to the problem of race in American churches. Theirs is a call for "multiracial congregations." They recognized that in the ministry of Jesus and during the earliest days of the church, the Christian tradition was multiethnic. For the church to recover its mandate is the imperative we face. The kingdom of God calls for heaven's ideal "on earth as it is in heaven" (Matt. 6:10 par.).

The researchers, however, are not naïve about the challenges that such a transformation would require. Nevertheless, their conviction

---

20. Emerson and Smith, *Divided by Faith*, 169–72.
21. Curtiss Paul DeYoung, Michael O. Emerson, George Yancey, and Karen Chiai Kim, *United By Faith: The Multiracial Congregation as an Answer to the Problem of Race* (New York: Oxford University Press, 2003).

is that the New Testament sets this reality before believers as the expectation for the church. They are not shy in calling for all racial groups, beyond black and white, to reconsider the racial profile of their churches. As Sydney, my coauthor, has quipped, "It's not just a white man's problem." That the situation is not hopeless can be seen in survey results, in particular the National Congregations Study directed by Duke sociologist Mark Chaves. He observed from 1998 to 2007 an increase of majority white congregations whose churches included Hispanics, Asians, and blacks.[22]

We hope that our study will stoke the fires for a renewed commitment to fulfill the calling of establishing the kingdom of God on earth. By looking at the Bible holistically—Old and New Testaments—we present the Bible's consistent teaching on the necessity of *striving* toward inclusive worship. We recognize, of course, that this is not always a realistic expectation since some church communities live in such isolation that the community at large is racially monolithic. We cannot be so idealistic that the pursuit of the perfect robs us of doing the good.

Nevertheless, churches hindered by natural demographic hurdles can take steps to reach out to other people groups. Start by examining the percentage of budgetary items given to evangelistic and missionary outreach. The biblical text calls us *all* to "seek justice," as the prophet exhorted his audience (Isa. 1:17). It is not enough to favor justice; we are expected to *seek* justice. If there is condemnation to be leveled against churches regarding race relations it is for the "Laodicean syndrome," which is a "lukewarm" attitude (Rev. 3:16).

We call for a godly realism without losing sight of the idealism of achieving the worldwide mandate. President Teddy Roosevelt's progressive yet realistic view of life captures what we intend. His exhortation to the nation's young people is inscribed on the wall of the Theodore Roosevelt Memorial Hall and Rotunda in the American Museum of Natural History (New York City). We quote in part: "Be practical as well as generous in your ideals/keep your eyes on the stars and keep your feet on the ground."

---

22. http://faithandleadership.com/blog/01-23-2009/mark-chaves-congrega-
tions-are-more-ethnically-diverse.

Giving an Answer

There has been an uptick in debates regarding the moral and intellectual advantages of atheism over religion. Celebrated books by Richard Dawkins and Christopher Hitchens have put religion in general and Christianity in particular on the firing line.[23] Among the chief criticisms is the charge that religion promotes racial intolerance and even genocide. Religious folk do not truly follow the morality espoused in the Old and New Testaments because it is totally unacceptable in civilized society, such as slavery, misogyny, and the like. Dinesh D'Souza responds that their arguments are skewed by attributing too much blame on the church for the troubles the world suffers and by neglecting the good will that Christianity has fostered in society, especially in Western civilization.[24]

On the surface it would appear that religion was the fundamental cause for the unspeakable crimes committed against the Jews and other racial groups by Hitler's regime. This can be extended to recent conflicts where ethnic wars have occurred, including Europe and Africa. Further inquiry will uncover, however, that the root causes were economic and political. In fact, Hitler's regime practiced too little religion instead of too much. By this we mean that a facile reading of Christianity, especially its sacred book, the Bible, has suited the political aims of power mongers and bigots who use religion for their own interests. A fair reading of the Scriptures shows that the Christian tradition has been the source of what both Christians and secularists value—personal human dignity and equal rights.

We present our book to demonstrate that the Bible does not advocate racial bigotry. On the contrary, it fosters equality and gives the best rationale for defending the unique value of human life. We want to assure the present generation of Christians that their faith is not tainted by the unseemly racism attributed by detractors to the Bible. When the Scriptures are interpreted properly, they do not

---

23. Richard Dawkins, *The God Delusion* (Boston: Houghton Mifflin, 2006); Christopher Hitchens, *God Is Not Great: How Religion Poisons Everything* (New York: Twelve, 2007).
24. Dinesh D'Souza, *What's so Great about Christianity?* (Washington: Regenery, 2007) 67–79, 204.

justify slavery and racial segregation. Our book will equip the reader with a clear picture of the Bible's teaching on human equality, racial integration, and personal liberty and freedom.

"WE ALL HAVE ISSUES"

Our colleague Patricia Outlaw, who teaches pastoral counseling, frequently says to her students by way of introduction, "We all have issues. I have issues. You have issues. All God's children have issues." Life is made up of challenges that no one can escape. There are contemporary issues that we as writers—and you as the reader—cannot escape. Four issues in particular reappear throughout the book, especially in the "Thought Provokers" that conclude each chapter: What we think about (1) multiethnic worship; (2) evangelism and missions; (3) immigration; and (4) racial intermarriage. These are not comfortable issues to take on since they challenge us to examine ourselves and to act upon the questions that arise. How we respond tells us something about ourselves as human beings, as members of the redeemed, and as witnesses to the lordship of Jesus Christ. The study and its implications may be calling us to make lifestyle changes that will move us out of our comfort zone.

First, multiethnic worship poses challenges for us because we must decide if it is crucial to the mission of the church at large. What specifically should we and our local churches do or not do regarding it?

Second, matters pertaining to the task of evangelism and mission naturally emerge from our study and are fundamental since the biblical portrait of the church is a worldwide ingathering of peoples into the kingdom of God. Do we have any latent bias for or against one group or another that hinders an all-out effort to reach certain peoples? We must take an honest self-examination of our lives and our churches to prioritize our commitment of resources and personal involvement.

Third, immigration will inevitably touch every aspect of a country's social fabric. This is especially true for the church since its very constitution is to disciple all nations. Are we open to the newcomers? Is our response to public policy regarding immigration consistent with our Christian witness?

Last, as different ethnic groups increasingly live together in proximity, interracial marriage inevitably becomes more common. What is God's view on the matter? We must view it from sound biblical instruction.

Keep these four issues in mind as you read the book and prepare yourself to consider *and* act upon what you and your church congregation decide is the direction God would have you follow.

SCRABBLING OVER TERMS

"Scrabble" is a verb and noun meaning "to struggle/struggling" toward a goal, like a cat clawing and scratching a door. Social scientists, historians, and linguists have "clawed" ("scrabbled") their way toward defining the lexicon of racial terms which we hear in everyday conversation and in the media. There is only one thing that modern scholars agree on—no one definition of a term satisfies all. We offer a few guidelines to assist readers.

Race and Ethnicity

"Race" and "ethnic" are often used as synonyms, but each has a different nuance.[25] "Race" refers to inherited physical traits that characterize peoples, such as facial features and skin color. "Ethnic" (Greek, *ethnos*) identifies an affiliated "people group" who share history, traditions, and culture, such as familial descent, language, and religious and social customs.

"Race" in the modern sense may imply a distinctive people group whose lineage comes from a common source. It is often associated with the idea of pure lineage.[26] It is not a useful term since peoples do not in reality descend from a shared ancestor. Ancient peoples were of

---

25. See especially D. J. Wiseman, ed., "Introduction: Peoples and Nations" in *Peoples of Old Testament Times* (Oxford: Clarendon, 1973), xv–xxi.
26. Benjamin Isaac, *The Invention of Racism in Classical Antiquity* (Princeton: Princeton University Press, 2004), 25–26, 33–34, prefers "people" since there is no true biological descent. He observes that the Greek Athenians were the exception in classical times since they considered themselves a pure lineage and who had dwelt only in their native homeland, thus making them superior to all other peoples (p. 165).

blended ancestral lineage (see chapter 3), such as King David, whose ancestry was both Hebrew and Moabite (Ruth). One of the unique features, however, of the Bible's genealogies is the interdependency of the human family, which had its origin in Adam (see chapter 2). We can truly say that there is a human *race*.

"People" (Hebrew, *am*) is the common term used by God in referring to the Israelites. With the possessive forms (e.g., *ammi*, "my people"), it captures the personal, relational aspect of the Lord and the covenant community, Israel (e.g., Exod. 3:7).[27] "Nation" (*goy*) is primarily a political term, describing a geopolitical state in a specific locale whose citizenship consists of interconnected communities. Peoples of the ancient Near East perceived family derivation, shared history, traditions, and customs as the primary means of distinguishing ethnic groups. Race as we think of it was not important for ancient peoples, including the Hebrews, and rarely appears in ancient texts or the Bible (e.g., Jer. 13:23). The ancients in Greco-Roman society did not have the concept that we usually think of today as "race," although many of their views were later adopted by modern racism in the eighteenth and nineteenth centuries.[28] Typically, the Hebrews, like the peoples of the ancient Near East, identified foreigners in terms of their language, locale, religion, and customs (e.g., Num. 21:29; Isa. 33:19; Amos 1:5).

This book often uses "people(s)" and "people group(s)" for an ethnic group but not exclusively. When we use the word "race," such as the Jewish race versus the Gentile race, we do not mean race in the technical sense of a pure racial group.

Racism and Ethnic Prejudice

In a repartee between Alice and Humpty Dumpty in Lewis Carroll's beloved *Through the Looking Glass*, the two characters passionately pursue the subject of what words mean: "'When *I* use a

---

27. E. A. Speiser, "'People' and 'Nation' of Israel," *JBL* 79 (1960): 157–63.
28. Ibid., 15, refers to Greco-Roman culture as promoting "proto-racism" by its sharing in some of the same opinions as modern racism, such as environmental determinism and heredity of acquired characteristics, 163.

word,' Humpty Dumpty said, in a rather scornful tone, 'it means just what I choose it to mean—neither more nor less.'"

The word "racism" is putty in the hands of the user. The key ingredient in the definition of racism, according to the study by Benjamin Isaac, is determinism whether biological, environmental, or astrological.[29] By determinism Isaac means that the individual does not have control over his intellectual and moral capacities. Biological determinism, for example, holds that there is a genetic connection between the physical genetics of a people group and features that are physical, mental, and moral belong to all individuals who make up that group. These traits cannot be changed or modified.

That these attributes are hereditary is based on an "imagined" belief (Isaac's term), not on facts; thus individuals are "doomed," so to speak, to continue these traits. This is often connected in ancient society and more centrally in modern racism of the eighteenth and nineteenth centuries with environmental determinism, which contends that climate and geography dictated physical, intellectual, and moral traits (see chapter 2). These acquired traits were inherited through biological descent. Thus, it was contended that the peoples from the lower hemispheres and in the warmer climates were not progressive intellectually or morally, while those of the European and North American habitations developed superior "races." Common to antiquity and modern racism was fear that the mixing of "races" by intermarriage would result in the superior races degenerating.

Ethnic prejudice, however, works differently, according to Isaac, who distinguishes prejudice from racism. Racism assumes that individuals cannot change whereas ethnic prejudice does not accept the notion of inherited, *unchanging* qualities held by all individuals in a group. In other words, an individual's traits cannot represent a group or, reversely, a group cannot be treated as though it were an individual.[30] Prejudice, of course, is just as damaging to an individual's self-understanding and life but it is technically not the most viral form of racism. Both racism and ethnic prejudice are held by persons in American culture, and we must be aware of both without confusing them.

---

29. Ibid., 23. Also see his summary of the principles of racism, 505.
30. Ibid., 23–25.

We do not draw a technical line between our use of the words "racism" and "prejudice" since the latter can be a "racial prejudice." They are interchangeable in our usage.

Multiethnic Church

Exactly what constitutes a multiethnic church? Some may think that a worship service in which more than one ethnicity participates is multiethnic, whereas others would require that the church be truly integrated in pastoral and elder leadership. Others would require that it include a variety of distinctive cultural features, such as language, music, liturgy, and dress.

Sociologist George Yancey defines a multiethnic church by percentages of ethnic representation in worship services: No one ethnic group has more than 80 percent of the *regular* (emphasis mine) congregation at worship.[31] We are not speaking of a shared worship service on an occasion when two congregations come together for a special event. Yancey's definition, in our estimation, is not especially rigorous, yet he found only 8 percent of U.S. churches are racially integrated. The number of churches that are fully integrated in leadership and worship style is significantly lower. Multiethnic worship is rare in the evangelical church, although there is a trend toward more communities turning to multiethnic inclusion. (We use "multiethnic" ["multicultural, multiracial"] as a general description with no technical definition in mind.)

On Ethnic Names

That we live in a pluralistic society is readily evidenced by the diversity of terms used to designate peoples of major ethnic groups. We offer a few comments to help readers understand our practice of naming people groups. In naming a few we run the risk of offending some by omission, but we have selected these because they are commonly used in America's public discourse. There are technical

---

31. George Yancey, *One Body One Spirit: Principles of Successful Multiracial Churches* (Downers Grove: InterVarsity, 2003), 15.

versions given in the classification of the U.S. Census and Education Department, as we have noted above.[32] The difficulties that government agencies face in attempting to categorize individuals by ethnicity alerts us to the vastness of the pluralistic society we live in.

Hispanic and Latino. One of the most challenging ethnic designations in American culture is the difference between "Hispanic" and "Latino" (feminine "Latina"). There is no consensus regarding the use of these terms among those who are considered Hispanics/Latino(a)s. We will use them as synonyms, since doing so is widespread, although we recognize that there is a historical difference in their origin.

The word "Hispanic" refers to peoples of descent from Spain whose language is Spanish. It includes peoples of the Americas and the Caribbean. The peculiarity of "Hispanic" is its official adoption by the 1970 U.S. Census Bureau to categorize the ethnic group from Latin American countries. It is an American designation, and thus should not be used of peoples living *in* Latin American countries. The word "Latino(a)" derives from the word "Latin" and is considered the broad term to designate all peoples from Latin American countries without reference to any connection to the European country Spain. The prevalent term is "Hispanic," although there is a trend toward using "Latino(a)." The preference of most Hispanics/Latino(a)s is specific country of origin, such as Costa Rican and Dominican.[33]

The Hispanic/Latino(a) community is not a uniform ethnic group in regard to country of origin, race characteristics, or language (not all speak Spanish, for example).[34] Common life experiences and social concerns regarding their full rights as citizens and their retention of identity and heritage have cultivated the development of a panethnic identity for the Hispanic/Latino(a) community. Recently there has been greater acceptance of the broad, encompassing terms

32. For the working definitions of people groups see the official National Center for Education Statistics' Web site: https://surveys.nces.ed.gov/ipeds/VisInstructions.aspx?survey=10&id=466&show=all#chunk_370, accessed 8 October, 2009.

33. Zaida Maldonadao Pérez, "U.S. Hispanic/Latino Identity and Protestant Experience: A Brief Introduction for the Seminarian" in *Perspectivas: Occasional Papers* (Princeton: Hispanic Theological Initiative, 2003), 96–98.

34. Benjamin Valentine, *Mapping Public Theology: Beyond Culture, Identity, and Difference* (Harrisburg, PA: Trinity Press International, 2002), 5 (footnote 5), 31–37.

"Hispanic/Latino(a)" by members of this group, motivated by the pressing need to address the same minority issues.

Black and African American. A 2007 Gallup poll asked blacks/African Americans which of the two designations they preferred; they included the option "doesn't matter." The results showed no consensus. The polling suggested that "a clear majority of blacks say that they don't care which label is used."[35] Those who showed a preference, however, leaned toward "African American" rather than "black." We use the terms interchangeably.

THOUGHT PROVOKERS

1. What do you predict will change or stay the same regarding racial issues since the election of President Barack Obama?

2. How do secular society and the church overlap and differ in their respective views of race relations?

3. How should Christians answer the charge that Christianity historically encouraged racism?

4. What do you or your church think is the best way to address racial tensions? Individual by individual? Or by social action changing systemic racism? Why?

5. Are you or your church ready to seek inclusion of different ethnic groups? Why or why not?

6. What should a multiethnic church look like?

7. How much emphasis should your church place on achieving a multiethnic church?

---

35. Frank Newport, "Black or African American? 'African American' slightly preferred among those who have a preference," September 28, 2007. http://www.gallup.com/poll/28816/black-african-american.aspx, accessed 6 October 2009.

Chapter 1

God's Design for Creation

STEREOTYPING. **WE ARE ALL** guilty to some degree of stereotyping groups of people. Stereotypes are simplistic generalizations, based on assumptions, regarding a group and applied to all individuals that make up that group. Some of the more benign are "all blondes are stupid" and "all men are pigs," unless of course you are a blonde or a man! The most egregious stereotypes are commonly ethnic, such as "all Muslims are terrorists." Cartoon caricatures perpetuate these false images. We each need to consider how we would answer this question: "What stereotypes do I carry with me?"

Veronica Chambers, author of *Mama's Girl* and children books *Celia Cruz* and *Queen of Salsa*, gives a first-hand account of how she has been stereotyped and the hurt that has come with it. She, an African American, is married to Jason, who is white, and they have one daughter. She tells of one incident that sums up what the pain is like for people who are the objects of stereotyping: "When we lived in a fancy condo building, I was mistaken for the maid and pointed to the service elevator. It hurts—all of it [stereotyping], every time. . . . [But] Even on the toughest days, I know that Jason is not responsible for the ignorance of others."[1]

Stereotyping is at best a lazy way of dealing with people who are not racially or culturally like us. But the Bible tells us that each person has value in God's eyes and should be respected by us. The importance of every person has its fundamental roots in the beginning of

---

1. Veronica Chambers, "Love in Black and White," *Real Simple* (March 2009), 48.

God's story of reconciliation. The story of God's plan for reconciliation begins at—well, at the beginning!

THE MASTER DESIGNER

Oops! God has no "beginning." But he chose to reveal himself in the dimensions of time and space—"In the beginning, God created the heavens and the earth"—which is how we understand ourselves. God introduced himself in these terms so that we might know him. God is the author, facilitator, and perfecter of the Bible's story of reconciliation. In other words, he is the Great Reconciler.

God is also the Master Designer who alone can bring reconciliation in the world that he has created. People, however, both in antiquity and in the present, have attempted to remake God's design for creation.

Distorting the Master Plan

In ancient times, humanity was diminished to the rank of servants to the gods.[2] The gods made the world for their own pleasure and created men and women to do menial tasks. Class systems mirrored the deities. The closer a person was thought to be to the gods, such as king and priest, the higher a person stood in the social order. Peasants and slaves were the lowest of the low and did not receive the same level of dignity and value.

Deification of the created order, such as sun and stars, and the various creatures, such as land and sea animals, was standard. A god who was independent of nature was seldom contemplated. Especially important was the king who was recognized as either divine in person (Egypt) or a sacral son of the gods (Canaan and Mesopotamia). The ancients believed that the institution of kingship was a creation of the gods, which mirrored the hierarchy of the pantheon of gods ruled by the creator-god. For example, in

---

2. For a useful study see John H. Walton, *Ancient Near Eastern Thought and the Old Testament: Introduction to the Conceptual World of the Hebrew Bible* (Grand Rapids: Baker, 2006), esp. 97–98, 214–15, 280–81.

Babylonian religion the creator-god Marduk was elevated by the gods as king over the pantheon.

The Bible's creation account, however, shows that human life is valued on the basis of being created by God, not a person's place in the social order. The creation of all men and women in the "image of God" teaches that all have equal footing. The creation account presented a view counter to the prevailing thought. There is a democratizing of all people, meaning no person is inherently more important than another.

Certain practices today also defy the Master Designer. Surgical sex change, unisexual dress, and homosexual relations, for example, oppose the heterosexual nature of human creatureliness. Pedophilia and even bestiality are part of the modern scene worldwide. Ethnic bigotry played out in genocide and sex slavery continues. Although some strides have been made to manage environmental resources, the West and burgeoning countries, such as China and India, continue to exhibit poor supervision of our God-given resources.

Restoring the Master Plan

The Great Reconciler, however, has a plan that will bring all creation into perfect harmony with himself (Isa. 11:1-9; Rom. 8:18-23). This is accomplished on our behalf through the death and resurrection of Jesus Christ (e.g., 2 Cor. 5:17-19; Col. 1:19-20). Through the church, the Lord brings our world into closer conformity with his ethical ideal. The church is the chief witness to the Master Designer's perfect plan. We are ambassadors from the court of Christ, calling "Be reconciled to God" (2 Cor. 5:20). Our charge is to pray and work toward the goal that Jesus taught us to pray, "Thy kingdom come. Thy will be done in earth, as it is in heaven" (Matt. 6:10).

DESIGNED FOR LIFE

The Bible's creation story indicates the incomparable value of life—life in all its expressions. To best understand the message of creation, we must consider the literary features of the story as well as its contents.

Six Days for Life

The six creation days show that God made and ordered the universe so that there might be sustainable life (Gen. 1:3–31). The six days of creation entail God's making of the cosmos as we know it, beginning with an incomplete and lifeless universe: "Now the earth was without form and empty and darkness was over the surface of the deep, and the Spirit of God was hovering over the surface of the waters" (Gen. 1:2). Precisely what elements are meant in this description is disputed, but there is much that can be learned from this verse. The "earth" was not yet in the condition that we know and understand. It could not sustain life and therefore was characterized by cosmic barrenness—the absence of life.

In the first panel of three days, God gave order resulting in vegetation where none had been (day 3). In the second panel of three days, paralleling the first panel, the Creator filled the organized earth with teeming life forms, where no life had been. The conclusion was the greatest creation achievement, the making of man and woman on the sixth day. All was prepared for sustaining life and establishing humankind as the stewards of the terrestrial world. As the luminaries ruled the skies on the fourth day, humankind was appointed by God to exercise dominion over the earth and its creatures.

Day 1	light/darkness	→	Day 4	luminaries
Day 2	water/ atmosphere	→	Day 5	fish/birds
Day 3	seas/land vegetation	→	Day 6	land animals/ humankind

The Pattern for Life

The two chief features of God's design are *diversity* and *unity*. These two characteristics are reflected in the nature of human life, making them important features in our pursuit of racial integration.

The striking patterns of diversity provide a dense texture in creation. There are endless minute and vast configurations, most of which appear infinite to the human eye and mind. Yet all is enfolded into a unity of form and function. Coordination and cooperation produce controlled emergence and development.

The creation of the human family involves both diversity and unity. Our diversity is obvious and should be prized as the way God made us. When I (Mathews) attended a racially diverse church in Princeton, New Jersey, for a Sunday morning worship service, I was struck by the power of a gathered body praising God in a racially mixed, multicolored audience. I sat between an African American woman and an Indian family. Although white members dominated the leadership, the congregation was not predominantly white. When I looked across the congregation I saw many Asians and Indians, and fewer Hispanics and African Americans. The service was conducted in English but had Chinese and Spanish translations. There was also an interpreter for the deaf. What held this congregation together—their unity—was the common commitment to Christ. We were all image-bearers, all carrying the scars of sin and sorrow, but also all looking confidently to our Lord Jesus Christ as our one blessed hope (Titus 2:13).

DESIGNED FOR BLESSING

The creation account tells us that God is not only all-powerful and all-wise but also all-benevolent. The Lord blessed all his creation with favor, although human life was the object of special endowment.

Blessing for All

The creation of the human family reflects creation's two principles of diversity and unity. The human family exhibits unity in personhood and diversity in gender and role. The unity of humankind is grounded in its personhood—"the image of God" (Gen. 1:26–28). This is the chief distinctive of humanity. That the blessing for the human family is for all persons is indicated by the interplay between the singular (unity) and plural (diversity) references in 1:26: "Let us make man in our image, in our likeness, and let them rule. . . ." The rendering "man" (*adam*) is singular in number but generic in reference, meaning a whole class—translated "mankind" or "humankind." It is followed by the plural pronoun "let them rule."

Verse 27 especially exposes the unity and diversity of humanity. The verse has an inverted repetition (known as chiasmus) that creates a parallel between the parts of the verse (emphasis mine).

> So God created *man* in his own image,
> In the image of God he created *him*;
> Male and female he created *them.*

The last line clarifies that "man(kind)" consists of "male and female." Diversity within the human family is noted by the gender specific terms "male" (*zakar*) and "female" (*neqebah*), not the marital terms "husband" (*ish* or *baal*) and "wife" (*ishshah*). Gender is intrinsic to personhood, whereas the relational terms "husband" and "wife" identify human roles in the context of human interaction. The reason for the gender-specific terms is to underscore that all members of humanity are recipients of the blessing. Also, "male and female" anticipates the blessing of human procreation (v. 28).

The meaning of "the image of God" historically has been a theological and exegetical challenge to interpreters. Although the text does not necessarily restrict the meaning to one feature, the aspect that is actually explained in the text itself is the *functional* outcome of human creation. Humanity was made for the blessing that God conferred uniquely on humankind. God assigned humanity two tasks: procreation and dominion (1:28). This is the blessing that God has for all humanity.

Blessing of Procreation and Dominion

"Blessing" is the key term in the book of Genesis, occurring more often in this book than in any other. Its general meaning when used of God blessing others is divine favor. Typically, the favor was prosperity and well-being.

Procreation. Prosperity included procreation. God blessed

crawling creatures, fish, and birds, enabling them to be "fruitful and multiply" numerically (Gen. 1:22). Those whom God created in his image he also blessed with the divine enablement to procreate. The same language occurs for the blessing of the human family, "Be fruitful and multiply and fill . . ." (1:28).

Dominion. There was, however, substantive difference in the blessings bestowed on animals and humanity. The human family received the mandate to "subdue" the earth and "have dominion" over the animal creatures (1:28). It is apparent from the context that the commission to rule reflects the superiority of the human species over that of all other creatures. The context clarifies that the human family must be accountable to God for their stewardship over his creation. Authority over life resides with God, who zealously guards his prerogative of giving and taking life.

There is no biblical justification for men and women to abuse creation or to harm one another. The typical social system in the ancient world reserved the role of "rule" for kings, which resulted usually in intimidation and coercion. Although the Hebrew words "subdue" (*kabash*) and "have dominion/rule" (*rada*) may describe the rule of a monarch (e.g., 2 Chron. 28:10; 1 Kings 4:24), the context of the creation account tells us that the representative rule of God is by *all* human beings, all those made in the "image of God," not exclusively a social class of kings and bureaucrats. The biblical perspective is all men and women function as "royalty" with its privileges and its responsibilities.[3]

But what about the institutions of kingship and slavery that existed in Israel? The establishment of a human king over Israel was a temporary measure whereby the Lord secured for his people well-being. Psalm 72 describes the ideal king who rules in righteousness, assuring justice for all and providing for all. The institution of kingship foreshadowed the perfect rule of God through his son, Jesus Christ. In God's eyes, all men and women have equal worth and

---

3. The case for the rule of a husband over his wife in Gen. 3:16 is not to be understood in the same sense as humanity exercising rule over the earth. For a fuller discussion see Kenneth Mathews, *Genesis 1–11:26*, NAC (Nashville: B&H, 1996): 250–52.

privilege, for the Lord "shows no partiality" (Acts 10:34; Rom. 2:11; cf. 2 Chron. 19:7; Luke 20:21).

The idea of "rule" in the creation story does not give license for slavery or oppression of any sort. Where the Bible addresses slavery, it assumes it exists as part of a fallen, sinful world and places restrictions on it. We can liken it to Jesus' comment on the institution of divorce, which he attributed to the sinfulness of humanity, not God's ideal. Slavery was not part of the Creator's original design.

In the ideal beginning, there is no human subjugation of one another. There is no "Master Race" concept in the Bible that excuses racial superiority, because the theology of creation undercuts the ideology that one race is inherently superior to others. There is no hierarchy of racial superiority or of individual superiority in the eyes of God.

DESIGNED FOR RELATIONSHIP

The creation story shows that humans have the capacity to enjoy a *relationship* with God and with one another. A personal relationship exists because both God and humans are living, personal beings.

Relationship with God

From the blessings spoken by God directly *to* the human family, we infer that humans can relate to God personally (Gen. 1:28); this detail differentiates the human family from all other creatures. The Lord "blessed" the animal world but the text does not say that he addressed animals directly as persons (1:22). God related to humans by honoring them with a direct spoken word. This presupposes that they could receive, understand, and respond to the mind of God.

The parallel account of creation in Genesis 2 shows specifically the capacity of humans to relate to God and to one another in a way unlike the rest of the created order. The Lord "formed the man of dust from the ground and breathed into his nostrils the breath of life" (2:7).

Body and Soul. Humans are complex beings, consisting of both material and immaterial. Corporeal existence and the inbreathing of

God result in a unified being—"and he became a living person" (2:7). The traditional rendering "a living soul" can be misleading to readers who interpret "soul" as the ancient Greeks did. In Greek thought, the "soul" was conceived of as eternal and preexistent; the essence of a person was immaterial, and the body was dispensable as a shell or container.

But the Bible teaches that people are not "souls" but "soulish," meaning that we are whole persons with body and soul. Christian teaching is that the unity of the body and personal essence are separated at death on a temporary basis (1 Cor. 15:42-55). The resurrection of the body insures the reunification of the whole person. The body is precious in the sight of God.

The description of "dust" from which the Lord "formed" humanity indicates the material nature of humanity. The term "formed" describes the work of a potter (Jer. 18:4-6), depicting God giving focused attention and care in the creation of the man. This picture corresponds to the contemplation and intentionality reflected in the phrase "Let us make man . . ." (Gen. 1:26).

Human life received the breath of life *directly* from the Creator, "And [God] breathed into his nostrils the breath of life" (2:7), whereas the animal world received the life force through the intermediary of the "ground" (2:19). The production of animal life is told in an impassionate way. Nevertheless, humans are creatures who share in the properties of other creatures.[4] Human life is not divine. We are not miniature gods and goddesses. No person is by nature superior to another person.

Man and Woman. The Genesis narrative reinforces the distinction between human life and all other life. The animals are subject to the man and the woman, who correspond to one another in their fundamental being. She is "suitable" (NIV) for the man whereas the animal kingdom is not (2:18). The Hebrew expression *kenegdo*, literally, "like what is in front of him," is a linguistic invention that

---

4. "Living creatures" describes both humans and animals (e.g., 1:20-21, 24; 2:7; 9:10; Ezek. 47:9), and both receive the "breath of life" (e.g., 2:7; 7:22). Although "breath of life" in Hebrew slightly differs in the respective descriptions of humans (*nishmath chayyah*) and animals (*nishmath ruach*, 7:22), they have parallel meaning in other passages (e.g., Isa. 57:16).

highlights the equality and alliance of the first couple. The first man made this clear at the introduction of the woman:

> The LORD God made the side (rib) which he had taken from the man into a woman, and he brought her to him. And the man said, "This one is bone of my bones and flesh of my flesh. This one will be called 'woman' for out of man this one was taken." (Gen. 2:22–23)

The man immediately recognized the woman as made of the same "stuff" as himself in contrast to the animals over which they were to rule. There is a sound play between the Hebrew words "woman" (*ishsha*) and "man" (*ish*). English has the same sound allusion in "man" and "wo-*man.*" The play reiterates that the man and woman are alike in their personhood.

The act of "making" the woman is another picturesque way of describing God's investment in her creation as being the same as the man. The word "made" is used of building, such as Noah's construction of an altar (Gen. 8:20). God then is the divine potter and builder of the man *and* woman. They each possess dignity and value not given to any other in all of creation.

Thus, the man and woman are sufficiently differentiated from one another to be recognized as separate persons, but the unity of human beings shows that the commonality of human life exceeds their differences. In other words, diversity functions under the umbrella of an encompassing unity—a unity grounded in each person's essential being as human.

Relationship with Others

Another implication of the teaching of "image" is the interpersonal relationship of the male and female. If the two are to exercise dominion over the created world in a responsible manner, the couple must work together in an informed and coordinated way.

Dignity of the Man. The man received the assignment "to work and keep" the Garden of Eden which the Lord had prepared for him (2:15). "Work" (*abad*) and "keep" (*shamar*) are terms that share in the description of the Tent of Meeting (tabernacle). Moses erected the Tent of Meeting in the center of the twelve tribes of Israel, symbolizing God's dwelling among them. "Work" and "keep" describe the "service" (*abad*) and the "keeping guard" (*shamar*) by the Levitical priests in the Tent of Meeting (e.g., Exod. 38:21; Num. 1:53).[5] That priests held a lofty dignity is reflected in the relationship they exclusively enjoyed with the Lord, for "the LORD is [their] inheritance" (Deut. 10:9).

Eden and the Tent of Meeting were the places where God and humanity communed. The Lord placed Eden under the charge of the man. There could have been no greater duty entrusted to humanity than the management of the garden where God "walk[ed] in the cool of the day" (Gen. 3:8).

Dignity of the Woman. The woman, too, had an indispensable role in the garden as the childbearer whose duty was to join with her husband in bringing in the blessing of rule through human procreation. The man could not achieve the blessing apart from the woman nor the woman apart from the man. The apostle Paul referred to this codependency when he taught that "in the Lord a woman is not independent of man or man of woman, for as the woman came from the man, likewise the man comes through woman. But all things are from God" (1 Cor. 11:11–12).

God has made men and women for community. We are social beings. We can't go it alone, either as individuals or as communities. This is more true today in our global village than ever before. Like a kaleidoscope where not bit of glass functions independently of the whole, the experiences of one part of the human family affect the whole human family.

The people of God must be rightly related to God and rightly related to one another. A multiethnic church is a reflection of God as the Master Designer of creation, displaying diversity and unity. A church that accepts ethnic isolation, intentionally shut off from other racial groups, is a sham of church, not an authentic functioning and worshipping body of Christ followers.

---

5. "Work" and "keep" occur again in tandem in Num. 3:7–8 and 18:7, which describe Levitical oversight of the Tent of Meeting.

DESIGNED FOR WORSHIP

Creation theology also teaches that the human family (and all creation) was designed for the worship of God. Creation has an eschatological dimension, pointing ahead to the culmination of God's design for worship at the throne of the Lamb, which is surrounded by believers from every nation (Rev. 5:9; 7:9–10; 14:6–7). The culminating day in the creation week is the seventh day (Gen. 2:1–3). It is the only day on which God "rested" (*shabbath*) and the only day that is "blessed" and "consecrated" (v. 3). This was the prototype of the "Sabbath day" in ancient Israel which was a regular feature of weekly worship (e.g., Exod. 20:11).

Another striking distinctive of the seventh day is the absence of the closing refrain, "and there was evening and there was morning, the first day, etc." This omission serves a metaphorical purpose, indicating theologically that the seventh day has no end. God as the Eternal One has made available to his creation an eternal rest. By implication the Lord is inviting his creation to enter into this rest with him. This is achieved through worship. By celebrating the seventh day as holy, fully consecrated to the Lord, we recognize the Lord as the Lord of all creation. The writer to the Hebrews (4:3–10) referred to the "eternal" seventh day when he admonished his Christian readers to enter into God's perfect salvation "rest."

It is only fitting that human life as the pinnacle of God's creative word and as sole "image of God" should enter into the Sabbath rest through faith and offer sacrifices of praise (Pss. 33:1; 147:1). Adam and Eve's sons, Cain and Abel, were the first in recorded Scripture to bring offerings to the Lord (Gen. 4:1–4a). Formal worship characterized early humanity: "At that time people began to call on [or publish] the name of the LORD" (4:26). From the beginning, the worship of God was the experience of being human—individually and collectively. Worship is for all peoples and for all times.

Our Creator is also our Redeemer. The Sabbath teaching not only celebrated the Creator (Exod. 20:8–11) but also reminded Israel of the great salvation that God had provided the enslaved Hebrews in Egypt. The people were liberated from their bondage on the basis of the Passover provision (Exod. 12). The redemption achieved in Egypt was the motivation for the worship of God (see Deut. 5:15). Sabbath observance then brought together the recognition of God as Creator *and* as Covenant Redeemer.

The Lord has made and redeemed all who are the "image of God" for the purpose of worship. To the degree that the church mirrors this creation purpose in our worship we meet our Master's design. Multiethnic worship testifies that God is Creator and Redeemer of *all* humanity who stand in solidarity under the lordship of Jesus Christ. John's vision of multiethnic worship indicates it is a property of the "new creation"—now and in the eternal state to come—when "an innumerable multitude . . . from every nation, and all tribes, and peoples and languages" (Rev. 7:9) worship the Lamb of God in choral synchrony.

DESIGNED FOR FREEDOM

God also designed human life to enjoy freedom. By this we do not mean freedom in the typical way we moderns think of human freedom. For many today, "freedom" means self-rule and autonomy. From the Bible's perspective, however, this is slavery to one's self without regard to God and to others. Genuine freedom means liberty to love and live with God, to be what God intended for us. The Lord did not create men and women to be slaves to themselves or to one another.

Freedom to obey was the first choice that our parents in the garden faced. But they made the wrong choice and became enslaved to sin with its selfish appetites, fear, and hostility. What happened? Why have human relations departed so far from the Creator's purpose for us?

The Tree of Decision

In the idyllic garden of Eden, which abounded in beauty and bounty, stood two trees that represented the generosity God bestowed on our first parents (Gen. 2:9). The tree of life provided human life when accessible to the man and woman. The tree of knowledge of good and evil provided the opportunity to enjoy genuine freedom through choosing to obey God's command: "And the LORD God commanded the man, saying, 'You may surely eat of every tree of the garden, but of the tree of the knowledge of good and evil you shall not eat, for in the day that you eat of it you shall surely die'" (2:17). "*Every* tree of the garden" was theirs except the one tree. The tempter tricked the woman into thinking that God held back something from her (3:1–5). He disputed her belief that God was good. Eat of the tree and they would be like gods!

The Wrong Decision

Their disobedience resulted in death (3:6–8), although even in judgment the Lord showed mercy by postponing their death (cf. Gen. 5:4–5). By choosing wisdom independently of God, they lost the opportunity of life (3:22–24). Human history has testified to the sad reality of this choice, and all humanity has followed suit, choosing our own way and suffering the consequences.

When we compare Genesis 2 and 3, disharmony replaced harmony in the created order. First, the man and woman separated themselves from God. They fear him. Although they retain their unique person-hood as the "image of God," they no longer can carry out their created purpose in the freedom that God had intended for them. They are en-slaved to sin and its passions. Second, the man and the woman compete for dominance. Jealousy takes the place of joy (Gen. 3:16b). And third, humanity will be at war with the good world that the Lord entrusted to their oversight (3:17–19). From creation's bliss to sin's burden, they now struggle to bear children (3:16a) and to farm the land (3:17).

The Human Dilemma

This is the Bible's story of the human condition. This is the lot of humanity. Everything from petty selfishness to the horror of genocide can be explained by the wicked nature (capacity) of human beings. What we touch we taint, if not destroy. The zeal for domi-nance over others, the wanton disregard for our environment, and the evasion of moral conscience are the bitter fruit that we have gained for ourselves. Yet, by God's grace, humanity still bears his "image," and he has placed deterrents to curb the voracious appetite of sin.

Humans, as seen vividly in racial strife, compete for dominance.

The Bible's view of reality explains most satisfactorily why racial integration remains a "dream," as Martin Luther King Jr. famously remarked in his "I Have a Dream" speech.[6] Humanity's better moments have humans striving to attain the goal but it cannot be satisfactorily achieved because human sin will finally get its way. The goodwill of humanity will succumb to the impulses that drive the wicked to succeed at any cost to human life and well-being.

DESIGNED FOR RECONCILIATION

Although the man and woman in the garden rebelled against the Master Designer, they remained the objects of God's special grace. The Master Designer promised a savior and continued to bless the human family.

The Promise of a Savior

God's love assured a savior, a deliverer who would rescue sinful, fractured, egocentric humanity. In Genesis 3 we read of God's judicial punishments pronounced against the serpent and the man and woman. In each case the punishment relates to the crime committed by these culprits. In the case of the serpent, an offspring of the woman will defeat the serpent on her behalf. "And I will cause hostility between you and the woman, and between your offspring and her offspring. He will strike your head, and you will strike his heel" (3:15 NIV).

This announcement of a future deliverer foreshadowed salvation through Jesus, the perfect God-man (cf. Rom. 16:20; Gal. 4:4; 1 Tim. 2:5-6). Jesus' incarnation and sacrificial death was the basis for the reconciliation that we experience as spiritually regenerated persons.

The Promise of Continued Blessing

The promised blessing of procreation and dominion over the terrestrial world continued, though only partially. The divine judgments

---

6. Delivered on the steps of the Lincoln Memorial in Washington, D.C., on August 28, 1963.

against the woman and the man contained rays of hope. The punishment of painful labor in childbirth was the hearkening of grace, for by means of giving birth, she would provide the future savior. There was life for humanity, although death reigned until the coming of the deliverer (cf. the refrain "and he died," Gen. 5; see Rom. 5:14). For the man the toil of the land by which he gained livelihood also contained a ray of blessed hope. Although exiled from the garden, he would have arable ground for a harvest.

God delivered imprecations against the serpent (Gen. 3:14–15), yet he did not utter curses against the first couple. This implies that God viewed them as salvageable, so to speak, that is, *reconcilable.* He did not curse the woman, because she was central to the redemptive plan God had for creation. The man, too, did not receive a curse, because as a person created in the "image of God" the Lord had endowed him with value. Rather, the Lord cursed the ground (*ad-amah*), from which the man (*adam*) was taken: "cursed is the ground because of you" (3:17).[7]

That the man had confidence in the Lord's promise of reconciliation is seen in the name that he gave his companion. The name "Eve" (*chawwah*) means "life" (*chay*) (3:20).[8] Expulsion from the garden on the one hand sealed the doom of the first couple, but on the other hand also delivered them from living in their sin perpetually (3:22–24). Since they no longer had access to the tree of life, they would die as warned by the Lord (2:17). Yet God gave the man the continued task of working the ground and the hope of reconciliation continued by virtue of the survival of the woman.

Keeping Watch Over Others

Expulsion meant they faced life *outside* the garden (Gen. 4). What became of humanity? Eve gave birth to two sons, Cain and Abel, but the sin of their parents *inside* the garden had poisoned

---

7. The Hebrew wordplay *adamah* ("ground") and *adam* ("man") conveys that the man was responsible for the sorrow that the creation experienced, although the man himself was spared a direct imprecation.

8. The Hebrew wordplay of *chawwah* ("Eve") and *chay* ("living") expresses the origin of all future human life.

the well. The egregious sin of Cain killing his brother Abel was the horrendous fruit of their parents' decision. Cain was not absolved of his responsibility, however. He was the first person in the Bible to receive the "curse" of God, for he was an "image-killer" (4:11). When God questioned Cain about his brother's whereabouts, Cain answered with the reverberating question we must all answer: "Am I my brother's keeper?" (4:9).

Cain's responsibility toward Abel was grounded in their relationship as brothers. From the perspective of the author and readers, kinship was highly honored in Hebrew culture. Tribal affiliation marked the psyche and identity of a Hebrew person. The crime of fratricide was unthinkable! The underlying reason for kinship loyalty was the common source from which family members descended. This goes to the heart of what personal responsibility toward one another means. All men and women have common parentage in that all human life comes from God as Creator. Today's common aphorism, "we're all God's children," acknowledges our common creation (cf. "Adam, son of God," Luke 3:38).

Jesus explained the extent of human responsibility when he taught our care for a "neighbor," an exhortation found in the Mosaic covenant law: "Love your neighbor as yourself" (Lev. 19:18). When asked, "Who is my neighbor?" Jesus answered with the most remembered parable in Scripture. We call it the parable of the good Samaritan (Luke 10:29–37). The original context of "Love your neighbor" was the Hebrew community of faith, but Jesus drew out its implications and taught his followers that there were no ethnic boundaries to keeping watch over others. When we realize that all people are our neighbors, we will strive to accept and love, not reject or ignore.

Yet God showed mercy even on the criminal Cain by granting him a protected life. Cain feared that his expulsion from society would subject him to retaliation. Once the human family grew, he feared he would be an object of vengeance (Gen. 4:13–14). But God warned that anyone who took vengeance against Cain would be subject to a greater act of vengeance (4:15a). The Lord therefore marked Cain, not to punish him but to protect him (4:15b).[9]

---

9. The passage does not explain the nature of the mark. The word "mark" (*oth*)

Reinventing the "Mark" of Cain

In the sordid history of racism, Cain's "mark" (Gen. 4) was interpreted as punishment of black skin. Nothing could be further from the truth. This viewpoint assumed that the mark was punitive. Actually, it was the opposite; it was an act of mercy extended toward Cain.

If it is so transparent to modern interpreters that the biblical Cain was not black nor did he become black as punishment, how did the notion gain acceptance in Europe and America in the seventeenth to nineteenth centuries? Moreover, since slavery is not a factor in the biblical story of Cain, how could slavery become attached to the idea of Cain's blackness?

David Goldenberg, based on his extensive study of the connection of Africans, black, and slavery in biblical and postbiblical times, suggested that the origin of the misinterpretation was a mistaken understanding of the ancient Syriac translation (known as the Peshitta from the second to third centuries A.D.).[10] The Hebrew of Genesis 4:5 concludes with this description: "and his [Cain's] face fell." The Syriac translators in interpreting this phrase rendered it "and his face became sad." But the Syriac term "sad" is also related to the root word meaning "to be black," and later Armenian interpreters (fifth to sixth centuries) took the version to say "black."

This confusion of "sad" and "black" generated a tradition that connected Cain's mark with blackness. To connect slavery and blackness, slave traders and owners justified their actions by appealing to the errant view that Ham was black *and* that his descendants were condemned to slavery (9:22-27; more on the racist interpretation of Ham follows). It was reasoned therefore that Ham must have married a descendant of (black) Cain, making Ham's son Canaan both black

---

is the most general term for a "sign" or "pledge." The traditional belief that the mark was placed on Cain's forehead is a speculation derived from a different passage and a different Hebrew word. Ezekiel's vision of the purging of idolaters in the temple includes placing a "mark" (*taw*) on the foreheads of those who were innocent of idolatry (9:4-6).

10. David Goldenberg, *The Curse of Ham: Race and Slavery in Early Judaism, Christianity, and Islam* (Princeton: Princeton University Press, 2003), 178-82.

and slave. Goldenberg shows that the popularity of these misinterpretations was due to the rise of the African slave market in the Near East, Europe, and America. The Bible was used to excuse slave trade as a fulfillment of God's will for the nations.

THE "SAME OLD" NEW WORLD

The words "Same Old" and "New" side by side in the heading capture what followed the flood. The post-flood world of Noah and his sons was new in some ways but regrettably the same in the most important way—a sinful fallen humanity. The human dilemma of inevitable sin among human beings and its threat to the fulfillment of the blessing continued in the family of Noah who was the same old Adam.

The Old World

Even though Cain was a murderer, God still granted him an offspring, for he fathered an extensive lineage that is described in Genesis 4. Also, his family was instrumental in developing civilization's urban life, sciences, and arts. Despite these achievements, Cain's family continued his moral impunity. The epitome of his family immorality was Lamech, who was a polygamist and murderer (4:19-24). But standing opposite the lineage of Cain was a righteous lineage, the descendants of Seth, whose prolific line resulted in the righteous Noah (5:32), the savior of the human family.

As the population exploded numerically, wickedness also increased—more people, more wickedness (6:1-8). Intermarriage between the lines of the Cainites and Sethites led to the ancient world's worst moment of wickedness and the moral dissolution of the Sethites. Humanity became so wicked that the Lord purged them through floodwaters. It was *not* due to ethnic integration but to the immoral behavior of the two families. Only Noah received God's favor (6:8), and through him the Lord preserved the human family. From the floating ark that rode out the floodwaters, the inhabitants emerged, making Noah the "new Adam" whose sons received the promised blessing anew (1:26-28; 9:1).

The New World

But did the world change for the better? Did hatred and violence come to an end? No. Human proclivity to intolerance and injustice persisted. The flood and the safeguards that the Lord instituted only restrained human sinfulness. Emerging from the ark, Noah built an altar for sacrifice to appease God and also offer thanksgiving for deliverance. God accepted the sacrifice and promised never again to destroy humanity in this way (8:21–22). Nevertheless, the flood's purging did not change the wicked nature of humanity. The Reformer John Calvin observed that if God were to wipe out sinners on the basis of their collective sinfulness, we would need a "daily deluge"![11] God granted stability in the natural world (8:22), but perverse human conduct continued to sabotage community harmony.

The Lord put in place two protective measures after the flood to tame the violence that had become so fierce (9:2–6). The blessing initially given to humanity was altered to cope with the realities of the post-flood world which would be characterized by violence and killing.

The first safeguard for human life pertained to animals (9:2–3). God puts in the hearts of the beasts an intuitive fear of humanity. This assisted human beings in escaping the carnivorous instincts of undomesticated animals.

The second safeguard is important for our study. Human life above all must be protected (9:5–6). Divine retribution demanded the life of a murderer, an "image-killer." The Lord gave humanity the exacting task of carrying out capital punishment (by judicial process, Deut. 17:6–7). The capital offense of murder is logically grounded in the constituent nature of human life as uniquely created "in the image of God" (Gen. 9:6). Despite human sin committed in the garden and the subsequent escalation of human sin, the "image" was not eradicated. Even the worst human beings *are* image-bearers, though their actions may be utterly despicable in our eyes.

---

11. John Calvin, *Commentaries on the First Book of Moses, called Genesis*, tr. John King (Grand Rapids: Eerdmans, 1948), 284.

When I hear of grave atrocities, such as violence against children and genocidal pogroms, I sometimes feel ashamed to be human. I feel as a member of humanity that I am soiled, needing a "moral bath." This was brought home to me again when I saw a documentary of the Karl Höker collection of photos taken in 1944 at the Nazi death camp at Auschwitz. Höker was adjutant to the commandant of the camp. The collection was a rare find because it showed the SS officers and their families smiling and at play when away from their duties as mass murderers! Little known to the public is that there was a German resort community on the grounds of the camp. The documentary concluded with these comments by staff members of the United States Holocaust Memorial Museum in Washington, D.C.:

Judy Cohen, Director of the Photographic Collection:
We all know that monsters do monstrous things. But when you see people who look like they're nice guys, in a fairly benign setting, and we know for a fact that they were doing monstrous things, then it raises all sorts of questions about what's man's capacity for evil. In a different setting would they still be monsters?

Joseph White, Research Assistant:
They were all too frighteningly human.

Rebecca Erbelding, Archivist:
It makes you think about how people could come to this. That they don't look like monsters. They look like me. They look like my next door neighbor. Is he capable of that? Am I?[12]

Yes, as sinful human beings we have the potential of committing the most depraved crimes. This is why reconciliation can only be fully and finally achieved by a Savior who redeems and transforms the human state.

---

12. "Auschwitz through the Lens of the SS: Photos of Nazi leadership at the Camp," United States Holocaust Memorial Museum, http://www.ushmm.org/museum/exhibit/online/ssalbum/video/ (accessed 29 June 2009).

The Old World Déjà Vu

Yogi Berra, the hall-of-fame baseball player, quipped, "It's like déjà-vu all over again." The New World is the Old World again. The Lord promised Noah and his descendants, as well as the whole created order, that his future disposition toward the world would not be destruction (Gen. 9:8-11). The rainbow in the sky was a sign that universal destruction by flood never again would occur, thus evidencing a (partial) reconciliation of the world to God.

The depiction of Noah reminds us of the first man, Adam. Both were farmers and both received the charge to procreate and populate the earth. Both also, sadly, stumbled in their tasks. Adam ate of the unlawful tree, and Noah became drunk by imbibing the fruit of the vine. Noah was "Adam revived."

> Then Noah began farming and planted a vineyard. He drank of the wine and became drunk, and uncovered himself inside his tent. Ham, the father of Canaan, saw the nakedness of his father, and told his two brothers outside. But Shem and Japheth took a garment and laid it upon both their shoulders and walked backward and covered the nakedness of their father; and their faces were turned away, so that they did not see their father's nakedness. When Noah awoke from his wine, he knew what his youngest son had done to him. So he said, "Cursed be Canaan; a servant of servants shall he be to his brothers." He also said, "Blessed be the LORD, the God of Shem; and let Canaan be his servant. May God enlarge Japheth, and let him dwell in the tents of Shem, and let Canaan be his servant." (Gen. 9:20-27 NASB)

The curse that Noah spoke against Canaan was related to the nature of the crime that Canaan's father, Ham, had committed against his own father, Noah. Ancient and modern interpreters have found in the expression "saw the nakedness" an act of homosexuality. However, the phrases "to see nakedness" and "uncover nakedness" are figures of speech referring to heterosexual relations not homosexual acts (e.g., Lev. 18:6-19; 20:10-21). Moreover, the reaction of the two sons in covering up their father's nakedness shows us that the expression is not a figure of speech but a recounting of Noah's literal nakedness.

What then was the severity of the crime? Ancient cultures understood the act by Ham as a heinous offense. He dishonored his father by ridiculing him publicly. For this reason Noah condemned Ham by shaming his son, Canaan—thus, a parallel between Noah and his son Ham. Ham's crime was a transgression against what later was codified in the fifth commandment, "Honor your father and your mother" (Exod. 20:12). Dishonor against a person's parents called for execution in ancient Israel (Exod. 21:15, 17).

The author also created a literary echo of the sin committed by the serpent against Adam, whose nakedness was shameful in the garden (Gen. 3:6, 11–13). Thus, the crime of Ham may be likened to the sin of the serpent. The cohesion of the Noahic family and thus postdiluvian humanity fractured as a result. The brothers were set on a course of warfare and servitude. This is reminiscent of Adam's family whose son Cain murdered his brother, Abel.

The special interest of the Israelites in the inhabitants of their possession, the land of Canaan, explains why the curse against Canaan was particularly relevant to their setting. History shows that the relationship between the Canaanites and Israelites was a struggle for supremacy. At the rise of David's monarchy, however, the Israelites achieved the upper hand and broke the influence of the Canaanites in the land.

Was it right that Noah cursed Canaan when it was Canaan's father, Ham, who transgressed? Did Israel take this prayer as license for committing genocide against the peoples of Canaan? On the face of it, Canaan appears to have had no part in the matter. Some interpreters have theorized that Canaan must have had a role in making the incident known. The Bible teaches that people suffer for their own crimes and not that of their parents or of another person (Deut. 24:16; cf. Ezek. 18), but there is another principle at work here. Because of the social cohesion that characterized family life, children tended to imitate their parents' behaviors. Corporate personality was an accepted idea. Parental influence typically held sway, it was thought, in deciding the future of a descendant. Morally, then, the failure of Ham most likely would recur among his lineage.

This proved true when the Israelites encountered the immorality of Ham's Canaanite descendants (e.g., Lev. 18 and 20). So bereft of moral civility were the Canaanites that the Lord judged Canaanite society and eventually broke their hold on the land. This was not genocide committed by Israel because of racial fear or ethnic supremacy; God made the sad pronouncement against his own covenant people for the same immorality. If the Israelites acted as decadently as their predecessors, they too would be expelled from the land (e.g., Lev. 18:28).[13] History shows that this happened to Israel in the eighth and seventh centuries B.C., and the nation never fully returned.

The Blessing of Ham?

The history of interpretation has shown that the "curse of Ham," as it was called, was used as biblical justification for grievous crimes against black-skinned ethnic groups. Edwin Yamauchi said it well when he observed, "No other verse in the Bible has been so distorted and so disastrously used down through the centuries for the exploitation of Africans and African Americans."[14]

When most readers of the Bible today think of "Ham," they probably equate his descendants with the populations of black-skinned Africans. Also, we don't first think of Africans historically as people of blessing. But Keith Burton, in his volume *The Blessing of Africa*, breaks through these stereotypes by showing that members of Ham's descendants settled in areas beyond the continent of Africa, including countries of the Middle East.[15] The title, *The Blessing of Africa*, has two sides. The first is the idea that Africans were the recipients of God's blessing. The reverse side is that as the recipients of blessing they were also the conduit of blessing. This corresponds to the Abrahamic blessing, which concludes, "and all the families of the earth will be blessed through you [Abraham]" (Gen. 12:3).

---

13. The Israelites are warned that they too will be "put under the ban" (i.e., destroyed) as were the cities of Canaan (e.g., Deut. 7:1-2) if they sinned in the same way (e.g., Deut. 7:26; Josh. 6:18).
14. Edwin M. Yamauchi, *Africa and the Bible* (Grand Rapids: Baker, 2004), 19.
15. Keith A. Burton, *The Blessing of Africa: The Bible and African Christianity* (Downers Grove, IL: InterVarsity, 2007).

On this latter aspect of blessing, Burton traces the importance of Christianity in the history of Africa and observes that African peoples were indeed major players in the early history of the church, especially North Africa. The Western church was indebted to the North African Augustine, the bishop of Hippo (fourth century A.D.). Before the inroads of Islam from the seventh century A.D., African peoples were receptive to the gospel. Today, dramatic changes are underway among African peoples as the rise of Christianity is reaching unimagined heights. To make this point, Burton asserts that "Africa soon will have the highest concentration of Christians in the world."[16]

We can point to the Bible itself to show that the blessing was intended for *all* of Noah's descendants: "And God blessed Noah and his sons and said to them, 'Be fruitful, and multiply, and fill the earth'" (Gen. 9:1; cf. 1:28). Isaiah's vision of a reconciled world, naming Israel's archenemies, is startling when he recounts God's future blessing: "Blessed is my people, Egypt, and the work of my hands, Assyria, and my inheritance, Israel" (Isa. 19:25; cp. Deut. 4:20).

Because many, though not all, of Ham's descendants were located in black Africa (Gen. 10:6–20), interpreters attributed the skin color of black Africans to the curse. If we measure by the geographical distribution of Ham's offspring, this is not even logically reasonable since his lineage included non-black African and Middle Eastern members. His sons were Cush, Mizraim (Egypt), Put, and Canaan. Cush and (perhaps) Put, whose location is uncertain, parented black Africans, but Cush's descendants included Arabian tribes and areas we know as the Middle East, including Nimrod's Babylon (Iraq) and Assyria (Syria) (10:8–12). Mizraim and Canaan's descendants were not black, though darker skinned than Caucasians (European, Asian).

If we understand that the biblical reference "Mizraim" included parts of modern Sudan, at least on a geographical basis, this would include black-skinned peoples. The descendants of Mizraim (Gen. 10), however, are not confidently located, and the origin of the Egyptians

---

16. Ibid., 16.

is disputed.[17] Canaan's descendants lived in what today are contemporary Israel, "Palestinian" areas, Jordan, Iraq, and Lebanon.[18]

More importantly, nothing in Genesis suggests even vaguely that the "curse" entailed a skin color alteration or any distinctive ethnic or physical feature. As in the case of Cain, the passage focuses on the behavior of the offender, not a genetic biological trait. Racist interpretations—either specific or inferential—contradict the clear teaching in Scripture regarding the equal value of every human being created in the image of God. They also conflict with New Testament teaching.

As in the case of Cain, we must ask how a misreading of the "curse of Ham" could have originated and gained such currency in Europe and America. Goldenberg's historical study shows that the key to understanding is the combination of two factors: slavery and blackness.[19] The idea of slavery is decidedly in the Ham story, but blackness was not a natural feature of the story. Therefore, it was gradually introduced into the story and reached its acceptance in coincidence with the increasing connection of Africa and the slave trade in the Near East. Although slavery through conquest was not selective, a prolific number of Africans became slaves, and blackness and slavery were commonly associated.

What further fueled the association was the commonly believed etymology of the Hebrew word "Ham," which was thought to be derived from Semitic roots that mean "dark," "black," or "hot." Here we have a combination of features coming together, says Goldenberg. Since Canaan's descendants were located in the hotter regions of Africa and Arabia, it was easy to combine the notions of black and hot. Moreover, the word for "hot" had sexual implications. This coincided with the legend that Africans were unusually sexual in their nature. Modern philological studies have not convincingly shown the etymology of "Ham," and therefore we are on safer ground to say that the etymology of the term is not and probably never will be known with certainty.

Goldenberg did not discover signs of the "curse of Ham" myth

---

17. J. Daniel Hays, *From Every People and Nation: A Biblical Theology of Race* (Downers Grove, IL: InterVarsity, 2003), 39–42, concludes that the original Egyptians were "probably a mix of Asiatic and Black African," 45.

18. Burton, *The Blessing of Africa*, 19.

19. Our following comments draw on many different sections in Goldenberg's study. He offers a succinct statement as his conclusion on pages 195–200.

in the early post-biblical period among Jews and Christians. Not until the seventh century did the "curse of Ham" tradition appear in Christian Syriac and Muslim Arabic. As the African slave market became a reality, first in Europe by the fifteenth century and then in America by the seventeenth century, the idea of Canaan's perpetual slavery and black skin color was taken up. Jewish writings followed suit in Europe, making all three major religious bodies purveyors of the fiction. This tradition was imposed on the biblical account to justify the flourishing slave market.

One of the arresting observations made by Goldenberg was the pervasiveness with which the myth had become dogma. Proslavery and abolitionists accepted it, and African American authors also passed it on along with the "Cain was black" myth.

In conclusion, the biblical evidence and the early centuries of late antiquity show no efforts to denigrate others on the basis of ethnicity or skin color. It was not until the seventh century when there appeared among Muslims a clear acceptance of the matrix of "slave and black African." It took 1300 years before the myth was exposed for what it was, but the damage done by the folklore still lives.

WHAT THE STORY TELLS US

According to our understanding of God's reconciliation for his creation, four fundamental teachings undergird the remainder of what the Bible tells us about his plan.

First, human beings are creatures. God "alone has immortality" (1 Tim. 6:16), meaning that God in his essence has immortality (cf. 1 Tim. 1:17).[20] Christians *receive* immortality as a consequence of faith in Christ who bestows immortality at the resurrection of the body (2 Tim. 1:10; 1 Cor. 15:53). The importance of this for the story of reconciliation is that all men and women as creatures have a derived value by virtue of their dependent relationship with their Creator. No person has an inherent value apart from the benevolence of God ("image of God"), and this means no person can count

---

20. George W. Knight III, *The Pastoral Epistles*, NIGTC (Grand Rapids: Eerdmans, 1992), 269-71.

himself or herself more worthy than another person. The apostle Paul urged his readers to consider others' interests above their own and to consider others "more significant" (Phil. 2:3–4). He pointed to Christ, who took on the form of a human servant despite his right to display his deity (2:5–11).

Second, God gave the human family the charge to exercise rule over the lower creatures, not to rule over one another. The passage shows that a human was not charged to exercise dominion over another human in the same way that humanity was to rule over the terrestrial sphere. Human oppression denies the Creator his rightful due as the Master Designer. Freedom is a creation blessing, and we must strive to preserve it where possible.

Third, creation in the image of God was for *all* humanity, both male and female. Although we may not know definitively what the "image" is, we can confidently conclude the following: *If you are human, you are created in God's image. If you are created in God's image, you are human.* This applies to all individuals and people groups without prejudice: male and female, young and old, the intellectually capable and incapable, the physically sound and impaired, and *all* people groups (cf. Gal. 3:28). All persons have the responsibility and privilege of exercising dominion as their divine assignment. But no one person or group can achieve this. We need one another. The differences among the collage of humanity must not distract us from our unity as the "image of God."

Finally, God's plan of reconciliation includes those who have been marginalized or discarded by society. The so-called cursed peoples were not intended for perpetual "curse," for God has a blessing for them, and he is carrying this out perfectly through the gospel of Jesus Christ and his church. If we have a disparaging attitude toward, or if we mistreat a person or a people group, we fail to acknowledge the Lord as our Master Designer.

THOUGHT PROVOKERS

1. What steps can your church take to "recover" the Bible's teaching on human dignity?

2. Why are racial stereotypes destructive to God's plan for racial integration? What are some of the racial stereotypes that you have heard from your youth? Why do we sometimes hang onto them?

3. How can your church provide opportunities for people to join in the worship of God across ethnic lines?

4. How and why do we sometimes fail to appreciate the worth of human life?

5. How would you respond to someone who resurrects the erroneous interpretation of the "curse of Ham"?

6. What is so wrong with human nature that suspicion of and hatred for others, especially those who are not like us, is common?

7. How has the Lord provided a path to reconciliation among members of fractured humanity?

Chapter 2

God's Blessing for *All* Nations

GENEALOGIES AND FAMILY MIGRATIONS are important to all of us because they tell us where we came from and in part who we are. This is why people whose past has been lost or forgotten desire a history to provide a "centering" in the world. My father's family moved from Mississippi to Texas to find work during the depths of the Great Depression in the 1930s. Typically, families move because of threat or trauma, such as economic necessity, war, captivity, or escape from prosecution or persecution. Others move for adventure or to make a better life. The Bible attributes the emergence of nations to a confluence of factors, including pride and linguistic chaos. The family joke in the Mathews clan is that somewhere between Mississippi and Texas a "t" was lost in our name. The Mississippi branch spells our name "Matthews," and the Texas branch spells it "Mathews." My brother's genealogical research led him to conclude that the Texas version is the authentic spelling. I don't think the Mississippi folk were convinced!

The contemporary craze in America regarding oral and genealogical history was fueled by the TV mini-series *Roots* (1977), which was based on Alex Haley's prize-winning novel by the same name (1976). The book tells the story of Haley's family based on oral family memories and his research. Haley proposed that his African-American family's roots could be traced to Kunta Kinte, a boy captured by slave traders and sent to America on a slave ship from his native Africa.

If we seriously pursue avenues of racial integration in American society and in the church in particular, we have to look at the broad historical context of who we are and how we came to be neighbors.

That we humans are absorbed with discovering our past has been shown again in The Genographic Project, popularized in the *The Human Family Tree* produced by the National Geographic Channel.[1] As the project's name indicates, the attempt is made on the basis of DNA samples from around the world to trace the migratory movements of the human population from its common birthplace (East Africa) and to explain the genetic makeup of the world's various ethnic groups. Readers may or may not be sympathetic to the presuppositions regarding societal evolution and concomitant theories of migratory patterns, but what is important for us to recognize is that knowing our origins is crucial to understanding our racial relationships in light of history. Genealogies and various ethnic listings were common in antiquity. The Hebrews had their national history and traced the fathers back to their beginnings in the context of the world of nations. By the genealogies of Noah's three sons in the Table of Nations (Gen. 10), the Israelites could locate themselves in terms of their relationship to others.

The Human Dilemma and the Nations

We discussed in the previous chapter that God had inaugurated the creation plan to bless the human family and was not deterred despite the disobedience of the man and the woman in the Garden of Eden. What had been fractured, he would repair through a Deliverer born of the woman (Gen. 3:15). Despite encroaching sin in all the earth (6:1–8), the Lord's mercy was extended by delivering a remnant of the first creation through Noah and the inhabitants of his ark (Gen. 6–8). Again, however, we met with the sad tale of the continuing sin of humankind by the sin and its consequences for his sons (9:20–27). Noah and his family replicated Adam's sin. The human dilemma of sin continued among the nations who were the offspring of Noah's three sons.

But the Lord blessed the "new Adam" and his sons as he had the first Adam (9:1). To demonstrate this hope, the author of Genesis constructed his narrative to make prominent the descendants of one of the

---

1. *The Human Family Tree*, National Geographic Channel (2009), http://channel.nationalgeographic.com/channel/human-family-tree, accessed September 17, 2009.

brothers, Shem, from whom the family of Father Abraham descended. God's promise of blessing for all humanity would be facilitated through one family, the offspring of Abraham. By means of creating a nation, God brought salvation to all people groups. In this episode we see the tapestry woven by God as the Master Designer. The plurality of the nation groups still possessed a unity by virtue of their common human nature. The people who made up the nations were created in the image of God, receiving their value from the Lord God.

The different identities of the people groups were not subsumed under one privileged ethnicity, such as under the Israelites. The nations maintained their distinctive histories. This is the principle of *diversity* that we discussed in the chapter on creation. The unity of the peoples of the nations resides in their common parentage and, more importantly, their shared creatureliness and personhood. The continuing challenge for nations today is to discover what they can draw on to maintain unity without sacrificing their distinctive purposes and contributions. The resolution is at an unexpected level—not in global economy, common language, united politic—but in the unity bestowed through the lordship of Jesus Christ. Our ideological commitment to Jesus is what transforms and undergirds a true kinship not hindered by geography or language.

Creation Blessing and the Nations

That God determined the identity and the number of the nations is reflected in the New Testament as well as the Old when the apostle Paul argues that "From one man he [God] made every nation of people to dwell upon all the face of the earth, having determined set times and fixed boundaries for where they live" (Acts 17:26). Unfortunately, this passage and the "curse of Ham" (Gen. 9:24–27) spurred the attempt to distinguish superior and inferior people groups. The assumption was that God had established the locations of peoples and thereby predetermined their social and moral standings. In the mid-nineteenth century, clergyman F. A. Ross published *Slavery Ordained of God* (1857) in which he contended that geographical locality of groups, such as those in Africa, were inferior to those whose origins were in Asia and Europe, when he argued, "That

Europe, indented by the sea on every side, with its varied scenery, and climate, and Northern influences makes the varied intellect, the versatile power and life and action, of the master-man of the world."[2] In *Earth and Man* (1849), noted French geologist and cartographer A. H. Guyot proposed a correlation of physical geology and climate with a people group's social and moral character, concluding,

> It results from this remarkable distribution of the races of man, that the continents of the North, forming the central mass of the lands, are inhabited by the finest races, and present the most perfect types; while the continents of the South, forming the extreme and farsundered points of the lands, are exclusively occupied by the inferior races, and the most imperfect representatives of human nature.[3]

Strikingly, Guyot is not malicious in his intention; rather, he used his study to prod his readers who were of the favored regions (Europe and North America) to assist the rise of the less favored.

We will discover, however, that the Table of Nations does not in any way indicate that God has unalterably determined the moral nature of the nations. It does not suggest that God has ordained certain groups to achieve greatness and others to follow behind or serve the interests of the superior peoples. The Table of Nations tells us, on the contrary, that God's creation blessing is for *all* nations. The table's picture of a numerous and dispersed human family corresponds to the Creator's intent for human life (Gen. 1:28: 9:1). Even the classic enemies of Israel appear in the table (e.g., Egyptians).

THE NATIONS: CURSE OR BLESSING

There is no small irony in the name of this institution: "United Nations" (UN). The nations that convene in the General Assembly,

---

2. F. A. Ross, *Slavery Ordained of God* (Philadelphia: Lippincott, 1857), 50–51.
3. A. H. Guyot, *The Earth and Man: Lectures on Comparative Physical Geography in its Relation to the History of Mankind*, trans. C. C. Felton (Boston: Gould and Lincoln, 1860), 262.

192 member states, are hardly united when it comes to most global matters. It begs the question, "Why is the number of UN-sponsored peacekeeping operations as many as sixteen (as of this writing)?"[4] We do not mean to disparage the purpose of the UN, whose founding in 1947 was to promote international peace. The sad reality is that world peace requires "promotion" at the tune of an annual budget of 4.171 billion dollars (2008-2009 budget, not including the peacekeeping operations whose annual budgets vary significantly). Although we applaud any effort to achieve peaceful international relations and to serve as a watchdog on international crimes, such as slave trade and genocide, the task cannot be realized fully because of the inherent nature of the people who make up the nations. Peace is cheaper, but war satisfies the human appetite for power and oppression. Peace satisfies the nobler spirit in us, but rarely do we humans rise to it.

The biblical story of reconciliation between people groups begins with the origin of the nations whose inception was the result of willful rebellion against God's purpose of blessing. The divine blessing involved procreation but also included geographical dominion in order for humanity to exercise rule over the world. God's blessing was re-issued to Noah after the flood catastrophe: "Then God blessed Noah and his sons and said to them, 'Be fruitful and multiply and fill the earth'" (Gen. 9:1). The Babelites, who had congregated on the plain of Shinar (Babylonia), chose to cluster around the Tower of Babel in a defiant coalition against God's command instead of disseminating around the globe. Ironically, the nations' formation and fragmentation began in entrenched unity.

The narrative of Genesis 10-11 consists of three major parts: the Table of Nations (Gen. 10), the Tower of Babel (11:1-9), and the genealogy of Shem (11:10-21). The Table of Nations occurs first, and the explanation of the emergence of the nations follows (11:1-9), with reports of the building of the city Babel and its tower. In other words, the arrangement of the chapters produces a *dis*chronologized timeline, placing the consequences before the cause. The cause for

---

4. The number sixteen does not include peace-building missions in nations recovering from warfare that are administered by another UN commission office. http://www.un.org/en/peacekeeping/bnote.htm#minurso (accessed 3 July 2009).

the breakup at the tower was the pride that the Babelites flaunted. Although the explanation for the world's dispersed nations (11:1-9) is essential, the author is looking forward. The resolution is in the Shem genealogical record, for it ends by pointing to his descendant Abraham (11:26). He arranged the stories out of temporal sequence so that the outcome of and the resolution to the disunity among the nations are highlighted. It is with the tower story, however, that we begin, which logically explains the division of the nations.

The Tower of Pride

The builders of the tower at Babel constructed it to impress future generations with their autonomy, ingenuity, and ability. But for the author of Genesis and his readers, it held significance only as a tribute to human pride.

After the sons of Noah disembarked from the ark (Shem, Ham, and Japheth), the brothers produced offspring who remained united in a common cause. They wanted to establish "a name" for themselves (11:4a). On the face of it, the reader is troubled, because the mention of the word "name" reverberates the rebellious sentiment first expressed in the Garden of Eden. Wisdom in the ancient world was greatly sought and generally believed to be a divine possession. The garden residents desired wisdom apart from God (Gen. 3:5-6). The temptation in the garden was planted in the couple's minds by the satanic serpent who got them to doubt God's goodness by suggesting that God was withholding wisdom and eternal life from them. Coupled with the Babelites' desire to make "a name" (recognition) was their determination to remain unified geographically around the tower—a unity generated by fear. We are reminded again of the ugly past. Cain was troubled by fear of isolation (4:14), and the Babelites desired the security that a uniform humanity provided (11:4b). The cohabitation of the peoples in the same location at Shinar was emblematic of the uniform viewpoint and goals that they held in common.

You may ask, "Isn't the unity of nations what your book is campaigning for?" Yes and no. Genuine unity must be predicated upon a commitment to the Lord God, not based on anything or anyone else. Otherwise, the unity is circumstantial, which means that it is superficial and fragile. When the Lord "came down to see" their building efforts, he observed their cooperative efforts and was alarmed at what sinful endeavors a unified humanity could accomplish. The language "see" reminds us of the flood narrative when the "LORD saw that the wickedness of man was great" (6:4). This is the understanding that we should give to the Babel event. In God' eyes, the building of the city and its tower was motivated by self-serving ambition. The author's way of telling the Babel incident lampoons the puny efforts of these urban planners. Their goal of reaching to the heavens (11:4) is satirized when the story says that God "came down" to investigate their bustling activity (v. 5). Their goal was a feeble effort in comparison with God's truly towering magnitude. He created linguistic havoc, which in turn led to the progressive dispersal of the Babelites geographically into various people groups. What they had hoped to avoid became their destiny—they scattered over the face of the earth.

Once they set a common goal, their industry could accomplish almost anything. The story does not denigrate human industry or innovation; it only condemns the wicked motivation of the Babelites. But what does independent, autonomous, determined humanity accomplish? With the modern marvels of human ingenuity comes the inevitable corruption of invention. The power unleashed by splitting the atom resulted in the creation of weaponry that can destroy millions and pollute the earth for generations to come. Unity based on the human spirit, without regard to divine accountability, cannot be left to its own devices, lest the world meet with self-inflicted destruction. A completely secular (nontheistic) endeavor has no moral base to transcend cultural prerogatives. Medical ethicists face this problem when considering the social questions of our times as science progresses faster than moral persuasions (e.g., cloning, stem cell research, end of life). Racial bigotry has also been rife with immoral standards that do not answer to higher Authority. Oppressive regimes and movements typically make up their standards of conduct on the basis of self-interests and power.

The Pride of the Nations

The fall of the Babelites was their pride, which was the chief sin of the nations. Repeatedly, the Hebrew poets and prophets decried the pride of the nations, including the people of Israel when they defied the word of the Lord (e.g., Ps. 10:4; Isa. 2:12; Jer. 48:29; Ezek. 28:2; Amos 6:8). The tower narrative is a parody on the pride of the nations. In the Babylonian creation myth, known as the *Enuma Elish*, demigods constructed a sanctuary of bricks for the chief deity Marduk. The specific reference to the technology of brick masonry in Genesis 11 mimics the industry of the Babylonians, whereas in Canaan, stones were the building material. As a final jab at the nations, their striving for "a name" leads only to the despicable name "Babel," which means in Hebrew just that—"babble, confusion." The Hebrew text creates a play on the words "Babel" (*babel*) and "confusion" (*balal*) (11:9). The Babylonian myth describes the origin of the city Babylon as divinely inspired and built. The name "Babylon" meant in the Akkadian language "gate of the gods."

But in the biblical account, the city was anything but a divine achievement. The story emphasizes that the builders were no more than mortal people (lit., "sons of men," 11:5). The Babelites forever would be known for their confusion, not their achievements. Verses 1 and 9, which bracket the story, pointedly present the irony of the story's outcome by the repetition of the phrase "whole earth." The "whole earth" that had "one language and one speech" (v. 1) now was scattered upon the face of the "whole earth" by the confusion of the "language of the whole earth" (v. 9). Independence from moral restraints was reversed by divine intervention.

The Theology of Geography

The Table of Nations reflects a "theology of geography." It lists the distribution of the nations primarily in terms of their ethnic and geographic features. We can learn about God's plan for the reconciliation of all peoples when we are attuned to the message of the Table of Nations. We learn important theological lessons from the literary features of the story.

The most important feature of the Table of Nations is its ethno-geographic nature.[5] The listing identifies the ethnicity of Noah's

---

5. D. J. Wiseman, ed., "Introduction: Peoples and Nations" in *Peoples of Old*

descendants in terms of their geographical distribution. The table is unique from other genealogical and ethnic listings in the ancient world. It is a complex and diverse collection that puzzles scholars. Nevertheless, our present knowledge is sufficient to understand the essential factors that underlie the list, enabling us to hear its theological message. Genealogies are constructed for the living, not the dead. The purpose of the table is not only to satisfy the author's antiquarian interests but also to communicate a message for the Israelites as they prepare to enter the land of Canaan.

The structure of the table consists of three parts: (1) the descendants of Japheth (10:2-5); (2) Ham (10:6-20); and (3) Shem (10:21-31). The geographical distribution is wide-ranging. *The Macmillan Bible Atlas* depicts the three geographical arcs reflected in the table, with the intersection of the three arcs appearing at the land of Canaan.[6] We can summarize the three geographical spheres as these:

- The lineage of Japheth is located fundamentally in Asia Minor (modern Turkey) and Europe.

- The Hamites settled in ancient Canaan (e.g., Israel and Palestine), Egypt, and other parts of Africa, Mesopotamia (such as modern Iraq), and parts of the Arabian Peninsula.

- The geography of the Shemites included northern sites of Mesopotamia, Syria, and also parts of Arabia.

More attention in the table is given to the Hamite and Shemite lines since Israel had far more contact with them than with Japheth's descendants.

We are wrong to think of the list as a solely genealogical record of individuals—fathers and their children. The selection of the nations listed is based on diverse criteria: "lands," "families," "languages,"

Testament Times (Oxford: Clarendon, 1973), xv–xxi, discusses this feature of the table.

6. Y. Aharoni and M. Avi-Yonah, *The Macmillan Bible Atlas*, rev. ed. (New York: Macmillan, 1977), 15.

and "nations" (Gen. 10:5, 20, 31). Also, the collection includes individuals (e.g., Nimrod, 10:8-12), people groups (e.g., Jebusites, 10:16), and geographical locations (e.g., Mizraim [Egypt], 10:13). The language "sons of" and "father of" in the Bible is not always to be taken literally as direct offspring. For example, the person Salma is said to be the "father" of the town Bethlehem (1 Chron. 2:51). Sidon (Gen. 10:15, 19) may name an individual or the Phoenician city that bore his name. The word "daughters" was used to refer to "villages" that were attached to a major urban site (e.g., Num. 21:25). The word "metropolis," meaning "mother city" in ancient Greece, referred originally to a state or city that produced dependent colonies. We do not mean there is *no* genealogical connection between the entities named, for the table presupposed that there were real familial relationships involved. Nonetheless, the precise familial linkage may not have been uppermost in the mind of the author, who thought chiefly of the economic and political ties that resulted.

Another important aspect of the table is its limitations. It does not attempt to name every people group. The table's nations are representative of the whole. This is shown in two ways. First, the table implies this. The phrase "islands of the nations" (Gen. 10:5) describes unnamed distant places that emerged from the Japhethites named in verses 2-4. Second, the table's total number of nations is seventy, which, as a multiple of seven and ten, may be symbolic of "completeness" (e.g., Gen. 46:27; Deut. 32:8).[7] A noticeable feature is the absence of the name "Israel" in the list. This is because the whole of the table is told from the perspective of and assumption of Israel's settlement in Canaan. In other words, since the Israelites were the intended audience, Moses could assume that they would include themselves. Moreover, Genesis 11:10-26 lists Abraham's ancestors. Also, the count of seventy members may reflect the importance of seventy in the history of Israel. Seventy descendants of Jacob took up residence in Egypt (Gen. 46:27; Exod. 1:5). Israel was represented by seventy elders in its desert sojourn (Exod. 24:1, 9). The table may

---

7. The count of seventy names is achieved by omitting the individual "Nimrod," or more likely omitting the name "Philistines," which is a parenthetical aside (Gen. 10:14).

be arranged with seventy nations to reflect the organization of Israel (Deut. 32:8).8 In other words, the nations were created in the image of Israel.

The theological significance of this is staggering. Rather than Israel and the nations isolated and at enmity, Israel and the nations are destined for integration. Israel will have a ministry to the nations who will eventually take on the character of Israel's special relationship with the Lord.

A Theological Compass

Although the table is historically important and accurately reflects the complexities of the nations' identities and relationships, its theological message is the focus of the writer's attention. The background information and historical specifics were designed to establish the framework for the theological significance of God's work in history. The authors of Scripture wrote "theological history"—God's viewpoint on historical events. The Bible's authors believed that historical events had a divine *telos* (end, goal). The table's preamble (Gen. 9:20-27) is the key to understanding the theological message of the table. It describes the curse and blessing that Noah sought for his three descendants. The table provided theological and moral pictures that enabled the Israelites to understand the world into which they were born as a nation. The theological message of the table is God's purpose to bless every nation through a newly created nation descended from Shem (Gen. 10:21-31 with 11:10-26). God did not cancel his creation blessing for humanity despite the scandalous sin in the garden; rather, he bestowed them anew upon Noah and his sons (Gen. 9:1). *All* of the sons of Noah, including Ham and Japheth, received God's blessing and commission. This blessing was based on creation and was expressed through the universal covenant

---

8. Deuteronomy 32:8 may make an explicit connection between Israel and the number of nations in the table. God established the number of nations "according to the number of the sons of Israel." There is however a different textual reading in the Greek Old Testament: "according to the number of the sons of God" (i.e., angels) (see NRSV, ESV, NLT).

established by God with the post-flood families of Noah and all creatures (9:1–17).

A Moral Compass

The moral dimension of the table is anticipation of the moral
behaviors of the three sons' descendants. By "moral behaviors" we
mean the different moral *choices* made by the sons, not that the sons
had inherent moral qualities that were inevitably passed down from
one generation to another. Rather, the basis for judging moral character was individual moral decisions (Jer. 31:27–30; Ezek. 18). We
addressed this issue in the previous chapter when we examined the
story of Ham's curse (Gen. 9:20–27). Ham chose to act defiantly
against his father, whereas Japheth and Shem exhibited wisdom and
deference by honoring Noah as their father. Noah called for retaliation in a divine curse against Ham's son Canaan. The incident was a
microcosm of what their descendants proved to be like. As mentioned
in the previous chapter, the ancient tradition of family solidarity helps
us interpret the moral relationship of an ancestor and his descendants. Parental behavior, such as child abuse or addictions, often re-
curs in subsequent generations until the social and psychological cycle
is broken. The assumption was that the Canaanites would make the
same deviant choices as had their ancestor Ham. This was proven true
in the case of the Canaanites whose godless culture was the most immediate threat to the Hebrew people's fidelity to God (Gen. 15:16b;
Lev. 18, 20).

The issue was not God's disdain for certain ethnic peoples and
his subsequent judgment that doomed certain groups to an inferior
intellectual and moral status. God did not show favor toward Israel
because of its superior knowledge or special God-given abilities (cf.
Deut. 7:1, 6–9, 17; 9:1, 4–5; 11:23). God's continued grace toward Israel was conditioned on its conduct, not ethnicity alone, for
the Hebrews were also subject to God's judgment if they acted as
wickedly as the Canaanites whom they had supplanted (Deut. 8:20;
18:9–12; 28:15, 37; cf. Lev. 18:28). Israel's history demonstrated
that when Israel acted wickedly they too were expelled by the Lord at
the hands of foreign enemies.

Summary

We have said that the purpose of the table was to orient the Israelites to the nations with whom they would come into contact. Especially important was the theological message showing that the sin at Babel affected all peoples. All were in need of salvation, and God set about to achieve this through Abraham. We might say that God had to save the nations from themselves by dispersing them. The same can be said for the nations today. Left to ourselves without restraints we would bring about cataclysmic self-destruction. God had a remedy for the divided nations, a blessing for all peoples—including the archenemies of Israel, such as Egypt, Assyria, and Babylon, which are named in the list. The list of seventy nations represents all peoples and conveys that all peoples are the objects of God's love and salvation. The table also warned the Israelites to avoid the moral decadence of the Canaanite culture.

The racist idea that peoples were predetermined to be superior or inferior based on divine selection does not reflect the purpose of the table or correlate with what actually occurred in the history of Israel.

The New "Babel"

The very mention of Babel brings to mind the reputation of the Babelites as disobedient and proud. But we wish to turn the word "Babel" on its head by speaking of a "new" language. The people at Babel possessed one language (Gen. 11:1, 9) and worked harmoniously to achieve a unifying goal. Their wrongdoing was building the city and its tower for their own selfish gain. But the "new Babel" is a unity that is *bestowed*. Those who make up the "new Babel" have received a unifying purpose that transcends human circumstances or barriers such as race, language, and culture. Their unity is for the higher purpose of serving the one Lord God, the Father of our Lord Jesus Christ. That unity is the gift of the Holy Spirit, who can be received only by the bestowal of God. The result is "the bond of peace" (Eph. 4:3). As the apostle Paul explained, "There is one body and one spirit, just as also you were called to one hope of your calling—one Lord, one faith, one baptism, one God and Father of all, who is over all and through all and in all" (Eph. 4:4-6). This unity is founded upon a common redemption, the creation of a new people who hold to a common devotion to the Lord Jesus Christ.

Acts 2 depicts the redemptive response of God to the fragmentation of the nations at Babel. The Holy Spirit came upon the congregated apostles and disciples in Jerusalem during the annual Jewish celebration of Pentecost. The Jews and Gentile proselytes who had gathered for the Feast were pilgrims from the scattered nations. Many of those nations and regions named in the Acts account are listed in the Table of Nations. Luke's report on this momentous founding of the church by the baptism of the Holy Spirit is a literary echo of the events at the Tower of Babel. The gospel of Jesus Christ as preached by the apostle Peter and the founding of the church on that day formed a community that rose above the languages and cultures of the nations represented by the celebrants at Pentecost. Although the apostles received the same Spirit in the name of the same Lord, they spoke the gospel in languages that were indigenous to the countries of the pilgrims (Acts 2:11). The Spirit overcame the diversity of languages, not by creating one language but by announcing the gospel through assorted languages. The cacophony of so many different dialects produced such aural confusion that bystanders thought the Christians were drunk on wine. The nations and their languages did not become one ethnic people speaking a *lingua franca* (a common language).

Belief in the message that the pilgrims heard in their native tongues created a uniquely "new people." The glue that held the people together was their devotion to Jesus as savior. They communally received the instruction of the word of God and worshipped the Lord in a gathered body (Acts 2:41-47). What melded them together was the saving grace and lordship of Jesus Christ. The call for the church today is to provide a place where genuine solidarity in the communion of the saints is a transformative factor in the local and national communities that they serve. *This is what makes church, the church.*

CREATING A NATION FOR THE NATIONS

Racial profiling has been a source of racial distrust. The rhetoric stepped up when the celebrated Harvard professor Dr. Henry

Louis Gates Jr. was arrested for disorderly conduct (subsequently the charges were dropped) at his own home. He and his driver were struggling with the back door to enter his home upon his return from a trip overseas. A neighbor called the police thinking that a burglary was underway. The stories by the arresting white officer and the African-American scholar differed significantly, and no one will know with certainty exactly what was said. Supporters of the professor contended that racial profiling was the cause of the disturbance. Friend and fellow Harvard professor Lawrence Bobo commented, "Ain't nothing postracial about the United States of America."[9] And those who supported the arresting officer argued that he followed procedure and was anything but a rogue cop. Such are the diverse viewpoints among us when we consider life's experiences—baggage from the ugly past. If you have never been intimidated by an officer, it is hard to accept that it happens. If you have been a victim of profiling based on skin color or know a family member who has been, then it is easy to attribute all incidents to racist motives.

Chosen for a Purpose

The history of the Jewish people shows that they were at times guilty of bigotry and at other times were victims of it. We suppose the same could be said about any people group that rubs shoulders with another. We need only mention the expression "chosen people" and the issue of profiling comes front and center. Understanding the place of Abraham and his descendants as a privileged people must be set in the proper context.

First, it is true that biblical texts refer to Abraham and Israel as the chosen people of God. The explicit statement "my chosen people" occurs only in Isaiah 43:20, but the sentiment is well documented in the Old and New Testaments (e.g., 1 Kings 3:8; Pss. 33:12; 105:6, 63; 106:5; Isa. 43:20; 45:4; 65:9, 15, 22; Acts 10:41; 1 Peter 2:9). The Lord fondly called Abram his "friend" (Isa. 41:8; 2 Chron. 20:7; James 2:23), treating him as his confidant (Gen. 18:17–19), and

---

9. Lawrence Bobo, "Scholar Meets 'Postracial' America," *The Birmingham News*, July 26, 2009, 5F. His column was published in the Washington Post and republished in newspapers nationwide.

names Israel his "treasured possession" (e.g., Exod. 19:5). Israel is even identified as the "apple of [God's] eye" (Deut. 32:10; Zech. 2:8). Jesus distinguished Jews and Gentiles on occasions in his public ministry, such as in healing the daughter of a woman from Syrophoenicia (Mark 7:24–30 par.; cp. "a daughter of Abraham," Luke 13:16). When sending out the disciples to proclaim the kingdom, he forbade them from going to the Gentiles and Samaritans (Matt. 10:5–7). Yet, he commended those among the Gentiles who exhibited "great faith," such as the Syrophoencian woman (Matt. 15:25) and the centurion whose servant was healed (Matt. 8:10 par.). The apostle Paul plainly noted the profit of the Jewish people over the Gentiles: "What then is the advantage for the Jew? Or what is the benefit of circumcision? Greatly in every way. In the first place, the Jews were entrusted with the oracles of God" (Rom. 3:1–2).

Second, the election of Israel was not an end in itself. It was a means to serve the nations. The story of the rise of the nations ends with the genealogy of Shem whose offspring concludes with the name "Abram," the son of Terah (Gen. 11:26). The Lord promises Abraham a blessing that includes three features: land, a great nation, and blessing (12:1–3). The syntactical structure of the decree makes it clear that God will bless Abraham for the purpose of blessing all peoples. The initial phase of the blessing is focused on the individual Abraham by the use of the singular pronoun "you": thus, "I will bless you" (12:2).

The promise is expanded by the following clauses which turn the focus transitionally from Abraham the man to the role of Abraham the benefactor: "so that you will be a blessing" (12:2). Then the relationship between Abraham and the others is explored. Those who choose to receive Abraham as God's appointed servant will receive God's favor, but those who reject him will be cursed by the Lord (12:3ab). "Bless" and "curse" are technical covenant language, meaning that Abraham was the sole conduit of grace for those who desired to enter into a favored relationship with the Lord. In other words, only by means of Abraham's message could the nations come into right relationship with the Lord as Creator and Savior. And the finale of the covenant echoes the Table of Nations, "in you [Abram] all the families (*mishpekhot*) of the earth will be blessed" (12:3c) and "these are the families (*mishpekhot*) of the sons of Noah" (10:32; also 10:5, 18, 20, 31).

To reinforce the theological message, the author of Genesis arranges the telling of Abraham's family history to show that the patriarch was the necessary link in God's plan of reconciliation for the disbanded nations. There is an overlap in the stories of the Tower of Babel and the calling of Abraham as God's ambassador. This intersection occurs by repeating the genealogy of Shem twice, first in 10:21-31 and again in 11:10-26 (although in a different format).[10] Sandwiched between these is the Tower of Babel debacle (11:1-9).

Shem Genealogy	Tower of Babel	Shem Genealogy
10:21-31	11:1-9	11:10-26

This arrangement emphasized the Shem genealogy but also indicated that the Babel story was not the last word, so to speak. God set in place the series of events that would eventually come full circle, resulting in the salvation of those very nations who had experienced the disfavor of God. As mentioned above, this would occur through the line of Shem whose lineage ended in Abraham (11:10-26). The universal blessing for all humanity would be accomplished through the family of Abraham. Abraham's role was to serve the nations, integrating them into the one family of God. Abraham's story then is set in the wider context of the family of nations. If anything, we can think of his family as instrumental in facilitating God's favor toward the nations. If Israel failed to turn outward toward the full sweep of people groups, they would fail to achieve the purpose for their existence.

10. Genesis 10 is a "branched" form of genealogy that gives more than one descendant per generation; 11:10-26 presents the genealogy in a linear form which provides only one descendant for each generation (also Gen. 5). The linear form focuses on a single line of descendants, such as Adam's lineage through Seth (not Cain) and Noah's lineage through Seth (not Ham or Japheth). Together the two genealogies convey complementary messages. The branched form indicates inclusiveness and the linear form designates the specific line though whom God will achieve the salvation of all nations.

What's in a Name?

Another sleight of hand by the author was the play on the word "name." Later, the story tells of the change in name from "Abram" to the covenantal name "Abraham" (Gen. 17:5). The meaning of "Abram" is "father" (*ab*) and "exalted" (*ram*), which can be translated in different combinations, e.g., "exalted father" and "[my] father is exalted." The name "Abraham" is given an explanation in the text, "father of a multitude." By playing on the name "Abraham" the Lord declares that he will be the ancestor of "many nations." The purpose of the name change reinforced God's promise that he will make Abraham and Sarah "into a great nation" (12:2; 18:18). The prophet Isaiah acknowledged this centuries later when the Lord exhorted Israel, "Look to Abraham your father and Sarah who gave you birth, for he was but one when I called him, and I blessed him and made him numerous" (51:2). Although he had a small beginning, his progeny proliferated beyond counting. His future was bleak initially, for Sarah was barren (11:30), but Abraham believed the Lord's promise and afterward he and Sarah bore Isaac, the promised seed (15:6; 21:12).

That Abraham would be the ancestor of many people groups did not refer solely to the Hebrew people descended through the favored son, Isaac. Abraham was also the ancestor of other tribes, such as the Arab tribes of Ishmael and the Edomites through Esau (twin brother of Jacob). Moreover, after the death of Sarah, Abraham took Keturah as his wife, and she gave him six sons (Gen. 25:1-4; 1 Chron. 1:32-33) whose geographical locations are in the general area of the Arabian Peninsula. When we remember that the Lord promised Abraham that his firstborn Ishmael would also be the father of a great nation (Gen. 17:8; 21:18), we can appreciate more the significance of the name "Abraham—father of a multitude." Abraham was the ancestor of both the twelve Hebrew tribes and many non-Hebrew peoples.

The Gift of a Name

The literary arrangement of a second Shemite genealogy

following the Babel story communicates another message. It shows that the disgrace at Babel was followed by God's grace in providing for a righteous family. From the one family of Abraham would come the future savior of all nations. We know that the Lord also promised Abram that he would make his name great (Gen. 12:2). People today typically do not know the names of the powerful pharaoh or the kings of the east of Abraham's times, but they know the name Abraham. The three great religions of the Book—Judaism, Christianity, and Islam—trace their roots to Abraham. Yet much more is in view in our story when we see that there is a subtle play on the word "name." The tower builders hoped to make a "name" (*shem*) for themselves, that is, a reputation. But they sought this independently of the Lord. Ironically, God had already bestowed "Shem" (*shem*), meaning "name" (*shem*), on his lineage whereby he would raise up a "name" (*shem*) for Abraham (12:2). In Hebrew, the personal name "Shem" sounds like "name." From this person came Abram who *received* a name from the Lord. Divine bestowal, not selfish independence, was the plan whereby the nations might receive the blessings of God intended for all humanity. We see this in Abraham's descendant, Jesus. Jesus humbled himself, carrying out the Father's will. And by his perfect obedience, Jesus received from the Father the name "Lord," which is "the name above every name" (Phil. 2:9).

The story of reconciliation does not end with Abraham because we do not yet see the salvation that the promissory blessing in Genesis anticipated. We must look beyond Abraham to the history of his people to learn how God chose from the descendants of the patriarch a family of kings, the house of King David. In giving David this special commission, the Lord used the same language that he had spoken to Abraham centuries earlier, "I will make you [David] a great name" (2 Sam. 7:9). And we know from the New Testament writers that the messiah-king, who achieved the spiritual salvation of all peoples that believe, was the Lord Jesus Christ. We sometimes overlook that the New Testament begins with this all-important first announcement, "The book of the genealogy of Jesus Christ, the son of David, the son of Abraham" (Matt. 1:1). In Jesus resides the culmination of God's age-long plan of reconciliation.

Father Abraham

After hearing that my fourteen-year-old granddaughter's class in church had learned about the (near) sacrifice of Abraham's son, Isaac (Gen. 22), I asked, "Jessi, do you remember the song 'Father Abraham Had Many Sons'?" We sang it together, and I followed with the question, "Why do we call Abraham, 'Father Abraham'?" It gave me a chance to pursue an important theological truth in a simple way. Abraham is called the father of the Jews in the Bible (e.g., Acts 7:2), but he is not solely a biological ancestor. He is the spiritual father of those who place their faith in his descendant Jesus. "*We* are the children of Abraham!" I emphasized with Jessi.

The promissory blessing of Abraham has a direct spiritual application to the church. The apostle Paul referred to the promise as the "gospel foretold to Abraham" for the salvation of Jews and Gentiles (Gal. 3:8; cf. Rom. 4:17–18). Those who trust Christ are Abraham's spiritual descendants, "for it is those of faith who are the sons of Abraham" (Gal. 3:7; also Rom. 4:16). This is what God had in mind when he promised a future progeny for Abraham. The promise has been accomplished through Abraham's one perfect offspring, "who is Christ" (Gal. 3:16). By Abraham's descendant, Jesus, we are saved from our sin by virtue of a right relationship with him. Our spiritual kinship in the family of God is established through our kinship with Jesus, for "both the one who sanctifies and the ones who are sanctified, all are from one, for which reason he [Jesus] is not ashamed to call them brothers" (Heb. 2:11; Rom. 9:8). Thus we are given the global assignment, "go therefore and make disciples of all nations" (Matt. 28:19) and to serve as his witnesses "to the end of the earth" (Acts 1:8). If Jesus is not ashamed of us as brothers and sisters, how can we clash with a Christian brother and sister regardless of ethnic derivation if we claim we know God, for "if someone says, 'I love God,' but hates his brother, he is a liar!"(1 John 4:20)?

Abram the Hebrew

Since Abraham is the father of all who believe, what is the significance of his ethnicity as a "Hebrew"? One of the most common

oversights that readers of the Bible have regarding Abraham's ethnicity is his parentage. In the individual person of Abraham there
is a unique ethnic connection between the nations and the Hebrew
people. We know that Abraham's family migrated from Ur in the
southern Mesopotamian region, known as Chaldea, to the Upper
Mesopotamian city Haran (Gen. 11:28, 31; 15:7; Neh. 9:7; Acts
7:3-4). Although we don't know whether or not Abraham's actual
birthplace was Ur, we can be certain that his family connections are
Mesopotamian.[11] Abraham had Mesopotamian parents, meaning that
they were non-Hebrew; his family came from the members of the
"nations" listed in the Table of Nations. The location of the Tower
of Babel at Shinar was the general area from which Abraham migrated
to Haran (Gen. 10:10; 11:2). This geographical connection brings to
the fore the crisis that the Babel incident had created for the nations.
Abraham, who came from that same region, was God's answer to the
confusion that reigned among the nations. The patriarch Abraham
was God's essential link between universal humanity and the particular family of the Hebrews.

What was the source of the ethnic name "Hebrew"? And how
did it come to designate the family of Abraham? We should clarify the
meaning of the terms "Jew" and "Hebrew." The word "Jew" (*yehudi*)
derived from the word "Judah" (*yehudah*), who was a son of Jacob and
the ancestor of one of the twelve tribes of Israel ("Judahites," 2 Kings
16:6).[12] "Judah" also designated the southern region of Israel's land
which was geographically dominated by Judah's tribe. It became more
regularly used from the eighth century B.C. on. Outside the Bible it first
appears in Assyrian texts. The term came to refer to the descendants
of Abraham in general, especially during the Babylonian exile of the

---

11. The matter is the subject of scholarly discussion and need not concern us
in detail. It is sufficient to say that the Scriptures may point to two different
sites as the family's ancestral home—Ur in southern Mesopotamia (Gen.
11:28, 31; Neh. 9:7; Acts 7:3-4) and Haran in northern Mesopotamia
(Gen. 12:1; 24:4, 7). Moreover, it is further complicated by the meaning of
the Hebrew word *moledet* which is typically understood as "birthplace" or
"native land"; however, the term can be a general one for the place where
one's kinfolk lived without regard to a family's specific birthplace. Since
migratory patterns were common at that time, the Terah clan could have
migrated to Ur from other sites, even back and forth between Haran and Ur.
12. Most of the standard Bible dictionaries provide the information in our text.

sixth century and afterward. Judah was the chief tribe that was exiled, and its members made up the majority of the returning Jews (e.g., Ezra 6:14; Neh. 13:23). Also, it named the Jews who remained behind in Babylon and Persia (Esther 3:6). The terms "Jew" and "Hebrew" could be equated when referring to an ethnic body (e.g., Jer. 34:9; Acts 6:1; 2 Cor. 11:22). The "language of Judah/Judahite" referred to the Hebrew language (2 Kings 18:26, 28; Neh. 13:24).

"Hebrew" (*ibri*) has a complex history since it conveyed both an ethnic group and perhaps a social class.[13] The first use of the term in the Bible occurs in Genesis 14:13, where Abraham is distinguished from his ally "Mamre the Amorite." The origin of the word "Hebrew" is uncertain, but we do know how it was used in ancient sources. In the Bible, it typically is used as an ethnic marker, differentiating the Hebrew people group from others (e.g., Exod. 1:15–16). It was also useful to designate the homeland of the Hebrews (Canaan); when Joseph was in Egypt he named Canaan as "the land of the Hebrews" (Gen. 40:15). "Hebrew" could also refer to the Hebrew language, which was identified as the language of Judah (2 Kings 18:26). Perhaps "Hebrew" was also a term that functioned as a social designation apart from ethnicity. In some biblical passages the "Hebrews" appear to be differentiated from the "Israelites" (e.g., 1 Sam. 13:3, 6–7; 14:21; 29:3). The idea that the word could refer to a social class is built in part on the name *Habiru/Apiru* who were a social class of troublemakers for Canaanite chieftains during the late second millennium B.C. Since Abraham and Joseph were called "Hebrews" by non-Hebrews, such as the Philistines and the Egyptians, the word may have had at one time the idea of a migratory alien. This corresponds well with the constant reminder in the Bible that the fathers of Israel were foreigners to Canaan (e.g., Gen. 23:4; Exod. 6:4; Deut. 26:5).

The "Mark" of Covenant Blessing

The story of Abraham shows us that the Hebrews had their beginnings from among the nations, and that the nations in the

---

13. For a useful survey of the issues, see Eugene Merrill, *A Kingdom of Priests*, 2nd ed. (Grand Rapids: Baker Academic, 2008), 117–25.

land of Canaan considered Abraham and his family foreigners and aliens. In other words, they were "outsiders." The fathers did not claim ethnic superiority, and they exhibited tolerance toward other people groups (e.g., Philistine king Abimelech, Gen. 21:22-34). They did not set out to abolish cultural differences with the indigenous peoples of Canaan; rather, they acknowledged these differences. Especially important was their distinction as the recipients of God's promissory blessing. By accepting the mark of circumcision, Abraham and his household identified themselves as people in special relationship with *El Shaddai*, "God Almighty," the God of Abraham, Isaac, and Jacob (e.g., Gen. 17:1; 35:11-12; Exod. 6:3). Circumcision was not peculiar to the Hebrew people. It was practiced by others, notably the Egyptians as a puberty rite among young males. What differentiated the Hebrew practice of circumcision was its theological significance (Gen. 17). New meaning was given to the rite as a sign of covenant relationship. What is striking is its practice within the household of Abraham itself. Ishmael, the "also" son of Abraham, was the first to be circumcised in his family, even before the birth of Isaac (17:25-26). He too bore the mark of his father's covenant with God. Every male, whether native or nonnative, who identified with the household of Abraham and with Israel received the mark of covenant relationship (17:12-13; Exod. 12:48). Thus, the chief sign of special distinction was one shared with any and all who would accept the God of Abraham.

The Special Case of Abraham's Family

Abraham was both distinguishable from all peoples but connected at the same time to all peoples.

The rise of Abraham's family and the nation Israel was complex genealogically because of two opposite aspects—interdependencies and differentiations. The family tree possessed interdependencies with other people groups and differentiations within its own people group.[14] The Genesis account makes a remarkable claim when it

---

14. F. Crüsemann, "Human Solidarity and Ethnic Identity" in *Ethnicity and the Bible*, ed. M. Brett, (Leiden: Brill, 1996), 57-76.

shows that all human beings came from one ancestor, Adam. The Hebrews realized that they were connected ultimately to all peoples. The expression "human family," according to Genesis, is literally true. Differentiation is also essential to understanding Abraham's family tree. For example, in the Table of Nations, Eber fathered two sons, Joktan and Peleg (10:25). Abraham's line originated in Peleg, not in his brother, Joktan (11:16–19; Luke 3:35). Although the lines of Joktan and Peleg produced different results, Abraham was related to both lines. More familiar is the example within the clan of Abraham. Isaac and Rebekah bore twin brothers, Jacob and Esau. Jacob/Israel became the father of the tribes of Israel, and Esau fathered the tribes of Edom. Although the two nations considered the other its archenemy, both nations could trace their ancestors back to closest of kin—even *twin* brothers.

The idea that the Hebrew people were of a pure ethnic race does not correspond to the biblical evidence. We don't have to stray from Abraham himself to see the principles of interdependency and differentiation at work. Abraham and Nahor were brothers whose households migrated with their father to the city Haran in the region Paddan Aram (e.g., Gen. 11:26–32). The Abraham branch was called Hebrew, and the Nahor branch was called Aramean. For example, Bethuel, the son of Nahor, is identified as "Bethuel the Aramean" (e.g., Gen. 24:15 with 25:20; 28:5). They were connected as blood kin, but their descendants parted geographically and linguistically. Just two generations later the two people groups spoke different languages, Hebrew by the Abraham branch and Aramaic by the Nahor branch (Gen. 31:45–49).

Marriage Practices

Another principle at work in the Abraham family tree was the common practice of endogamy, or marriage within a family group of kin. Religious motivations prompted the fathers' practice of endogamy, not ethnicity alone. Abraham married Sarah, his half-sister (Gen. 20:12). Moreover, Abraham ensured that his son Isaac married a daughter from the household of his brother Nahor in Aram. Rebekah was the granddaughter of Nahor, making her a second cousin of Isaac

(Gen. 24:15; 25:20). Isaac and Rebekah later insisted that their son Jacob marry one of their own lineage, sending him to Paddan Aram to marry a daughter of her brother Laban's house, meaning Jacob's wives (Leah, Rachel) were the nieces of his mother, Rebekah. Thus we again have a case of the patriarch marrying his cousins who themselves were sisters. One of the great ironies of Scripture is that the mothers of the twelve tribes of Israel, Leah and Rachel (Ruth 4:11), were born to women of Aramean identity. This means that so-called ethnic terms, such as Aramean, were not always based on a truly separate biological descent but could be used to distinguish a people by territorial associations or language.

Exogamy, or marriage outside the family group, was practiced too but was uncommon. For example, members of the early Hebrews married non-Hebrew peoples, such as Judah and Joseph, who married Canaanite and Egyptian women, respectively (Gen. 38:2; 41:45).

Culture and Ethnicity

People groups of the ancient past cannot always be identified today on the basis of a distinctive culture. I experienced this confusion first-hand in the 1970s when I joined my university friend who was of biracial descent. His father was a U.S. naturalized citizen who had emigrated from Mexico, and his mother was an Anglo from Arkansas. Because he exhibited many stereotypical Hispanic features, and because his last name was Martinez, many potential landlords assumed that he was a Mexican who struggled with the English language. "No, ma'am," he would say in his Arkansas drawl when asked about his language skills. He had been born and reared in Arkansas, didn't know Spanish, but did enjoy eating Mexican food. I was from the border state of Texas, and there wasn't a lick of difference between us culturally. Archeological remains in Canaan from the Middle and Late Bronze Ages (ca. 1500–1200 B.C.) show that there was no significant difference in the material culture of the indigenous Canaanites and the newly arrived Israelites. In other words, we cannot tell from material culture alone if an occupation layer from a village or town is Canaanite or Israelite. One specialist in the study of ethnography in Palestine concluded that the material culture of the Canaanites and Israelites was so similar that one could contend that the "early Israelites were a rural subset of Canaanite culture."[15]

Conclusion

The ethnic picture of the ancient world was too complex to make an ethnic identification on the basis of one factor alone, whether language, material culture, or geopolitical association. The Canaanites, for example, whose language and material culture were similar to the Israelites, came from a different line of decent (Hamites, Gen. 10:15-19), whereas the Arabian tribes (from Joktan, Gen. 10:26-30), who were of the same lineage as the Israelites (Shemites), differed more than the Canaanites in language and cultural tradition.

The nation Israel that emerged from the patriarchal past was also a complex of ethnic identities. We will attempt to answer the question of what held the tribes together, if not a pure genealogical lineage.

THOUGHT PROVOKERS

1. Do you have a complex genealogical history? Are you of mixed ethnic background? Do you even know what your ethnic genealogical tree is? Does it matter?

2. How would you answer someone, using the Bible, who claimed that the Bible teaches that the Jews, as "God's chosen people," are superior to other people groups? What would you say to someone who said that the Bible ("Table of Nations") proved that there are unalterable differences between the races and that these differences should be maintained by prohibiting mixed racial marriages?

3. Can you think of other occasions in world history when people

---

15. L. Stager, "Forging an Identity: The Emergence of Ancient Israel" in *The Oxford History of the Biblical World*, ed. M. Coogan, (New York: Oxford University Press, 1998), 137.

groups who considered themselves ethnically and socially superior to others claimed a pure race? What was the reason and outcome of their claims?

4. From learning that the Hebrew people were not racially pure, what are the implications for the way we see ourselves and others as part of God's kingdom? Since Jesus was the "one offspring" of Abraham that God ultimately had in mind when he promised blessing for the patriarch and his descendants (Gal. 3:16), what does this say to us about bringing the gospel of Jesus Christ to the nations?

5. How important to you is the geographical association of people you know who come from different parts of the world, such as Nigeria, Puerto Rico, and Bangladesh?

6. How can the church better educate its members on the complexities of ethnic history so as to avoid pigeonholing individuals ethnically or by social class?

7. Why do we place a higher significance on a person's racial characteristics, such as skin color and facial features, than the biblical authors did?

Chapter 3

"God's People" and the "Also Peoples"

THE CLASSIC WAR MOVIE "The Longest Day" (all 179 minutes of it!) is a 1962 re-creation of World War II's historic invasion of Normandy by the allied troops on June 6, 1944, now known as D-Day. One distinctive of the movie is that the actors spoke lines in their native language. Curd Jürgens, a noted German-born actor, played German general Günther Blumentritt (also a consultant for the film) who was chief-of-staff to Karl von Rundstedt, general commander of the forces in the west. In the film, the German generals, upon learning of the invasion, called for the formidable German panzer divisions to move up to the region of Normandy to impede the progress. But Hitler had chosen to center power in Berlin, making the generals on the ground turn to Berlin for approval. When Blumentritt's vital request arrived, Hitler was asleep and could not be disturbed. Blumentritt said in disgust, the war was lost because of "our Führer's" sleep. Then he added, "God must be against us!"

How, I wondered, could anyone with any moral sensitivity believe that God *could* be for the Third Reich? However, the proper question for all people groups to ask is not, "Is God for *us*?" but "Are we for *God*?"

WHO ARE "GOD'S PEOPLE"?

The Western world, informed by the biblical tradition, answers that the Jews are God's "chosen people." We saw in the previous chapter, however, that Abraham and his descendants were chosen by God for the purpose of serving God's greater aim of bestowing blessing on *all* nations. We found that the Hebrew people were chosen for a role and

that role could be perfectly fulfilled only by one offspring of Abraham—
the Lord Jesus Christ. Those who are rightly related to Christ through
faith therefore can be said to be "God's people." The apostle Peter
celebrated this when he said of Jews and Gentiles, "Formerly you were
not a people, but now you are God's people" (1 Peter 2:10; Hos.
2:23).[1] "God's people" are those who worship the God and Father
of our Lord Jesus Christ (e.g., Eph. 1:3). And who is this God, this
Father of Jesus? He is the God of Abraham, Isaac, and Jacob, the one
true God of Israel (e.g., Exod. 3:15; Matt. 22:32 par.; Acts 3:13).
What marks "God's people" is not ethnic descent but faith.

The Bible also shows, however, that certain peoples were deemed
unacceptable. These were the "Also Peoples."[2] All those who were
not part of Jacob-Israel could be considered the "Also Peoples,"
since they did not directly receive the same benefits extended by
God to the Israelites. The Hebrew people were prohibited from entering marriage with foreigners and were warned against trusting in
relationships with foreign nations (e.g., Egypt, Isa. 31:1-9). Some
of the "Also Peoples" were condemned to destruction, while others
could be treated better but still only under specific restrictions.
They were commonly differentiated by socio-economic classifications, such as "resident sojourners" and "foreigners." We use terms
today that have emotional baggage and class implications, such as
"illegal alien" versus "undocumented immigrant" or "unregistered
immigrant." The first underscores their status as lawbreakers, hence
criminals. Unlawful entry is a misdemeanor, however, not a felony.[3]
The latter elicits a gentler response, reflecting a sympathetic view of

---

1. The apostle Paul is specific in context when he applies Hosea 2:23 to Gentiles: "those who were not my people I will call my people" (Rom. 9:25).
2. We have modified for our purposes the expression "also sons" used by
R. Syrén, *The Forsaken First-Born*, JSOTSup 133 (Sheffield: Sheffield,
1993), 144-45. By this expression he refers to the firstborn sons who were
not the direct recipients of the bequeathed "blessing," such as Ishmael and
Esau.
3. See the U.S. Citizen and Immigration Services' homepage for the Immigration and Nationality Act, Title II, Chapter 7, Act 266. The penalty is a fine
not exceeding $1,000 or imprisonment not more than six months, or both.
http://www.uscis.gov/portal/site/uscis/menuitem.f6da51a2342135be7e
9d7a10e0dc91a0/?vgnextoid=fa7e539dc4bed010VgnVCM1000000ecd190
aRCRD&vgnextchannel=fa7e539dc4bed010VgnVCM1000000ecd190aRC
RD&CH=act.

immigrants as human beings, just like citizens but lacking formal recognition by government-issued documents.[4]

As we saw in the previous chapter regarding the complicated ethnic picture of the patriarchs, there is a complicated ethno-cultural milieu that explains why God commanded the Israelites to beware of the "Also Peoples." By "ethno-cultural" we mean that the people groups with which the Israelites rubbed shoulders were ethnically and culturally entangled, making them vulnerable to foreign religious and cultural persuasions. The Israelites were not xenophobic (i.e., fearful of or having intense dislike for strangers); rather, their attitude toward immigrants and foreigners was rooted in theological and moral differences. Moreover, their responses toward immigrants and foreigners were mixed—sometimes favorable and at other times restrictive. This was consistent with attitudes toward foreigners in the ancient Near East. Egyptians and Mesopotamians benefitted from the influx of foreigners. Egypt's policy was to accept and absorb newcomers. They supplemented the Egyptians as workers, educators, artisans, and domestic help. However, there were times when Egyptians and Mesopotamians aggressively opposed and denigrated ethnic immigration in reaction to periods when foreigners came to power (e.g., the Hyksos in Egypt and the Gutians in Mesopotamia). When threatened, whether the threat is real or imagined, native peoples fear the "invasion," and their attitudes toward immigrants change.

"GOD'S PEOPLE" AND THE QUESTION OF RACE

The fathers of the Israelites were not a pure race to begin with.[5] If Abraham were the first "Hebrew," we can hardly say that his parents

---

4. M. Daniel Carroll R., *Christians at the Border: Immigration, the Church, and the Bible* (Grand Rapids: Baker, 2008), 21-22. The author contends that the term "illegal" conjures up a pattern of criminality that is inappropriate for most Hispanic immigrants. He advises that the doctrine of the "image of God' should engender compassion and influence the "tone of Christian participation in the national debate" (p. 69).

5. "Pure race" is legal parlance that describes (in theory) the race to the courthouse to record one's legal claim of property ownership over other contenders. Of course, we do not mean this by the expression "pure race."

were "Hebrews" too. This would be an anachronism (i.e., out of chronological order or wrong historical setting). His parents were people of the Mesopotamian region (the land between the Tigris and Euphrates Rivers), probably Amorites, whose lineage could be traced back to the Shemites (Gen. 10:21–31; 11:10–26; 24:10; Acts 7:2). The early Israelites could not and did not claim that they were a pure race. Ancient peoples generally showed little interest in maintaining homogeneous race, unless a nation fell under the threat of invaders. Then steps were taken to disparage the invaders, usually along the line of their "barbaric" behaviors, not their race per se. Later, after the Babylonian exile (sixth century B.C.), the Jews claimed their ethnic heritage was a privileged position (e.g., Matt. 3:9 par.; John 8:42–59). That the Israelites maintained a pure race is a Sunday school myth that is heard from time to time. The biblical text describes the people who escaped from Egyptian bondage differently.

A Mixed Multitude

The exodus generation included a "mixed multitude" (*ereb rab*) of people (Exod. 12:38, 48; cf. Neh. 13:3; Jer. 25:20, 24; 50:37). The Holman Christian Standard Bible captures the expression's meaning: "an ethnically diverse crowd." Egypt had for centuries been populated by numerous ethnic groups who migrated due to famine (e.g., Jacob's family) or were captives from Egypt's many wars (e.g., 1 Kings 9:16; 2 Chron. 12:9). The various non-Hebrew groups who attached themselves to the Israelites must have been spared the final plague of death directed against the firstborn in Egypt; we presume they escaped because of their faith in the Lord, believing the Passover blood applied to the doorposts of Hebrew homes (and maybe their own homes) would save them (Exod. 12). It is not clear from the text to what degree the "mixed multitude" was integrated into the community of the Hebrews, although the statute of Passover observance provided for immigrants who had undergone the covenant sign of circumcision (12:43–51).

Moses himself had taken a wife of Midianite lineage (Zipporah, Exod. 2:21), whose father was Jethro,[6] a Midianite priest (Exod.

---

6. Douglas K. Stuart, *Exodus*, 2 (Nashville: Holman, 2006), 99 (footnote

18:1–12); Jethro also was identified as a "Kenite" (Judg. 1:16; 4:11).[7] Caleb, the renowned man of faith who exhorted the Israelites to enter the land of Canaan (Num. 13:30; Josh. 14:14), was of the tribe of Judah (Num. 13:6; 34:19) but also was acknowledged as the son of a "Kenizzite" (Num. 32:12; Josh. 14:6, 14; cf. "Kenizzites," Gen. 15:19). Moreover, the picture of Caleb's ancestry is complicated by the pedigree attributed to Caleb's younger brother, Othniel (Judg. 1:13), who is best remembered for his role as Israelite judge (Judg. 3:7–9). Othniel was recognized as the son of "Kenaz" (e.g., Josh. 15:17; Judg. 1:13). And "Kenaz" is the name of Caleb's grandson (1 Chron. 4:15). So, who was Kenaz? The name first appears for the grandson of Esau, who also was identified as the chief of an Edomite clan (Gen. 36: 15, 42; 1 Chron. 1:36, 53). The relationship of these various people groups can be explained in part by the migration of the Kenizzites from Edom to the Negev, where they integrated into the Judahites.[8] Assimilation of people groups in the ancient Near East was a common practice. Ezekiel reflected the mixed ethnic setting of Canaan when he condemned the people of Judah for idolatry: "your father was an Amorite and your mother a Hittite" (16:3, 45).[9]

However, some individuals and groups who affiliated with the Israelites retained their former identities. "Ruth the Moabite" (e.g., Ruth 1:22), an ancestress of King David (4:17), and "Uriah the Hittite," who was one of David's prized mercenary troops (2 Sam. 23:39), were two persons whose loyalty to the Hebrew people was praised in the biblical tradition. One people group that kept its ethnic distinctiveness was the Gibeonites, whose affiliation (ethnicity?) was Hivite and Amorite (Josh. 9:7; 2 Sam. 21:2); they became servants

---

146). Also named Ruel (Exod. 2:18, a clan name?) and perhaps Hobab (Num. 10:29; Judg. 4:11), although Hobab's identity is disputed.

7. Numbers 12:1 indicates that Moses' wife was a "Cushite" (lower Nubia), but the woman is not identified as Zipporah and may have been another wife taken by Moses.

8. E. C. Hostetter, "Kenaz" in *Eerdmans Dictionary of the Bible*, ed. D. N. Freedman, (Grand Rapids: Eerdmans, 2000), 763. An example is a clan of the Kenites who migrated to the Negev (Judg. 1:16); Heber the Kenite was an individual who moved north to Kedesh (Judg. 4:11).

9. For the significance of this statement, see Daniel Block, *The Book of Ezekiel Chapters 1–24*, NICOT (Grand Rapids: Eerdmans, 1997), 508.

to the Israelites after deceiving Joshua to gain protection (Josh. 9:3–10:14).

By these examples we can see that people groups and their complex identities mirrored a world of local and international interdependencies. These interdependencies included ethnicity but also could have been socio-economic without reference to lineage. As we saw in our previous chapter's discussion, language was not a reliable indicator of ethnicity (e.g., Jacob spoke Hebrew whereas his uncle Laban spoke the Semitic language Aramaic, Gen. 31:45–49).[10] The term "Semitic" may refer to a family of languages but not ethnicity. In the Table of Nations, the Elamites are descended from the Shemites (Gen. 10:22), yet they did not speak a Semitic language.

Covenant Faith

What then can we say was the glue that held the Israelites together? What made them the "people of God"? The answer lies in the biblical tradition itself: their common commitment to the "LORD" (Hebrew: *Yahweh*).[11] What made Israel's tribal system in Canaan connected was not a typical "social mechanism"[12] or "social program."[13] It was the people's agreement to serve the Lord as their God whom alone they would worship. Moses' speeches recorded in the book of Deuteronomy addressed the second generation of wilderness sojourners who were on

---

10. Daniel Block, "The Role of Language in Ancient Israelite Perceptions of National Identity, *JBL* 103 (1984): 321–40.

11. The Hebrew word *Yahweh* was regularly translated "LORD" (*kurios*) by the Jews in the Greek version of the Old Testament, known as the Septuagint (second century B.C.). English versions follow the same translation tradition and use capital and small capital letters, "LORD" (versus "Lord," the Hebrew word *adonay*). By the expression "Yahwism" scholars mean the authentic religious faith of the Mosaic tradition that recognized Yahweh as the true Creator and Redeemer, "the God of Abraham, Isaac, and Jacob" (e.g., Exod. 3:15).

12. F. Frick, "Religion and Socio-Political Structure in Early Israel: An Ethno-Archaeological Approach" in *Community, Identity, and Ideology: Social Science Approaches to the Hebrew Bible*, C. Carter and C. Myers, eds. (Winona Lake: Eisenbrauns, 1996), 465.

13. N. P. Lemche, "The Relevance of Working with the Concept of Class in the Study of Israelite Society in the Iron Age" in *Concepts of Class in Ancient Israel*, USF Studies in the History of Judaism 201, ed. M. Sneed, (Atlanta: Scholars, 1999), 97–98.

the precipice of entering the land of promise. His emphasis was the loyalty the people must show to the Lord upon entering the land. Because they would encounter peoples who worshipped Canaanite deities, they had to take extreme measures to avoid assimilation. The primary way they showed their loyalty to the Lord *and* to one another was obedience to the command to worship the Lord at only those places that "the LORD (*Yahweh*) your God will choose, to make his name dwell there" (Deut. 12:11). The designated places were the only authentic places of true worship. Also, the people showed their love for the Lord and one another by carrying out the demands of the covenant law revealed at Sinai ("Horeb" in Deuteronomy).

One of the interesting facets of Deuteronomy is the community solidarity reflected in the speeches of Moses.[14] Although his audience received the commandments of God at Sinai when they were young (or before they had been born), Moses used the plural "you" when referring to what occurred at Sinai, as though they were the original recipients of the covenant law (e.g., Deut. 5:2-3, 23-27). Continuity with past and future generations was based on their common submission to the revealed word of God (*Torah*). They shared in the life of obedience under the lordship of God as administered through the covenant law. They were marked as *Torah*-keepers. Each generation was to observe it and teach it. Theirs was not a community that transcended generations because of the same historical, social, or religious life. The first generation lived *outside* the land and experienced Sinai, whereas the second generation lived in the land and had received the covenant law at Moab bordering the land of Canaan. The covenant law then was adaptable to the new circumstances that the second generation faced as a newly sedentary people. What gave each generation its identity as "the people of God" was their common faith, not a specific historical setting or event.

Bond and Bondage

The institutions of temple or monarchy also bonded the Israelites together and preserved them for their long history. Temple and

---

14. Peter T. Vogt, *Deuteronomic Theology and the Significance of Torah* (Winona Lake: Eisenbrauns, 2006), 154-59.

monarchy perished when the Babylonians besieged Judah in the sixth century B.C. What could bond the exiles together if they were to survive as "the people of God"? At the death of Moses, the instructions of Deuteronomy became the gold standard by which the people measured their fidelity to God. The author of the book of Joshua repeatedly reported the Israelites' careful observance of the "commandments of Moses" (e.g., Josh 1:3, 5, 17; 3:7; 4:12, 14; 8:31, 33; 11:12, 20; 23:14, 33;14:2; 21:8). Although they left behind Sinai and Moses, they had and always would have *Torah*. During the exile era, *Torah* studies and the synagogue system distinguished the Jews from their Gentile neighbors. The practices of circumcision, food laws, and Sabbath keeping differentiated them. But it is important to remember that these were behaviors, not an inherent ethnic distinctive. Gentiles who were proselytes, too, could and did practice the same traditions.

Ethnicity, therefore, was never the determinative feature, not the make or break factor, in forming a person's identity as a person of faith. Acceptance and the role of non-Hebrews were anticipated in the covenant law, assuming their inclusion but also controlling it. They, too, entered into league with the Israelites when they submitted to the Lord by taking up the covenant law. This is what we read in the apostle Peter's understanding of "the people of God," when he alludes to the prophet Hosea: "Formerly you were not a people, but now you are the people of God" (1 Peter 2:10 with Hos. 2:23). Therefore, when Peter speaks of Christians as "a chosen race" (2:9), alluding to God's salvation of Abraham's "race" (cf. Isa. 43:20-21; Exod. 19:5-6),[15] he refers metaphorically to any person—Jew or Gentile—who comes to the Lord Jesus Christ by faith. *What creates the bond is bondage to Christ!*

The "Old Country"

When the exiled Jews faced the new setting of Babylonia, they did not abandon their culture, although it was necessary to adapt it to the new environment. All immigrant groups today, because of the power of culture, maintain features of the "old country," such as

---

15. D. A. Carson, "1 Peter," *Commentary on the New Testament Use of the Old Testament*, G. K. Beale and D. A. Carson, eds. (Grand Rapids: Baker, 2007), 1030.

ethnic food, dress, folklore, and language. Future generations who assimilate further to the new cultural situation typically modify and in some ways give up the cultural markers of their parents and grandparents. Although persons continue the inherited traits of race, such as cranial shape, facial features, and color, they are blended culturally by accommodating the old and the new. This adaptation to a new culture may work in the opposite direction, too. The new culture accepts some features of the immigrants' culture or by a dominating foreign influence. An example of this is the introduction of American baseball in Japan by a visiting American professor at the turn of the twentieth century (1900 A.D.). The presence of "G. I. Joe" during the occupation of Japan after the Second World War especially fueled the Japanese passion for baseball, and it became wildly popular in Japan. Today, baseball is a worldwide sport, and America's professional team rosters show it by the recent influx of Asian and Latino players. One of the bizarre examples in ancient history is the adaptation of Jewish tradition to the flourishing Greek culture (known as Hellenism) in Palestine which was especially promoted by the ruler Antiochus IV in the second century B.C. To adapt to the new influences of Hellenism, some Jewish men underwent a procedure reversing their circumcision.

Because of the constant exchange and migratory flow of peoples in the ancient Near East, every nation had expectations of assimilation by foreigners. For example, one way in which the Jews adapted to their new home was the adoption of Aramaic, a Semitic language, which was the diplomatic language of the Mesopotamian peoples in the first millennium B.C. (cf. 2 Kings 18:26) and was used in writing significant portions of Daniel and Ezra. Jews also translated the Hebrew Bible into Aramaic, known as the Targums. The Palestinian dialect of Aramaic was commonly spoken among the Jews in New Testament times, despite the rise of Greek after the time of Alexander the Great, and continued afterward in rabbinic literature, such as the Babylonian Talmud. Jewish tradition and some contemporary scholars believe that the people returning from exile did not understand the Hebrew Scriptures, making it necessary to translate them into Aramaic (Neh. 8:8).[16]

16. E.g., Charles Fensham, *The Books of Ezra and Nehemiah*, NICOT (Grand

Assimilation was an important goal of the political and social policies of the Egyptians. Foreigners were so thoroughly integrated that it
is difficult for scholars today to distinguish if a person had non-Egyptian
heritage. They became such a part of mainstream Egyptian culture that
scholars cannot confidently assert in many cases if a person had non-
Egyptian heritage. Foreigners adopted the dress, language, and religion
of their new country. Within a few generations the transition was virtually complete. A biblical example is Joseph, who took an Egyptian name
and an Egyptian wife and who spoke Egyptian. Joseph's demeanor did
not reveal to his Hebrew brothers his ethnic heritage. Assimilation was
also common in Mesopotamia. Like others, the Israelites were a nation
who safeguarded their borders and independence. They expected new
residents to assimilate into Israel's social and religious life, but it was
not required of all foreigners and not in every way. Especially important
from the viewpoint of the covenant law were the demands regarding
moral behavior and certain religious prescriptions.

The exiled Jews, however, faced the challenge of assimilating
during the Babylonian exile and retaining their cherished distinctive
heritage as "the people of God." If they failed to perpetuate their
faith in the God of their fathers, they had no reason for existing as
a unique people. By adopting the synagogue system, they preserved
their heritage as *Torah*-keepers. Daniel and his friends, for example,
learned the Aramaic (Chaldean) literature and language and accepted
new Babylonian names (Dan. 1:3–7), but they refused to eat the food
and drink provided by the king. The food probably reflected their
concern for its possible association with idolatry and pagan rites. He
and his friends drew the line where compromise imperiled their faith
in the Lord God (1:8–21).

That immigrants maintain remnants of their culture and adapt to the
new is a good thing today. Individuals and communities who migrate
must retain identity markers or they initially flounder in their new envi-
ronments. To surrender all of the "old country" may stifle assimilation
to the new because of a person's cultural confusion and sense of betrayal
to the homeland. To think that immigrants must automatically give up

---

Rapids: Eerdmans, 1982), 218. The opposing view, commonly reflected
in English versions, is that the verse refers only to explaining the text, e.g.,
H. G. M. Williamson, *Ezra, Nehemiah*, WBC (Waco: Word, 1985), 278–79.

their ethnic traditions upon residing in a new country is unrealistic. The same issue faced the early church as it expanded among Gentiles, which soon became the dominate population in the church. The early church conference in Jerusalem (Acts 15), in response to Gentiles who were unsure as to what degree they should become "Jews" after choosing to follow Christ, addressed the markers of "Jewishness" (food laws, circumcision, and Sabbath observance). They issued a compromise, urging Gentile Christians to maintain food laws, noting that other requirements would be "a burden" to them (15:28–29). This most likely was a transitional step, for the apostle Paul later taught his churches that adherence to food laws was unnecessary to maintain a relationship with God (Col. 2:16; cf. Rom. 14:20; Gal. 2:11–16).

Rejection or assimilation cannot be absolute but must be both/ and. It is impossible to replicate the "old country" in every way, and it is inadvisable to abandon it in every way. Because of the inevitable cultural tensions that occur when immigrants and persons of the dominant culture meet, ways of ethnic and racial reconciliation become critically important to the welfare of each.

Where does the Christian church come into play? We cannot be on the sidelines, waiting for some government or educational institution to provide a lasting resolution. As Joseph Henriques comments, "Christians are uniquely positioned for brokering and modeling intercultural reconciliation."[17] He favorably quotes Manuel Ortiz, who refers to the church as uniquely "Christ Culture."[18] God as Creator and Redeemer created a new "one man" through Jesus Christ that transcends all cultural differences. No ethnic group can make exclusive claims on "Christ Culture," for it is God's creation.

YIKES, "ITES"!

The biblical "ites" are various and numerous peoples named in the Old Testament. The Canaan*ites*, Edom*ites*, Ammon*ites*, and

---

17. Michael Pocock and Joseph Henriques, *Cultural Change and Your Church: Helping Your Church Thrive in a Diverse Society* (Grand Rapids: Baker, 2002), 103. The entire chapter (pp. 99–123) is helpful for understanding the role of culture and the church.
18. Manuel Ortiz, *One New People: Models for Developing a Multiethnic Church* (Downers Grove: Intervarsity, 1996), 132.

Hitt*ites* were but a few. (I sometimes tell students that these were the term*ites* in the life of the Israel*ites*.) The Israelites knew some of these peoples well and were puzzled by others. Their knowledge of some was skimpy because there was little contact. Others were so familiar that the authors of Scripture assumed that the reader needed no explanation as to their identity and history. Consequently our knowledge based on the Bible alone is spotty. Archaeological recoveries and extra-biblical texts add considerably to our knowledge.

Egyptologist James Hoffmeier has described the policies in Egyptian and Mesopotamian countries toward immigrants.[19] There are many similarities between ancient practices and the ones contemplated today in America. Immigration was commonplace in the ancient world, and countries upheld the integrity of their boundaries. They built garrisons at their borders to oversee traffic, supervising the entry points by requiring immigrants to declare their business and seek formal permission to enter. Foreigners could advance in their society economically and socially. In the case of Joseph, although a renowned leader in Egypt, he was still distinguished as a Semite and sought permission from Pharaoh to settle Jacob's family in Egypt. At times, host countries were resistant to immigrants, but they generally were open to those who came for employment and sought goods and services.

The "Assembly of the LORD"

In the Deuteronomic mandate to avoid pagan worship, Moses prepared the Israelites for dealing with the diverse people groups that they would encounter in the land. As mentioned previously, one purpose of the Table of Nations (Gen. 10) was to prepare the Israelites by informing them of the nations' origins and relationships to one another. Deuteronomy 23 details who can be accepted into the "assembly of the LORD" (vv. 1–8).[20] The "assembly" refers to the

---

19. James K. Hoffmeier, *The Immigration Crisis: Immigrants, Aliens, and the Bible* (Wheaton: Crossway, 2009), 29–57.
20. J. G. McConville, *Deuteronomy*, Apollos (Downers Grove: InterVarsity, 2002), 320–21. According to McConville, Deuteronomy 7 and 20 explain the policy of warfare. Deuteronomy 7:1–2 presents the course of action gov-

gathered community of Israelites for worship; it also indicates a mustering for military purposes, since the following instructions pertain to war (vv. 9-14).[21] The covenant law presented varied courses of action toward different people groups due to diverse criteria. There was no single policy that covered all groups.

What to Do With the "Ites"

The first guideline is the rejection of the Ammonites and Moabites in the assembly (Deut. 23:3-6). This is surprising in one way but understandable in another. It is surprising because their ancestors were ethnically related to the Israelites; they were the offspring of Lot, who was the nephew of Abraham (Gen. 19). Their restriction evidently was not due to ethnic bigotry since they were kinsmen of the Hebrews; certain groups ethnically unrelated, however, did have access. Exclusion must have been determined on some other basis. The Ammonites and Moabites were denied because of a severe offense committed against the Israelites. Moab (and presumably Ammon) had resisted Israelite passage through its land when they were en route to Canaan. They took an aggressive stance against Israel, hiring the sorcerer Balaam to call for curses (Num. 22-24). The theological factor underlying the grievous nature of the insult was the divine promise in the Abrahamic covenant: God "will bless those who bless" Abraham and "will curse the one who curses" him (Gen. 12:3). The rejection then was rooted in behavior, not ethnicity or racial characteristics. Another reason for their exclusion may have been in connection with prohibitions pertaining to ritual impurity. Any Israelite conceived by incest could not be accepted into the assembly (Deut. 23:2).[22] This,

---

erning the Israelites upon entering the land, whereas chapter 20 describes the policy after the victory and settlement of the land.

21. Ibid., 348.

22. Our moral sensitivities are rightly disturbed when we think of an innocent child, for no fault of his or her own, bearing the life-long taint of incest. But the prohibition is understood more acceptably when we remember that worship includes powerful symbolic images. Since the Lord God is complete in all of his perfections, it was necessary that all acts of worship exhibit perfection, too. Incest was morally repugnant in Israel; therefore, it was symbolically incongruous that anyone or anything associated with incest would be seen in the house of worship. This and other such kinds of ritual impurities

too, shows that the ban was not based on ethnicity. This specific ritual prohibition immediately precedes the prohibition against Moab and Ammon. That Moab and Ammon's births were the result of the incestuous unions of Lot and his two daughters may have been in mind (Gen. 19:30–38).

In light of the above, the more ready acceptance of the Edomites and Egyptians than the Ammonites and the Moabites is not surprising (Deut. 23:7–8). Although the Edomites were archenemies of Israel, they were not active participants in undermining the Israelites' journey. They were closer to the Israelites by birth since their ancestor Esau was the twin brother of Jacob, and the text specifically states that was the justification for their possible acceptance (Deut. 23:7). Moreover, Esau and Jacob reconciled over their past grievances before they finally parted (Gen. 32).[23] Reception of the Egyptians, however, was an amazing act of grace since they had enslaved the Hebrews. Yet their prior favorable treatment of their ancestor Jacob (for Joseph's sake) took precedence: "for you [Israel] lived as sojourners in their land" (Deut. 23:7). Unlike the Moabites and Ammonites, the Egyptians had initially practiced hospitality to the Hebrews which was a widely held virtue in the ancient Near East.

The probation period differed, too. The Ammonites and Moabites were shut out for ten generations, and the Edomites and Egyptians for three generations (Deut. 23:2–3, 8). The number ten could be symbolic for completeness, indicating that they were permanently excluded. Even if taken as a literal number, ten generations would effectively have had the same results.[24] Perhaps the period of time was for testing the loyalty of the parties to the Lord or for purgation of ritual impurities. Acceptance was by no means automatic. Ritual

---

were done away with for all time by the only One who is truly perfect in holiness and obedience to the Father, our Lord Jesus Christ. His perfections are now ours and we are forever welcomed into the presence of God (e.g., Heb. 10:1–10).

23. That the prophet Amos depicted the imminent judgment of God against the nations and their future salvation by the symbolic significance of "Edom" shows the prominence of Edom in the history of Israel (Amos 1:11–12; 9:12 with Acts 15:15–18).

24. Forty years per generation was generally used as the symbolic ideal, thus giving 400 years (Num. 32:13; Job 42:16); actually, a generation was probably closer to twenty-five years, resulting in 250 years.

stipulations concerning the camp of Israel generally involved an evaluation (usually by a priest), a time factor (determined by the nature of the impurity), and a ritual reinitiating act into the community.

Although the Lord commanded the Israelites to exterminate "the seven nations," they did not carry it out completely (e.g., Deut. 7:1-2; Judg. 1:1-2:6; cf. Acts 13:19). Pockets of Canaanite resistance remained, and in some cases the Israelites chose to make them forced laborers and slaves. Moses anticipated the influence of Canaanite idolatry and had no illusions about the challenges that Israel faced after the settlement (e.g., Deut 29:18-29). Exemptions were inevitable.[25] Exception to the Moabite ban, for example, was Ruth the Moabitess. In many ways Ruth proved herself to be more Yahwist in her commitments to the Lord and her husband's family than the wicked behavior of the native-born Israelites during the era of the Judges.

We conclude from our look at the "ites" that the basis for admission or rejection was behavior, not ethnicity. The worship of God was available to all.

"ALIENS" AMONG US

Israel's attitude toward "aliens" was mixed during its long history, but generally the Israelites favored aliens and foreigners until the collapse of the nation under Babylonian oppression, followed by Persian overlords, and finally Greek and Roman occupations. The long "times of the Gentiles" (Luke 21:24) set the stage for the New Testament picture of the Jews' strong anti-Gentile bias. The Hebrew people did not hate the nations. Reading their history solely through the lens of the New Testament skews the facts. An accurate and balanced examination is called for.

Who Are the Immigrants?

The extensive lexicon of terms found in the Old Testament to describe "aliens" is itself evidence of the importance they played in the

---

25. McConville, *Deuteronomy*, 153-54. The restrictions in Deuteronomy 23 were in actual practice not absolute.

life of Israel—including the religious, economic, and social dimensions of daily life. The chief term alongside which the others are best understood is the common word *ger*, usually translated in the different English versions by a variety of terms, such as "alien," "stranger," and "foreigner." The translation "resident alien" for *ger* has been suggested for two reasons.[26] First, its appearances in context in Old Testament passages reflect the idea of an "alien." For example, *ger* is often contrasted with the word for "native-born" (*ezrach*) Israelite (e.g., Exod. 12:19). Second, the translation "resident" indicates the idea of a *ger*'s permanency in the land. This is suggested by its occurrences as a compound expression with *toshab*, meaning "guest" when it occurs by itself (see below). But when *ger* appears in the compound *ger wetoshab*, the compound expresses a *ger* has settled in the land on a long-term basis (e.g., Gen. 23:4; Lev. 25:23, 35, 45, 47). Since a *ger* was an immigrant, he did not inherit family land. His livelihood largely depended on the largess of the indigenous Israelites who gave him opportunity to work and take up permanent residence in the land. He could become independently wealthy, even buying Hebrews as indentured servants (Lev. 25:47b). Resident aliens integrated into the fabric of Israelite society but retained distinctions in the eyes of the covenant law and society in general from the native-born population. The obligation of Hebrews to resident aliens extended to loving them by treating them with the same fairness as they would native-born "brothers" (Lev. 19:33–34).

"Temporary residents" (*toshab*) were "guests" who did not have the status of the permanent resident (*ger*); they were likely temporary hires (e.g., Lev 25:6), but they could be purchased as (indentured?) slaves and could be inherited by the slave-owner's children (Lev. 25:45–46). *Sakir* describes specifically the class "hired worker" who is paired at times with the "temporary worker" (*toshab*) (e.g., Exod. 12:45).[27] The hired worker evidently had provisional status, since the

---

26. Jacob Milgrom, *Leviticus 23–27*, AB (New York: Doubleday, 2001), 2187. Milgrom gives credit for this suggestion to E. Z. Melamed, "Hendiadys in the Bible," *Ta* 16:173–89, 242 (in Hebrew). A hendiadys is a compound of two words joined by the conjunction "and," which expresses one idea normally expressed by a noun and an adjective, e.g., "nice and mad" instead of "very mad."

27. Translators struggle to differentiate the terms at places in the text. NRSV

law required that workers receive their wages on a daily basis (Lev. 19:13). Workers' wages were the standard for calculating what was due an owner when an Israelite was released from his indebtedness (Lev. 25:50).[28] Israelite law required that owners of Israelites who had sold themselves into service were to be treated as hired workers (*sakir*), not as slaves, thus indicating that hired workers enjoyed better treatment and could not be sold as slaves due to their independent status (25:53).

Terms for "foreigner" (*nokri*) and "stranger" (*zar*) can appear as parallels (e.g., Job 19:15). Generally, they indicated persons and lands that were outside Israel. A "foreigner" was the most removed from native-born status (what we generally think of by "Gentile"). The term itself could express humility (Ruth 2:10) or humiliation (e.g., Gen. 31:15). There is a sinister aspect to the term; for example, it describes an adulteress or prostitute (e.g., Prov. 2:16; 5:20). "Stranger" (*zar*), too, usually had a negative connotation, such as a "strange god," meaning idol (Ps. 44:20), and often of occupying enemies ("strangers") from foreign lands (e.g., Isa. 1:7; Ezek. 28:10). The term often appears in the same vein as the word "foreigner" (e.g., Isa. 61:5). The common point of the two terms is their reference to what is unknown and unusual, and therefore suspicious and feared. The wide usage of the terms includes, however, a positive dimension, such as the "unusual" (*zar*) works of God who performs remarkable deeds (Isa. 28:21).

Today, the U. S. Citizenship and Immigration Services agency manages the legal immigration of foreigners to the United States. It presents a variety of classifications that categorize the legal status of immigrants. The most common categories include: (1) naturalized citizen; (2) legal non-immigrant (e.g., tourists, students, workers), legal permanent resident ("green card" recipients); conditional permanent resident (a two-year resident), refugee (resettled in the U.S.

---

translates here "bound (*toshab*) or hired servant (*sakir*)," suggesting by "bound" that the "temporary resident" was obligated to the landowner (an indentured servant?) and the "hired worker" was not.

28. An Israelite who sold himself to a foreigner for unpaid debts may be freed by a fellow Israelite or by himself at a later time; the owner received payment for the number of remaining years (whether few or many) until the next Year of Jubilee (Lev. 25:47–53).

due to or threat of persecution), and asylee (a resident who receives protection). The nonlegal immigrant is an undocumented immigrant (or illegal alien), meaning that he or she has no form of legal status as recognized by the U. S. government. Nevertheless, many undocumented immigrants are employed, receive wages (under the guise of a forged social security number), and pay income taxes. The labels "undocumented immigrant" or "illegal alien" are hot-button terms in the contemporary debate regarding illegal immigration and the host of related issues faced today, such as health care and public education.[29] The difference in the two phrases reflects our perceptions of immigrants.

The role of foreign-born populations in ancient Israel had importance for the well being of the nation, just as we find today that foreign-born populations have for American daily life—public and private. The relationship between indigenous populations and foreigners is an old one and will not go away. "Immigration Reform is a Christian Issue" is the title of an editorial by Pastor Gabriel Salguero, a member of the Latino Leadership Circle. In commenting on the need for responsible emigration policy, he referenced the National Hispanic Prayer Breakfast in Washington, D.C. (June 19, 2009), which was attended by 750 evangelical Latino pastors and leaders. He summarized what he believed was the main message of those gathered: "The millions of Latino/a evangelicals are calling for fair and humane immigration reform *now* [italics mine]. This is not just a political issue this is a moral, spiritual issue that cannot wait."[30] We, as the American church, must strive to discover how to deal with the issues that pertain to immigrants and minorities who make up our churches and neighborhoods. How did God view immigrants in Israel?

---

29. For detailed information, see the official Citizenship and Immigration Services Web site, http://www.uscis.gov/; for a lay discussion of the terms, see Matthew Soerens and Jenny Hwang, *Welcoming the Stranger: Justice, Compassion, and Truth in the Immigration Debate* (Downers Grove: InterVarsity, 2009), 64–81.
30. Gabriel Salguero, "Immigration Reform is a Christian Issue," *On Faith*, posted June 20, 2009; www.newsweek.washington.com/onfaith/panelists/gabriel_salguero/2009/06/national_hispanic_prayer_breakfast_evangelicals, accessed August 26, 2009.

The Compassion of God

The fair treatment of immigrants in Israel was grounded in God's own compassionate love and care for them (e.g., Lev. 19:33–34; Deut. 10:18; Ps. 146:9). The Israelites were to uphold the moral mandates of the Lord by showing compassion (Exod. 23:9; Deut. 10:19) and justice (e.g., Deut. 24:14, 17). If Israel failed to live out the ethical teaching regarding aliens, they faced the "curses" of the law, which meant expulsion from the land (e.g., Deut. 27:19). Also, the Lord directed Israel to be generous to immigrants because they too were once aliens.

(1) The history of Israel shows that they were foreigners, beginning with the patriarchs who were landless immigrants (e.g., Gen. 21:23; 23:4; 35:27; Exod. 6:4; Deut. 26:5; 1 Chron. 29:15). The Lord promised the patriarchs who once were landless that they would inherit the land of Canaan. This promise reminds us of the apostle Peter's exhortation to his Christian audience, who as spiritual strangers in the world were to live as citizens of the people of God (1 Peter 2:11; cf. Eph. 2:19; Phil. 3:20).

(2) Moses and the nation of Israel were birthed in the foreign land of Egypt (e.g., Gen. 15:13; Exod. 2:22; 22:21; 23:9; Lev. 19:34; Deut. 10:19; also Acts 7:6; Heb. 11:13).

(3) Finally, in God's view the Israelites *always* were landless aliens. They were aliens in the land because the land belonged to the Lord God: "Now the land must not be sold [to another] permanently, because the land belongs to me; indeed, you are [only] aliens [*ger*] and tenants [*toshab*] with me" (Lev. 25:23). This verse shows that the Hebrews were always to consider themselves as guests subject to the prerogatives of the Owner. What effect would it have on our attitude toward immigrants and people of color if we considered ourselves aliens to this world and that ownership (priority, property, possessions) is not the chief worry for a Christian (Luke 12:22–34; Phil. 3:17–21; 4:6)?

Protections

During the most contentious time of the contemporary immigration reform debate, Chuck Colson, founder of Prison Fellowship

Ministries, endorsed a proposed compromise between the polarized views of the day. He supported the two goals of securing the borders and "offering a humane way of dealing with illegal immigrants already living in the United States."[31] This often-cited compromise has analogy with the Bible's teaching about immigrants and native-born Israelites. Protections for immigrants reflect the idea of compassion, and obligations reflect the need for security. The immigrant population had obligations toward their new country, and the native population had ethical obligations too. Given that the goal of security in ancient Israel was to preserve and carry out their unique role among the nations, "a kingdom of priests and a holy nation" (Exod. 19:6), the covenant law called for ethnic policies that corresponded to that obligation.

Protections for immigrants were built into the governing constitution of Israel—the covenant law of Moses. If there is bias to be pointed out in the covenant law, it should start with the exceptions guaranteed the underclass poor—the widow, orphan, and alien (e.g., Exod. 22:21-22; Deut. 24:19-21; 27:19; Prov. 14:31; Jer. 22:3). The wicked took advantage of immigrants in the marketplace and at court. To ensure their just treatment, the law exhorted the Hebrews to go out of their way to protect the immigrants' interests (e.g., Exod. 23:12; Lev. 19:10; Deut. 14:21, 29; 24:14). Also, as noted above, aliens could obtain property, grow in wealth, and take native-born Israelites as indentured servants (Lev. 25:47). In other words, these populations were not held back; the covenant law provided for their immediate needs and gave them long-term opportunity to rise and achieve independence. Especially distinctive for their day was Israel's generous policy toward runaway slaves, who most likely were of foreign origin; they were given permanent refuge and offered the protections of hospitality (e.g., Deut. 23:15). This policy was rooted in the history of Israel itself who were runaway slaves from Egyptian captivity. Although the Israelites were not received with hospitality en route to Canaan, they were to behave ethically.

---

31. Chuck Colson, "An Immigration Compromise," BreakPoint (July 12, 2006); http://www.breakpoint.org/commentaries/5443-an-immigration, accessed August 26, 2009.

Obligations

The level of participation in the life of the community depended largely on the immigrants themselves, although they had specific obligations that were mandated for continued acceptance in the community. It was their duty to observe Hebrew laws or suffer the consequences as would the native Israelites for their transgressions (e.g., Lev. 17:10). The expression "one law" for the native-born and for the foreign born speaks to the equal standing they had before the Lord (e.g., Exod. 12:49; Lev. 24:22; Num. 15:16, 29). The point here is that foreigners had the same or less expected of them but usually not a more burdensome demand than that placed upon the Israelites. There were important exceptions, however, when the theology of Israel's election came into play (e.g., Deut. 14:2; 26:19). Although non-Israelites received privileges, the distinctive role of Israel historically as "the people of God' was maintained (Deut. 14:21). Thus, the Hebrews could not charge interest on a loan given to fellow Israelites; they were "brothers," kinsmen who received the protections of family (e.g., Exod. 22:25; Lev. 25:35–37; Deut. 23:19–20). Moreover, interest-free loans were designed to assist native Israelites to rise above their economic difficulties. This law attempted to create economic balance. But this need was not true of foreigners, who could be charged interest (e.g., Deut. 23:20; cf. 15:3). "Foreigners" (*nokri*), as noted above, were not resident immigrants (*ger*) but temporary guests who visited, for example, for commercial purposes.[32]

Resident immigrants (*ger*), however, did not live under the same obligations regarding the religious life of the Israelites. Jacob Milgrom contrasts the *prohibitive* laws that address the holiness of the land (e.g., blasphemy, Lev. 24:16) and the *performative* laws that concern religious rituals (e.g., Passover, Exod. 12:49) that did not deal directly with safeguarding the land from impurities.[33] The basis for this

---

32. The policy toward permanent resident aliens (*ger wetoshab*) is unclear; Lev. 25:35 indicates that indentured Israelites were to be treated as a resident alien, probably meaning that they were not subjected to slavery. See Milgrom, *Leviticus 23–27*, 2207.

33. Jacob Milgrom, *Numbers,* JPS Torah Commentary (Philadelphia: Jewish Publication Society, 1990), 398–402.

differentiation was the relationship of the land to the rule and presence of the Lord among the tribes of Israel. As we saw above, the land belonged to God. It was his "home." Inhabitants were only permitted residents, and therefore they had to acknowledge the holiness of God's presence (represented by the tabernacle sanctuary). In other words, the land was holy because of the Lord's presence, and the occupants were required to maintain its holiness. Any transgression against the ritual and moral purity required of the land's occupants was rebellion against the lordship of the Owner (e.g., Lev. 17:12; 18:26; 20:2). The result was the eviction of defiant tenants. This meant that native-born *and* foreign-born residents had a common stake in the perpetuation of the holiness of the land. The performative rituals were voluntary for the immigrant. But if immigrants chose to celebrate the performative laws, such as Passover or various sacrifices (e.g., Lev. 22:18-25; Num. 15:15-16), they had to abide by the same requirements. In the case of the Passover meal, immigrants and their households were obligated to undergo circumcision before participating in the Passover meal (Exod. 12:48-49; Num. 9:14-15). If they refused circumcision, participation was an offense to God. Other examples were the sacred days of Sabbath and the annual Day of Atonement, when immigrants, like the people of the land, did not work (Exod. 20:10; Lev. 16:29).

Exception from work on special days of worship is representative of the broad-based humanitarian factor in the laws regarding non-Hebrews, but all laws were understood to have been given on the basis of the relationship of God and his people. In other words, every demand and response was viewed under the governance of *covenant*. The law did not forge the relationship but *regulated* the redemptive relationship that had been established at the exodus from Egypt *before* the revelation at Sinai. Every aspect of life was under the covenant law and had a spiritual and moral significance. The modern idea of a secular law versus a religious law was unimaginable under Israel's covenant law. God gave the covenant law, not Moses, a king, legislative body, or judge. This is reminiscent of the New Testament's insistence that all of life for the Christian is under the rule of the Lord. We are to do all, even the routine things, to the glory of God, the apostle Paul tells us (1 Cor. 10:31). What we say about and how we relate to "aliens among us" makes a difference in what it means to be a Christian.

WHY NOT INTERMARRY?

When I was a teen, I posed a moral question that had arisen in the church during the Civil Rights Movement of the 1960s. At church camp one summer, my pastor and I bunked beside one another in the men's tent. Since I had publicly surrendered my life to full-time Christian ministry, I felt compelled to engage in "deeper matters" than chatter about ball games or the latest hit movie. My pastor was very personable and greatly esteemed. He was a great model for me, whether I was a "preacher boy" or not. But he was not the kind of guy who chatted about typical subjects heard around the water cooler at work or school. As we lay in our cots, I asked him what he thought of interracial marriage. Was it acceptable or prohibited? In a word, was it a sin for a Christian? No persons can free themselves completely from their culture, and my pastor was no exception. His answer rang true to my ears because it conformed to what my culture had taught me. Kindly, he refused to label interracial marriage a sin, preferring to put it in the "inadvisable" category. Since the Old Testament prohibited the intermarriage of Israelites with a different race, he reasoned that it was best that we too not do it.

Knowing "Your Place"

There was a day in America when racial intermarriage not only was inadvisable but also was prohibited in some states, until the Supreme Court established the constitutionality of interracial marriages in the famous case *Loving v. Virginia* (1967). The lower court's trial judge, who had sentenced the interracial couple Mildred and Richard Loving to a suspended one-year jail term, based his decision on the erroneous belief that "Almighty God created the races white, black, yellow, malay and red, and he placed them on separate continents. And, but for the interference of his arrangement, there would be no cause for such marriage. The fact that he separated the races shows that he did not intend for the races to mix."[34]

---

34. Legal Information Institute, Cornell University Law School. Opinion written by Chief Justice Earl Warren. http://www.law.cornell.edu/supct/html/historics/USSC_CR_0388_0001_ZO.html. Accessed August 20, 2009.

This popular interpretation of Scripture during that day had a bearing on the ruling of the judge, but his understanding was misguided. The Table of Nations (Gen. 10) and the reference to it perhaps by the apostle Paul in Acts 17:26–27 are not intended to separate the nations as though they received (deterministic) inherent intellectual and moral traits. The spreading of the nations from Babel was the natural by-product of confused languages. The blessing God planned at creation for the nations included human dominion over the terrestrial world through procreation and geographical distribution (Gen. 1:28). The dispersal of the nations made the blessing still possible. It was not so much a punitive reaction as it was deliverance from their evil intention. Paul's argument in Acts 17 is even more removed from any possible racial determinism. His statements were part of an extended argument with the Greek Epicureans and Stoics, contending that the one true Lord God was not anything like their understanding of deity or Reason. He was Creator and Master over "the rise and fall" (v. 26 NLT) of the nations, and the divine guide who sovereignly ruled over the histories of the nations, all for the purpose of making himself known to them. Paul pled that the opportunity for them to know God through his Son, Jesus Christ, was right then! His appeal was evangelistic; it was not a commentary on racial segregation.

Making the Right Choice

We have seen in our discussion that the fundamental attitude of the early Israelites toward non-Hebrews was favorable but guarded. What then was wrong about the "ites" that discouraged intermarriage by the Hebrews with non-Hebrew peoples? Exogamy is a technical term that describes marriage to someone outside of a person's family group. In Mesopotamia, for example, intermarriage was not expected, and in Egypt resident foreigners were encouraged to marry Egyptian women so as to foster a homogenous Egyptian culture.[35] In

---

35. For a discussion on attitudes toward foreigners and their social roles in the

Mesopotamia there was little racial bigotry based on physical features such as skin color. The greater tension was caused by cultural differences between the urban life of Mesopotamia city-states and the non-sedentary life of the bedouin nomads. Exogamy in Israel, however, was prohibited in most cases and controlled in others.

If the idea of race and ethnicity did not dominate the way ancient Near Eastern peoples viewed themselves and foreigners, why did Israel discriminate when picking marriage partners? God intended to redeem the nations through creating a new nation by choosing Abraham and his descendants. For this plan to develop across the ages it was necessary for Israel to retain its sole devotion to the one true living Lord. But Israel lived in a vast sea of religious pluralism. It was common for societies to accommodate religions of other peoples by expanding their pantheon of gods and goddesses. Polytheism was a device for inclusiveness. Monotheism obviously countered this cultural norm. When intermarriage occurred it was typical that the newly formed union would mean the acceptance of foreign religions. Solomon's multitude of foreign wives brought their religion with them, which resulted in the death of the nation (1 Kings 11:1-8). The author of Judges captures the scenario that the law of the land hoped to avert: "The [Israelites] married the [nations'] daughters and they gave their daughters to them for wives, and they served their gods" (Judg. 3:6; cf. Exod. 34:16; Deut. 7:4-5). In practice this prohibition was not meant to be absolute since intermarriage was accepted when a foreign wife had become identified with Yahwism (e.g., Deut. 21:9-14).[36]

As a consequence of the mandate that Israel was under—to be the conduit of "the way of the LORD" to the nations (Gen. 18:19)—it was necessary to practice marriage inside one's family group (endogamy). Preservation of their unique identity as the true worshippers

ancient Near East, see Anthony Leahy, "Ethnic Diversity in Ancient Egypt," *Civilization of the Ancient Near East*, ed. Jack Sasson, (New York: Scribner's, 1995), 225-34 and Henri Limet, "Ethnicity," *A Companion to the Ancient Near East*, ed. Daniel Snell, (Malden, MA: Blackwell, 2005), 370-83.
36. Permission to marry a foreign woman captured in war may assume her conversion to Yahwism or, in light of the prohibition against intermarriage (20:10-18), that she is not from the nations of Canaan. See J. H. Tigay, *Leviticus*, JPS Torah Commentary (Philadelphia: Jewish Publication Society, 1996), 194.

of the Lord God required it. It was not a policy of racial bigotry. If anything, Israel showed a preoccupation with the nations, attracted by their cultural achievements. The Israelites began with a migrating group of former slaves who were enticed by the powerful city-states of the Canaanites. Purely on economic and cultural bases, it was to Israel's political advantage to engage in multicultural relationships. Their continued existence as a nation, however, relied on their religious fidelity, for it was their love of the Lord God that provided the union of the diverse tribes that made up Israel (Deut. 30:20).

The clearest examples of endogamy for purposes of maintaining religious identity are the patriarchs. Abraham and Isaac insisted on wives for their sons from their relatives' household in Haran (Gen. 24:2-4; 28:2-5). Both fathers expressed their request in the religious context of the patriarchal blessing (24:7; 28:3-4). To obtain wives from the neighboring nations—as did Ishmael and Esau—invited polytheism. Another case was the wicked action taken by Jacob's sons who used circumcision as a deceitful tool to murder the Hivites in retaliation for the rape of their sister Dinah (Gen. 34). The brothers insisted that the male Hivite community undergo circumcision before they would give Dinah to the Hivite leader, Shechem, for marriage (34:14-17). In effect this meant a mass conversion, so to speak, to Israel's God. In effect however it was a plot to render the Hivites temporarily defenseless. Although it was a pretense on the part of Jacob's sons, it reflects their sense of national identity as "the people of God," not Hebrew ethnicity. Circumcision obviously was not an inherited trait but a ritual expression of the people's commitment to the Lord God from generation to generation.

Last, some have claimed that the Jews were xenophobic (i.e., fearful of or having intense dislike for foreigners). The chief examples put forward are the policies of Ezra and Nehemiah, who were leaders of the postexilic community in Judah. The resistance of Ezra and Nehemiah to foreigners only reflected the original Mosaic law's cautions against intermarriage for religious reasons and was not a new prohibition. They had witnessed firsthand the devastating results of intermarriage and its (virtually) inevitable sway of religious pluralism. They did not want to repeat the same offense in this struggling community whose enemies were pressing upon them directly through armed resistance and indirectly through cultural enticements. They took dramatic steps to purge the population of its interracial marriages with "foreign women," that is, women who were not members of the postexilic community, requiring Israelite men to divorce their foreign-born wives (Ezra 9:1–15; 10:10–11; Neh. 10:30; 13:23–28). Although Nehemiah took stern action (13:25), it is often forgotten that the reform movement under Ezra was generated by the response of the community, not imposed by Ezra (Ezra 9:1–2; 10:2–4). Theirs was not an anti-foreigner campaign based on bigotry but a religious reform to preserve the integrity of their faith, whether held by Jew or Gentile proselyte. Ezra and Nehemiah also instituted other religious reforms, not just ethnic segregation (Ezra 8:15–31; Neh. 13:10–22). Because of religious pluralism, the leaders took measures that were exceptional and extreme, not a regular practice.

We in the Christian community today are not surprised by the admonition in Israel to avoid foreign entanglements as a general principle. The apostle Paul warned his flock at Corinth not to entangle themselves in relationships with unbelievers: "Do not be mismatched with unbelievers" (2 Cor. 6:14 HCSB). The setting for Paul's remarks was the participation of Christians in pagan worship of idols (2 Cor. 6:14–18), but the teaching is applicable to marriage and business partnerships. At stake is Christian devotion to God, not ethnic segregation, for the same apostle Paul declared, "There is neither Jew nor Greek . . . in Christ Jesus" (Gal. 3:28; also Rom. 10:12; Col. 3:11). Of course, Paul in his letters did not deny ethnic differences; he only denied that they have a role in constituting Christian identity and community. Rather, he celebrated that the Lord alone could unify all peoples as "one new humanity" (Eph. 2:15 NRSV). Religious compromise was the culprit, not intermarriage of races.

THOUGHT PROVOKERS

1. In what way can someone rightly say that the Jews are "the people of God"? On the other hand, why is it accurate to say that all peoples in Christ, regardless of ethnicity or race, are "the people of God"?

2. What terms in the Old Testament refer to people who were not native-born Israelites? What are the diverse terms used today describing "aliens among us" and what do they mean? Are we put off (or angry) when we hear rhetoric such as "undocumented immigrant" or "illegal alien"? What does this say about our stance toward immigrants? What privileges and responsibilities did the "outsiders" have in ancient Israel toward the "host" country? What privileges and responsibilities do immigrants have today?

3. What is your personal view toward immigration, both legal and illegal? What factors should be considered in forming your view of immigration? How do you resolve the tension between the Bible's teaching on compassion and on honoring law-abiding behavior? What biblical principles should we apply in developing a Christian attitude toward immigrants? Do you know an undocumented immigrant as an acquaintance or friend? Do you know any immigrant? How important is it that we have personal knowledge of an undocumented immigrant when considering the issue of immigration? What steps can you take personally and collectively as a church to become familiar with individuals and families who have moved here from other countries?

4. Has your church formed a policy toward accepting immigrants? What steps might be taken for your church to consider a ministry to immigrants? What should be the policy of your church toward immigrants who live nearby or visit your church? What should be your church's view of public policies regarding immigration? Should your church take a clear stand on immigration policy? Why or why not?

5. More than thirty years ago I discovered a disappointing attitude that I had harbored. My wife and I had just bought a house. On the day we moved in I was surprised to discover that my neighbor (across two fences—his and mine) was African American. The first thing that leapt to mind, to my shame then and now, was the fear that more minorities were around or moving in and would bring down the value of my house. Coincidentally, my realtor was visiting

to wish us well as we moved in, and I asked her, in a muted voice, about the number of minorities in the community. Her reply was probably both morally appropriate and legally required: "I don't know." Later that day I was struck by what a poor witness I had been. I vowed never again to take such an unchristian attitude and pollute the minds of my family and others. As it turned out, I had a friendly relationship with my neighbor. How do you *really* feel toward people of a different color who move into your neighbor or attend your church? Have you had an eye-opening experience like mine that revealed, at least to yourself, the depths of your hidden prejudices? What do we learn from such experiences or from hearing of others who have experienced something similar?

6. Since the Bible shows a mixed picture of interracial marriage—skepticism toward the "also peoples" *and* compassionate acceptance of them—what does the Bible teach us as followers of Christ about interracial marriage today? About the children of such unions? I have heard it said that you do not know if you are in fact prejudiced until your daughter brings home a new boyfriend who is of a different color!

7. Children are typically "sponges" when it comes to learning right or wrong attitudes and practices. What are you teaching your children or grandchildren about the "also peoples"? If you do not have children, how are you influencing your circle of friends and coworkers?

Chapter 4

God's Welcome to All

WORSHIP OF THE LORD God—the God of Abraham, Isaac, and Jacob—did not begin with the founding of Israel. This is often overlooked. Before there was Abraham and Moses, there were people among the nations who worshipped the one true living Lord.

WORSHIP "BEFORE ABRAHAM WAS"

We have adapted Jesus' words in his dispute with the Pharisees, "before Abraham was, I am," when he claimed his superiority over even Abraham and his preexistence as the Christ (John 8:58). The worship of the true God was not initiated by Israel and was never limited to Israel. The worship of the "LORD" (*Yahweh*), the distinctive name of Israel's God, was practiced by people before the call of Abraham and the founding of the nation of Israel (Gen. 4:26). John Levenson observed that the unique role of Israel as God's means of revelation to the nations (Exod. 19:5-6) did not contradict the universal openness to the worship of God.[1] The special role of Israel, as discussed in chapter 3, was conditional to its faithfulness to the divine mandate to be "a light to the nations" (e.g., Isa. 42:6; Luke 2:32). Israel was to be the conduit whereby all peoples might know and worship the Creator and Redeemer. Israel never had exclusive rights to God. The failure of national Israel to achieve its task was resolved by the one true seed of Abraham, the Lord Jesus Christ, who was that true and shining light to the Gentiles (e.g., Isa. 42:6; 49:6; Luke 2:32; Acts 13:47; Rev. 21:24).

---

1. John Levenson, "The Universal Horizon of Biblical Particularism" in *Ethnicity and the Bible* (Leiden: Brill, 1996), 143-69.

The examples of those who knew and worshiped the Lord apart from Abraham and Israel include the patriarchal figures Noah and Job, and the Canaanite priest-king Melchizedek, a contemporary of Abraham. Noah, we are told, worshipped the Lord God. The narrative says that he built an altar to "the LORD" (*Yahweh*) (Gen. 8:20). Job, too, was not a Hebrew as the story's context shows. He and his friends were members of the nations (Job 1:1; 2:11). The setting of the story does not make reference to Israel or any of the distinctive traits of Hebrew worship, such as tabernacle, Aaron's priesthood, and Davidic kingship. Yet the story refers to his piety as one who "feared God" (*Elohim*, 1:1), meaning that he worshiped God. The identity of his "God" is *Yahweh* (the LORD), according to the narrative (e.g., 1:6; 42:12) and by Job's own use of the name, although rarely (1:21; 12:9).[2]

As for Melchizedek, even though he remains an obscure figure to us, the author of Genesis makes it clear that he knew the Lord God as Abraham did and they worshipped the same God (Gen. 14:18–20). The name under which the Canaanite priest knew the Lord was the general name for deity, *El Elyon* ("God Most High"). *El Elyon* is identified as the "Creator of heaven and earth" (v. 19). Abraham's response indicates that *El Elyon* was one and the same as *Yahweh* (see v. 22). This meant that there was worship led by this king-priest in the city of Salem (i.e., Jerusalem, Ps. 76:2). The legitimacy of Melchizedek's priesthood is shown by the offering of a tithe by Abraham (Gen. 14:20), and the order of priesthood by which King David's royal line held its priesthood (Ps. 100:4). The writer of Hebrews acknowledged Melchizedek's priesthood as superior to Aaron's priesthood when he identified the priesthood of Jesus with that of Melchizedek (Heb. 5:6, 10; 6:20; 7:1–17).

Worship of the Lord God was not narrow and parochial. The worship of God was always open to all people groups. The call in the New Testament to extend the gospel to the nations is not an innovation but a return to the ultimate purpose of the call of Abraham and the fulfillment of that role by Jesus and the apostles.

---

2. See also Ezek. 14:14, 20. Ezekiel groups Job with the righteous heroes Noah and Daniel, all three worshippers of the LORD God.

GOD'S WELCOME TO ALL

Welcome is a critical feature in understanding the nature of worship in the Bible. Worship entails welcome and our acceptance of God's invitation. The Lord extended his invitation to all peoples to know and worship him. In our study of creation (chapter 1), we learned that the Lord transformed what was an unproductive and uninhabited world into a thriving, productive cosmos. He gave the divine blessing of procreation to men and women, who were to exercise responsible dominion over the earth (Gen. 1:26–28). At the conclusion of the six days of creation, the Lord established a day of celebration, the seventh day, and he made it "holy," a special day devoted to him. By implication in the creation narrative, and as made clear in the law of Moses, creation was invited to join him in this celebration. The Sabbath was a day of worship.

We also discovered that God established a unique people, and he chose to make his "home" among them (chapter 2). The twelve tribes of Israel encircled the tabernacle sanctuary, the residence of God. They were invited to visit him daily and especially every seventh day to offer him expressions of worship. The Sabbath, like creation's seventh day, entailed an invitation "to enter into his presence with thanksgiving" (Ps. 100:4). The Sabbath was a day of rest for all, including resident immigrants, foreigners, and even animal life. In chapter 3, we examined the identity and place of the "stranger" in ancient Israel, and we discovered that Israel was charged with welcoming immigrants and treating them with *hospitality*, which meant favorably and justly. We gave special attention to the meaning of the "assembly of the LORD" (Deut. 23), which referred to the community's public worship. Because of the sacred character of the community as the people of God, divine directives instructed the people as to the level of participation allowed foreigners and resident immigrants.

THE SIGNIFICANCE OF HOSPITALITY AND WORSHIP

Since divine welcome (hospitality) is central to worship, we must explore the tradition of hospitality and what it means today for *genuine* Christian hospitality and its call for all peoples to accept the divine welcome. This is the basis for multicultural worship. We may be surprised to learn that Christian hospitality is not what we think it is. There are two levels of hospitality, and it is easy to confuse the two.

John Koenig, in his study of the church's teaching on hospitality, describes the two features as "blendings of the spiritual and moral" and as the "spiritual-material welcoming" of the church.[3] Romans 12:13, he explains, reflects the twofold nature of Christian hospitality, which is an "expanding category."[4] In other words, the idea of hospitality is fluid, sometimes used in a narrow sense of a table meal and at other times broadening to include the offer of the gospel. In this verse the terms that best describe the idea of hospitality, "fellowship" (*koinoneo/koinonia*) and "hospitality" (*philoxenia*), are found together: "Share (*koinoneo*) in the needs of the saints and pursue the practice of hospitality (*philoxenia*)." *Koinonia* means to share in, partnership, which refers here to the physical dimension and *philoxenia* broadens this endeavor in the context of hospitality.

In the 1920s and 1930s, John D. Rockefeller Jr. was the richest man in the world. He also was generous and kind. After inheriting the fortune of his father, who founded the Standard Oil Company, Rockefeller Jr. spent his life as a philanthropist. One of his favorite projects was the restoration of Williamsburg, the colonial capitol of Virginia (1699–1780). He restored the Bassett Hall as his personal residence for two months of the year. John and his wife, Abby, hoping to be accepted by the little community of Williamsburg, entertained the citizens in their restored, but modest, home. During the evenings the Rockefellers hosted dinner with the cultural finery one would expect from the privileged, spontaneously inviting local acquaintances in the city. Abby would call the local William and Mary College, inviting five young women to the house for an afternoon tea. This gesture was a generous and sincere expression, but its very nature prevented the Rockefellers and the neighbors from creating true community. This was a benevolent act of entertainment that may

---

3. John Koenig, *New Testament Hospitality: Partnership with Strangers as Promise and Mission* (Philadelphia: Fortress, 1985), 2, 110.
4. Ibid., 10.

have been fueled by Christian motivation, but it was not Christian hospitality at the proper depth.

The divine gift of welcome is participation in the life of the triune God. At Basset Hall, there was no confusion as to the status of the guests and the host. The invitation was for one night only, and the guests had no illusion that they were the new "soul mates" of the Rockefellers. Theirs was an offer of entertainment, perhaps even Christian entertainment.

The *totality* of Christian hospitality cannot be understood as Christian fellowship in a person's home or in the church's gathering. We must consider the spiritual dimension of *genuine* Christian hospitality to see the Bible's portrait of multicultural worship. Multicultural worship is not a matter of ethnic diversity for its own sake. Ethnic inclusion is a natural expression of the divine invitation of fellowship God has offered to all peoples, "For in one Spirit we were all baptized into one body, Jews or Greeks, slaves or free, and we were all made to drink of one Spirit" (1 Cor. 12:13). The custom of hospitality intersects with our study here because the Old and New Testaments frequently use the imagery of hospitality when describing the kingdom of God. The depiction of hospitality in the future kingdom, as in ancient Israel and in New Testament times, included a host and guests who feasted together on food and drink in joyful celebration. Events, parables, and images of feasting paint the climactic moment when those of all nationalities who answered the call to dine with God come together in the kingdom at his supper table. Our Lord established his Supper to present the divine welcome that is now ours through the death and resurrection of the Lord Jesus. We celebrate the bread and cup, remembering that our "daily bread" too is a token of the final day of feasting—feasting on the true Living Bread that comes from our Host.

Since God's creation and redemption plan always envisioned the inclusion of all people groups, we conclude our Old Testament emphasis by looking at what the Bible portrays as the destiny of the nations. The prophet Isaiah's visions depict a new creation in which Zion (i.e., Jerusalem) is exalted above all nations. Zion, the location of the temple, was the traditional setting for the worship of Israel's God. The nations will join the Israelites in acknowledging the reign of the Lord God over all the earth. The psalmist entreats the nations to unite in the universal praise of God's glorious rule (Ps. 67). The church's inclusiveness of all peoples in the worship of the Lord Jesus Christ demonstrates here and now the future new creation and prepares us for the final expression of his universal kingdom (e.g., Rev. 7, 21–22).

INVITATION TO WORSHIP FOR ALL

"Do not overlook to show hospitality to strangers, for by this some people have entertained angels, not knowing it" (Heb. 13:2). When was the last time that you were visited by an angel and you refused to take in this visitor? Never, for if we knew that the stranger was an angel we would be quick to receive him. The author of Hebrews alluded to the guests (three "men") received by Abraham. Two of them, later revealed as angelic messengers, were also welcomed by Lot (Gen. 18–19). It is striking that one of the messengers was the Lord God (18:1–2). When we remember the words of Jesus, "I was a stranger and you welcomed me" (Matt. 25:35), we must consider the custom of hospitality in ancient Israel and in the church (Matt. 25:34–46). Jesus spoke of care for the stranger as a criterion for entrance into his eternal kingdom. Could anything be more important? But the questions that immediately emerge for our purposes are these. What did receiving strangers consist of? What is the meaning of authentic Christian hospitality? And was Jesus speaking generally of all peoples in need or were "the least of these my brothers" referring only to Christians? What is the obligation of the church to itself and to others outside the body of Christ?

The Custom of Hospitality

By "custom of Christian hospitality" we mean the tradition of practicing hospitality in ancient Israel and in the church. We do not refer directly to the deeper theological level that calls for a hospitality that is possible only through the spiritual relationship of the believer to the Lord God. And, significantly, that rich fellowship of the believer with his Savior is of the same order as that of the triune God.

We will address this further below. Here, we want to make it clear that we are not minimizing the practice of material generosity toward others. This practice is critically important, for to fail to do so would be disobedience and an indication of a person's grim spiritual condition. The apostle John warned his readers, "if anyone has the world's goods and sees his brother in need, yet closes his heart against him, how does God's love abide in him?" (1 John 3:17). What we contend is that the custom of Christian hospitality is an expression of a spiritual fellowship that transcends all human barriers, because authentic Christian fellowship is born out of the fellowship experienced within the Godhead. When we come to recognize the transcendent quality of this hospitality, then human barriers such as race, gender, and economic status are silly walls that men and women have erected because of human sin.

But first, let's look at the two most important elements of the custom. Protection and provision capture the chief obligations of host toward welcomed strangers. The practice of hospitality was highly valued in the ancient Near East. By extending hospitality the host provided safe haven for the traveler who was typically subject to the threats of the wild and to robbers. Provisions often included water for refreshment (e.g., Gen. 24:14; Judg. 4:19) and for washing dusty feet (e.g., Gen. 18:4; 19:2; Judg. 19:21; Matt. 10:14 pars.; Luke 7:44-46 pars.; John 13:5). Lodging for the night (e.g., Gen. 19:2-3; Judg. 19:6-20; Acts 21:16), a sumptuous meal (e.g., Gen. 18:5; 19:3; 24:33; Luke 10:7-11), and care for the traveler's animals were features of a good host (Gen. 24:19, 32; 43:24; Judg. 19:21).

Such hospitality was not a matter of setting up a chain of hotels for travelers. It was not a commercial enterprise. Nor was it a matter of entreating nearby friends and members of one's extended family. Hospitality was meant for the unknown person who seeks refuge. Essentially, hospitality in ancient Israel was a practice indicating a change in the status of a stranger to become a part of the host's community.[5] That this social transformation occurs can be seen in the

---

5. T. R. Hobbs, "Hospitality in the First Testament and the 'Theological Fallacy,'" *JSOST* 95 (2001): 3-30. Hobbs describes the practices and role of hospitality in ancient Israel. His is a sociological analysis, explaining how hospitality as a social convention functioned in the ancient world.

example of Job, whose affliction meant rejection even by the guests and servants in his household. Using the imagery of host and guest, Job bemoans his plight. Although the host, he has been counted an outsider—a stranger and foreigner in his own home (Job 19:15).

The payoff for the host in entering such a transaction was not monetary or even a pledge to return the favor. The host and traveler probably never again came into contact. The motivation for the host was maintaining honor in the community. A refusal to accept the request of an outsider was shameful and injured his social standing. More importantly, however, the Mosaic law called this refusal a *sinful* act. But exceptions were made since all strangers could not be welcomed, such as fugitives, murderers, thieves, and dangerous mercenaries.

The traveler of course benefitted by receiving a welcoming community, such as he would receive from his near family members and tribe. As we like to say today, "home away from home." Sociologists point out that the relationship of host and stranger had the symbolic value of changing a stranger's standing as a potential threat to accepting him as family who received provision and protection. The potential danger to the host and his near community has been transformed. Descriptive of this feature is the story of Lot's two visitors who were threatened in the city by the residents of Sodom.[6] Lot went to great lengths to protect his guests, even to offering his two daughters as sexual surrogates. The custom of hospitality took precedence in Lot's mind over the protection of his daughters. Although this was a sordid incident, it shows how important the custom was and how the visitors had become prized members of the host's personal "community" (household).

A parallel story tells of a Levite and his companions who visit the city of Gibeah en route to their home (Judg. 19). The story is a theological exposé on the sinfulness of the people during the dark days of the Judges. It is about a breach of hospitality. The Levite was "sojourning"[7] in the region of Ephraim (northern Israel), and his concubine abandoned him for her father's home in Bethlehem (south). He successfully wooed her to return, but her father insisted

---

6. W. Fields, *Sodom and Gomorrah: History and Motif in Biblical Narrative* (Sheffield: Sheffield Academic, 1997).

7. The verb "to sojourn" (*gar*) is etymologically related to the word "alien, sojourner" (*ger*), a resident alien (see chapter 3).

that he remain for five days, despite the desire of the Levite to leave. This was an exaggerated picture of hospitality. It served as a contrast to the behavior of the men of Sodom. At last the Levite and concubine left and traveled in the vicinity of Jebus (i.e., Jerusalem), which they avoided because the city was a Jebusite (Canaanite) holding. Nearby Gibeah was more appealing since it was part of the Israelite tribal people, from whom they would expect to receive favorable treatment. The irony is, the trouble they tried to avoid by not going to Jebus, they found in Gibeah. Moreover, there is a symbolic irony in that a "city" in ancient times meant security against the threat of the unknown, untamed wild. But they met with hostilities as they moved deeper into the heart of the city. Another unexpected aspect of the story is that a resident alien (*ger*) in Gibeah, not a native to the city, was the only person willing to take in the travelers. When the men of the city demanded the visitors for their pleasure, the host refused. To appease their demands, the Levite's concubine was given to the men, who raped and murdered her.

Hospitality was a feature of a godly community, consisting of provision and protection for unknown travelers. It involved a social transformation from potential threat to time-honored guest and secured for the host his social standing as a righteous man in the opinion of his community.

The Heart and Hearth of Hospitality

Does the Bible call for the Christian community to respond to the needs of the immigrant population? What is the suitable application for today's church? What is the difference between modern and ancient concepts of hospitality? What is hospitality in the minds of most people today?

Hospitality Today

I grew up in the culture of "southern hospitality" and have lived the last twenty years in the heart of southern hospitality (Birmingham, Alabama). I had always thought that I was a product of the South until I moved to the real South, the Deep South, and realized that

I was from the South*west*, for the South has its own cultural stamp. Historically, southern hospitality involved openness to travelers and was characterized by presenting table meals and lodging. It developed into the fine art of proper etiquette, including cordiality in speech, graciousness in actions (e.g., opening doors for women), and inviting friends and acquaintances for a heartwarming meal adorned by the finest tableware in the house.

I once rented a car in Detroit. When the parking lot attendant handed me my paperwork and released me from the rental car parking lot, I chimed my warmest, "Thank you, ma'am." When she broke into a smile, I realized that I had been discovered as a "foreigner" of southern roots. I responded kindly, "And yes, I am from the South!"

In a word, southern hospitality is being and talking "nice." Some people from different regions don't understand the underlying good intentions and are put off—even offended—by it.

I like public civility, and I think that it is a good alternative to being curt, but that is a cultural prejudice on my part. Others prefer speech that is not "dainty," as a northerner once described southern politeness; they prefer candor and sincerity (the assumption being that the southern practice is insincere). But biblical hospitality, as practiced in ancient Israel and in the Greco-Roman world, was not a mere showing of proper decorum in speech, dress, and superficial niceties. It is misleading to measure Christian hospitality by Western standards of inviting friends or acquaintances to our homes for a meal. We can be fooled by the preponderance of table meals in the Bible, thinking that is what hospitality is in its totality. Table meals show how we as Christians understand ourselves and how we practice Christian welcome, but they are not the whole of hospitality. Sharing a meal and complimenting the host for setting a good table betrays a superficiality that is anything but authentic inclusion. Even in the church, hospitality as fellowship can be profitable for the inclusion of the community, but it must be more than a "grand time had by all."

Christian Hospitality and the Triune God

Many interpreters equate the Bible's teaching on hospitality with the modern trend toward openness and inclusiveness, especially to immigrants and people who are racially different from ourselves (i.e., strangers). An examination of the Bible's understanding of hospitality will show us that Christian hospitality is much more and requires much more. Hospitality is to know and worship the triune God—accepting and participating in his transcendent welcome. The subtitle of Elizabeth Newman's book *Untamed Hospitality: Welcoming God and Other Strangers* captures the essence of Christian hospitality.[8] It reflects the two dimensions of Christian hospitality: the divine quality of hospitality and the human aspect of shared life. Her definition plunges us into a world that is foreign to our typical thinking for it "names *our graced participation* in the *triune life of God*, an extraordinary adventure where *together* we discover how to live out of an abundance unimagined."[9]

I have italicized the points above that we should consider. Hospitality has its origin in the nature of the *triune life of God*; it is a divine quality and, as such, can only be bestowed, that is, *graced*, not gained by trade or achievement. The gift is our *participation* in the life of the triune God. We do this by worship, according to Newman. Hospitality is not collateral to worship or a by-product of worship. Hospitality *is* worship.[10] Divine welcome is the ultimate meaning of hospitality, for the Lord God extends a welcome to us as outsiders to live in his life—the fellowship of the Father, Son, and Holy Spirit. It is also *our* and *together*, indicating that hospitality means community in its fullest sense. I do not mean just any connecting of peoples, even the inherent bonding of human kinship. This "together" refers to the transcendent brotherhood and sisterhood that we have with the Lord and thus with one another. In other words, when we enter into the life of the Lord God, we immediately find that the "house," so to speak, is full of others too. When guests arrived at Rockefeller's Bassett Hall, they found other guests seated around the dining room table. Presumably, they enjoyed one another as well as the hosts.

But the fellowship we speak of is not being friendly or even delving into personal, heartfelt matters with others, even with old

---

8. Elizabeth Newman, *Untamed Hospitality: Welcoming God and Other Strangers* (Grand Rapids: Baker, 2007).
9. Ibid., 14.
10. Ibid., 18.

friends or beloved family members. Christian fellowship involves re-lationship that is birthed and nurtured in the Lord's love for us; we in turn love him and one another, for "we love because he [Christ] first loved us" (1 John 4:19; cf. John 14:34-35). In Jesus' parable of the great feast, the host instructed his servant to go into the streets and countryside, bringing in more guests "so that my house might be filled" (Luke 14:23). Can one imagine a guest entering the home of the Rockefellers, sitting in a treasured position and then saying to the host, "Why did you invite that person tonight, Mr. Rockefeller? If I had known that person was here, I wouldn't have come. I only dine with people who look and think like me." In my mind I see John expelling the guest, explaining to the others, "I guess he wasn't inter-ested in dining with Abby and me after all." This analogy perhaps casts some light on the absurdity of presuming on the fellowship of God by rejecting people of different ethnicity, gender, or status. When we realize that all of us in the household of faith come by God's welcome, we have no reason to demand anything of the Lord or of others.

Biblical hospitality therefore is not and cannot be an individual's choice and activity. It is not a matter of a person extending help to another person irrespective of the crowded "house" we just acknowl-edged. It is bound up in being and acting in the context of relating to others, both *relating* to the host and to guests, as well as *being* the host and guest. At the same time we are host and guest—guest in the Lord's house and host by offering to others in the house God's grace that we have received. Koenig explains the mission of the church in these terms as he finds Luke's Gospel emphasizing the connection of the table meal and the word of the gospel.[11] Jesus became the host where he had been initially the guest, extending to others the gospel of the kingdom (e.g., Luke 7:35-50). Luke saw the table as the means for bringing outsiders into the refuge of the kingdom. A contempo-rary example is my former student and his wife who were invited by new friends to break the Muslim fast of Ramadan. Although they are the honored guests, they pray as the salt and light to build a rela-tionship in which they also can be hosts, extending to their Muslim friends welcome to the gospel.

---

11. Koenig, *New Testament Hospitality*, 90-91, 110, 119-20.

Although hospitality transcends ethnic differences, hospitality is not merely acceptance of and engendering ethnic diversity. Interpreters often equate the Bible's teaching on hospitality with the modern trend toward openness and inclusiveness, especially welcome to immigrants and people who are racially different from ourselves ("foreigners" and "strangers"). The problem is that Israel usually regarded hospitality as a function of protection for those who were already members of the host's *wider* community, such as tribal affiliation or a resident alien who has received community recognition and protective status on other grounds (e.g., Exod. 22:21; Num. 9:14). Foreigners who were not member residents had a different status since they were visitors, such as those in search of trade or were prisoners of war.[12] Newman speaks of a modern "distortion" of genuine hospitality if we assume that diversity is the *goal* of hospitality.[13] Rather, she contends, true biblical hospitality is the *means* to a goal. In ancient Israel the goal was preserving the community and the honor of the host.[14] In uniquely Christian hospitality the goal is contributing to the kingdom of God and setting before the world a picture of the kingdom. Inclusion alone does not correspond to biblical hospitality. The Bible's understanding of hospitality shows us that Christian hospitality is much more and requires much more. Authentic hospitality is to know and worship the triune God—accepting and participating in his welcome.

Christian Hospitality and Mercy

Are we then to disregard any responsibility for the protection of immigrants? No, for the Bible makes it clear that benevolence toward the underclass undergirds the favorable treatment of others, regardless if they are in the household of faith or not. Although there is no one-to-one equation between what was meant by hospitality in ancient times and today's treatment of immigrants, we are responsible for the lowest social class, which often includes recent immigrants. Yes, the "least of these my brothers and sisters" is probably a reference to

---

12. Ibid., 20–21.
13. Newman, *Untamed Hospitality*, 30–33.
14. Hobbs, "Hospitality," 7–8, 28.

Christians (Matt. 25:40, 45; cf. "his brother in need," 1 John 3:17), but Jesus showed compassion to the needy, and he expected his disciples to do the same (e.g., Matt. 9:13; 12:7; 19:21 pars.; Luke 19:8).[15] We do not close our doors to others, but we must realize that the two differ. One expresses Christian humanitarian impulses, and the other is grounded in our life with the triune God. Both are connected, for ultimately meeting the needs of others is Christian.

By serving as host we address the needs of others, and it gives us opportunities to act as host in the kingdom by inviting our guests to accept the invitation of Christ that he offers them—to become joint heirs in the kingdom with him and with everyone in the household of faith. "In fact, together with Christ we are heirs of God's glory" (Rom. 8:17 NLT). At the same time we are host and guest—guest in the Lord's house and host by offering to others in the house God's grace that we have received. Jesus was both guest and host at the Lord's Supper, for the owner of the house where the disciples gathered had prepared "a guest room" for Jesus (Mark 14:14; par.), and Jesus was host to the disciples he had invited to celebrate, providing food and drink. Moreover, he took on the role of a host's servant by washing the feet of the disciples (John 13:5) and called upon them to do the same in his name (13:14–17). Christian hospitality means that *we are welcomed and we welcome.*

HOSPITALITY IN AN INHOSPITABLE WORLD

Repeatedly, Israel and the church faced hostilities in the world. Israel's enemies were many and formidable. Only during a brief period in the reigns of David and Solomon did Israel have the upper-hand over its neighbors, but never did Israel achieve or even seek an empire such as those of Egypt and the Mesopotamian countries of Assyria and Babylonia. Instead, the history of Israel was marked by two extended periods of exile, the Egyptian exile for four hundred years and the Babylonian exile for about seventy years, although in a sense it did not end for centuries as the Jews remained under the thumb of the

---

15. David L. Turner, "The Gospel of Matthew," *Cornerstone Biblical Commentary*, vol. 11 (Carol Stream, IL: Tyndale, 2005), 330.

nations during "the times of the Gentiles" (Luke 21:24). The church followed the course of its founder, Jesus, who knew only "trouble in this world" (John 16:33; cf. Matt. 10:22 pars.). We are indeed "strangers" in this world (Heb. 11:13; 1 Peter 1:1; 2:11), whose home is a heavenly citizenship (Phil. 3:20; cf. John 18:36).

The Kingdom's Homecoming for All

Although we are not welcomed in this world, there is a far greater homecoming awaiting us when we will hear the Master's voice, "Well done, my good and faithful servant. . . . Let's celebrate together!" (Matt. 5:21, 23 NLT). Hospitality does not know the time zones of the ages. It is spoken of in the Bible in the past, present, and future. This is because hospitality has its source in the Eternal—from the eternal past through the forever future. The fellowship within the Godhead—Father, Son, and Holy Spirit—is the proper dimension for us to consider the transcendence of invitation. The Lord's Supper reflects the transcendence of the Lord's welcome. The Lord's Supper was set in the context of the past, the Jewish Passover, which remembered the nation's liberation from slavery in Egypt. As Jesus served the bread and cup to the disciples, he expressed its meaning in the present tense: "This is my body" and "this is my blood" (Matt. 26:26, 28 pars.). And the Supper pointed ahead, for Jesus delayed drinking the cup, saying he will drink it "new with you in my Father's kingdom" (Matt. 26:29 par.). "With you," in the plural, corresponds to what we have said about communal hospitality as central to the kingdom.

Isaiah's vision of the climactic feast of the ages describes the Lord God as Host who provides a rich table of food and drink (Isa. 25:6-8). The feast is set in the context of Israel's worship "on this mountain," referring to Jerusalem's temple arena. The banquet will include an eternal respite from enemies, including sorrow and death. The nations who had oppressed God's people will be rejected by the Host. The psalmists depicted the Lord as perfect Host who provides and protects (Ps. 23; 39:12). Here, too, the psalmists refer to the threat of enemies whom they call upon the Lord to vanquish. That this eternal banquet is not limited to Israel is indicated in the phrase "all the nations will stream" to the house of the Lord like a flowing

river (Isa.2:4).[16] They will call out, "Come, let us go up to the mountain of the LORD, to the house of the God of Jacob" (v. 3) so that
they will receive the teaching of the Lord. It will be an unending
period of peace when the great Judge inaugurates the presence of the
kingdom, "a nation will not lift up sword against nation" (v. 14). The
reference to "Jacob" and to the "nations" reflects the particularity
of Israel and the universal invitation to the nations. By coming to
the temple, the nations acknowledge the identity of God in terms of
the patriarchal promises, the God of Abraham, Isaac, and Jacob. He
is the God of promise who will save those who confess him as their
God, whether Hebrew or of the nations.

This recognition of Israel as the unique means of God's salvation, however, will not diminish the place of the nations in the future
kingdom. The prophet also saw the full partnership of the nations
with redeemed Israel. He described the future conversion of Egypt
and Assyria, countries where Israel had once been enslaved exiles.
These two nations were representative of the nations, for they and
Babylonia were the most notorious enemies of Israel.

In that day there will be a highway from Egypt to Assyria,
and Assyria will enter Egypt, and Egypt will enter Assyria, and
the Egyptians and the Assyrians will worship together. In that
day Israel, a blessing in the midst of the earth, will be a third
member with Egypt and Assyria, whom the LORD of hosts will
bless—'Blessed be Egypt my people, and Assyria the work of my
hands, and Israel my possession.'" (Isa. 19:23–25)

The "highway" is a metaphor expressing the free exchange between peoples. Gary Smith captures the idea well when he observes
that walls separate people, but "roads connect people and allow them to
interact."[17] What is the interaction in view? Not crass geopolitical treaties
and commerce. It is the worship of the Lord God. The idea of highway
continues in his prophecy when the prophet announced the triumphant
coming of Israel's God: "make straight in the wilderness a highway

16. Micah 4:1–3 parallels Isa. 2:1–4.
17. Gary Smith, *Isaiah 1–39*, NAC (Nashville: B&H, 2007), 363.

for our God" (Isa. 40:3; also John the Baptist, Matt. 3:3 pars.). More compelling still in Isaiah's vision is the descriptions of the three allies. Descriptions used of God's people, Israel, are applied to Egypt and Assyria. Egypt is also "my people" (e.g., Isa. 10:24) and Assyria "the work of my hands" (e.g., Isa. 29:23). The nations are of equal weight with Israel who is God's prized "possession" (e.g., Isa. 63:17). At one time Israel as God's "people" could be contrasted with wicked Assyria and Egypt (Isa. 10:24), but now they are all three God's holy people.

Isaiah 66, the concluding chapter of the prophet's vision, ends on the triumphant note of the redeemed who will gather in the house of the Lord to worship. This chapter sets before the reader the world of the new creation, "the new heavens and a new earth" (65:17). The new creation will include judgment and salvation. The divine invitation was extended to all peoples to repent, but those who refused to answer the call will be under judgment (66:4). This judgment will not be exclusive; his fiery wrath will descend upon "all flesh," including Israel, whose religion was self-vindicating (v. 16). But salvation, too, will not be exclusive. The salvation of God will be for all "nations" and "tongues" (v. 18). What will it be that attracts the nations to the call? The "glory" of the Lord will be revealed for all to see (cf. Isa. 6:3; 40:5; 62:2). The Lord's judgment falls first upon Israel, but there will be survivors who will be purged through the fiery wrath. The redeemed survivors (remnant) will exhibit and publish to the world the Lord's glory.

This demonstration of God's glory will result in the conversion of the nations who in turn will escort the Jews living among the nations to their homeland, where they will all join together in the worship of the Lord God. Again, as we saw earlier, the two dimensions of God's salvific work are found—the vehicle of his grace through repentant Israel and the universal appeal to all peoples. But what is unexpected will be the mediating role of the nations. The nations will achieve an intercessory role but in reverse, bringing Israel's "brothers" to Jerusalem (v. 20). John Oswalt describes it as "a full circle."[18] To underscore the privileged role of the nations, the passage

---

18. John Oswalt, *The Book of Isaiah Chapters 40–66*, NICOT (Grand Rapids: Eerdmans, 1997), 689.

declares further that the nations will be priests who have the same stature as the Levitical tribe (v. 21). This portrait of the inclusion of the nations could not be more stunning to the readers. The nations will have received full acceptance and even an honored position in the household of faith, a place which had been restricted to one family (Aaron), from one tribe (Levi), and from one nation (Israel). "Foreigners" (*nokri*) will "join themselves" to Israel and worship the Lord, receiving acceptance by the Lord on God's "holy mountain" in the "house of prayer," meeting its purpose as a house of prayer "for all peoples" (Isa. 56:6–7). For this reason, our Lord cleared out the money changers from the temple, making way for the age of the new creation when all peoples would be welcomed (Matt. 21:13 pars.). Ezekiel's vision of the future restoration of Israel to the land adds to the image of the nations' full partnership in the kingdom. In an astonishing new way the "resident immigrant" (*ger*) will be integrated into the redeemed community. Aliens, too, will receive their own parcels of land, the promised land that had been limited to the tribes of Israel (Ezek. 47:23).

The Kingdom Now for All

What kind of world is this? This strange new creation? Peace will reign. Foreigners will join in the community of God's faithful people. They will receive the same privileges reserved for the people of God and will hold an equal share in the inheritance promised to Abraham and to his descendants, who at one time had also been aliens to the land of Canaan. The book of Revelation builds on the themes of feast and new creation that we have discovered in the prophets. The feast will be the marriage celebration of the Lamb, attended by all those who have been invited (Rev. 19:9). Those who worship the Lord will be from all peoples, "a great multitude, which no one could number, from every nation, tribe, people, and language" (Rev. 7:9; also 5:9; 14:6). John's vision of the new heaven and new earth included the dwelling place of the Lord, the New Jerusalem—"Look, God's home is among humankind ("men")! He will dwell with them, and they will be his *peoples*. God himself will be with them" (Rev. 21:3). I have italicized the word "peoples" to point out the plural. Here, John expands on the covenant language in the prophecy of Ezekiel (37:27), which originally referred to Israel, "they will be my people." The New Jerusalem will be inhabited by a new people, the new covenant people, who will include Gentiles and Jews (Rev. 21:24-26). These are the ones who have accepted the invitation to live with God forevermore. G. K. Beale points out that the reading of the plural was "in order to make obvious that prophecies originally focusing on Israel have been fulfilled in 'every tribe, tongue, people, and nation.'"[19]

But the future is now! When Jesus spoke the parable of the great feast (Matt. 22:1-14; Luke 14:15-24), it was one of several allusions he made to the kingdom, comparing it to a joyful feast in which his followers would participate (e.g., Matt. 8:11; 25:21-33). Jesus' own practice of eating and drinking contrasted with John's disciples and the Pharisees, who practiced fasting (e.g., Matt. 11:18-19 par.; Mark 2:18-22 pars.). Jesus announced that the "feast predicted by Isaiah (25:6-8) has already begun to appear in the present world order."[20]

Since the kingdom is in its spiritual, inaugurated form, we as the church must exhibit the marks of the kingdom's presence in the world. Worship must include the central idea of hospitality, the welcome of God to any and all who will answer the call. We must overcome the barriers of language, tradition, and the prejudice which we have wrongly held to. The task of bringing the gospel to all, and living as the redeemed community made up of all, is what we have received. Multicultural worship glorifies God by showing forth that he is the Master over all peoples, and that his kingdom's grace is available to all peoples whom he has created, loved, and for whom he made redemption possible through Jesus Christ. Let us pursue the worship of God united around the throne of God and the Lamb so that the world in our present hour might see what Jesus taught us to pray, "Thy kingdom come."

19. G. K. Beale, *The Book of Revelation*, NIGTC (Grand Rapids: Eerdmans, 1999), 1047.
20. John Koenig, "Hospitality," *Anchor Bible Dictionary*, ed. D. N. Freedman (New York: Doubleday, 1992), 3.300.

144 | *Chapter 4*

THOUGHT PROVOKERS

1. Why is it significant that worship among the nations occurred long before the founding of Israel? How do you view the universal invitation to worship God? How can your church strengthen its outreach to others, both locally and around the world?

2. What did "hospitality" mean to you before reading this chapter? How do you understand the biblical view of hospitality in contrast to today's idea of hospitality as entertainment?

3. What is the relationship between the fellowship within the triune God—the Father, Son, and Holy Spirit—and the call for hospitality in the Bible?

4. How does the Lord's Supper express Jesus' offer of the kingdom today to anyone who will receive his invitation?

5. Is there a difference between the shared spiritual fellowship of Christians in the household of faith and acts of mercy toward the disadvantaged? If so, how do they differ? What do they have in common?

6. Since God's welcome to know him as Lord is offered to all peoples, and since welcome is critical to worship, why has the church historically struggled to accept multicultural inclusion?

7. How can the church overcome man-made barriers of gender, race, and status to achieve racial integration in the church? How can your church establish a welcoming environment for minorities? What bridges can you and your church build with "strangers" to the way of the Lord so that you can present God's welcome?

Chapter 5

Jesus' Stories of Reconciliation

THE TENDENCY TO JUSTIFY racial discrimination based on Old Testament passages is indeed a *mis*interpretation of God's overall design and desire for all of humanity to worship him (see chapters 1 through 4). As we turn to the New Testament, several concerns will shape our discussion and examination. Is God's desire for worship from all peoples consistently portrayed in the New Testament? The answer is found in a familiar passage. After the resurrection, Jesus commissions his disciples: "Therefore, go and make disciples of all nations" (Matt. 28:19; cf. Mark 16:14–16; Luke 24:47; Acts 1:8). This passage, often cited in support of evangelism and missions, makes clear that Jesus desires disciples from all races. And since Jesus Christ, as the Son of God, reveals God the Father to the world (John 5:19, 30), the desire for followers from all nations is not simply Jesus' will, but ultimately the Father's.

But this mandate raises several questions. How does the command to make disciples of all nations relate to the gospel message? Does the Great Commission become significant simply on the basis that it is the last command of Jesus Christ before his ascension? Or, is this universal outreach somehow tied to the unique events of Jesus' death and resurrection? What precisely has happened in the death and resurrection of Jesus Christ that breaks open the doors of salvation to include not only Jews, but all people groups? The apostle Paul understands the cross as the place where discrimination among the people of God has been put to death: "There is neither Jew nor Gentile, slave nor free, male or female. For all of you are one in Christ Jesus" (Gal. 3:28). Indeed, all forms of discrimination—race, social status, and gender—are eliminated in Christ so that there is not "many," nor even "two," but "one" body of Christ. Paul explicitly and carefully explains how the cross procures reconciliation and integration among races (Eph. 2:11–22). His teaching is an important passage that clarifies why the church is most appropriately the place of racial reconciliation and integration. (See chapter 6.)

However, if Paul has accurately interpreted Jesus' final concern and commission for multiethnic disciples, was Jesus also concerned with racial reconciliation in his ministry? Wasn't Jesus *Jewish*? And didn't he have twelve *Jewish* disciples? According to the Gospels, Jesus' ministry concentrated primarily on the Jewish people and was, therefore, geographically confined to Judea. So, how does a Jewish Messiah become Savior not only of Jews, but also Gentiles? Is this shift toward a racially all-inclusive salvation to be credited to Paul's renowned zeal for the Gentiles? Did Jesus provide any hint of this boundary-breaking element in his proclamation of the good news?

JESUS AND THE GENTILES

Although Jesus primarily directed his attention to the Jews, the gospel writers provide clues throughout their stories that the implications of Jesus' ministry extended beyond the borders of Judea. These stories anticipate Jesus' command to his disciples to evangelize and make disciples of all nations (Matt. 28:19; Mark 16:14–16; Luke 24:47 and Acts 1:8). Here we direct our attention specifically to two stories.

Jesus' Praise of the Gentile: The Centurion

Both Matthew (8:5–13) and Luke (7:1–10) tell about a certain Roman centurion who sought out Jesus on behalf of his ailing servant. This Gentile understood Jesus' ability to heal as Jesus' absolute authority over sickness. Based on this all-powerful authority, the centurion knew that Jesus only needed to say the words for healing to occur (Matt. 8:8–9; Luke 7:6–8). According to Jesus, this Gentile's faith was singular and unparalleled in all of Israel (Matt. 8:10; Luke 7:9). The centurion received from Jesus commendation for his faith and healing for his servant. In this instance, Jesus warmly received the Gentile and provided at least one of the benefits of his messianic role usually reserved for Jews—healing (see Luke 4:18-19 and Isa. 61:1-2).

Was Jesus Racist? The Gentile Woman

Another story of Gentile inclusion is found in Matthew 15:21-28 and Mark 7:24-30. This time, a woman sought Jesus' healing for her demon-possessed daughter. Matthew identifies her simply as a Canaanite (15:22), but Mark is more specific: "And the woman was a Greek, Syro-Phoenician by race" (7:26). In this story, the woman's Gentile status is an issue. It is impossible to interpret Jesus' response to her request for her daughter's healing as racially friendly or ethnically sensitive: "Let the children first be fed, for it is not good to take the bread of the children and throw it to the dogs" (Mark 7:27; Matt. 15:26). Today we would recommend that Jesus attend a workshop on racial sensitivity for making that remark. Although Jesus does not directly call her a dog, the innuendo is unmistakable: she is a Gentile, therefore a "dog." While "dog" has gained a positive sense in modern American pop culture (Randy Jackson's now famous "Dawg!" on "American Idol" comes to mind), in the first century, "dog" was negative and meant "animal, less than human," and "dirty." In the ancient world, dogs were city scavengers, not pets.[1]

The woman does not argue the matter, apparently accepting the "children-dogs" analogy for the Jew-Gentile distinction: "But Lord, the dogs under the table eat from the crumbs of the children" (Mark 7:28; Matt. 15:27). Regardless of the woman's savvy comeback, Jesus' reference to Gentiles as "dogs" is troublesome for obvious reasons: Was Jesus racist? Can we legitimately take away from this text that racism can be valid and Christ-like? And if this passage serves as evidence of Jesus' endorsement of racism, how does it fit with Jesus' last commission to his disciples (Matt. 28:16-20)? Is this passage truly a story of Gentile inclusion?

---

1. See also Exod. 22:31; 1 Kings 22:38; Ps. 22:16; Luke 16:21; Phil. 3:2; and Rev. 22:15.

At the most basic level this passage confirms that racism is not merely a modern invention; it is a long-standing issue and apparently the status quo in first-century Judea. Racism in the first century needs to be explored further, but for now, it is sufficient to note that racial discrimination *was* an issue during Jesus' time.

Just prior to Jesus' encounter with the Gentile woman, he had a confrontation with the Pharisees on the issue of purity (Matt. 15:1-20; Mark 7:1-23). While the Pharisees and the scribes define purity as cleaning hands before eating (external), Jesus defines purity as an issue of the heart (internal). The Pharisees and the scribes criticize Jesus' disciples for eating with unclean hands (Mark 7:1-2, 5; Matt. 15:1-2). Jesus, however, points out that while the Pharisees may fastidiously clean their hands, they leave aside the more serious matter, the commandments of God (Mark 7:6-13; Matt. 15:3-9). Jesus teaches his disciples that it is not what goes into a person that defiles, but what comes out of the person (Mark 7:14-16; Matt. 15:10-11). Food goes into the person and passes through, but what comes out of the mouth comes from the heart (Mark 7:18-20; Matt. 15:17-18). Defilement comes from within: evil thoughts, murder, adultery, sexual immorality, theft, false witness, and slander. (Mark adds greed, wickedness, deceit, licentiousness, evil eye, pride, and foolishness.) Jesus concludes, "But to eat with unwashed hands does not defile the man" (Matt. 15:20). The significance of Jesus' words is difficult to miss—Gentiles who do not follow purity or dietary rituals are not "unclean" by virtue of what and how they eat. Mark makes this meaning of Jesus' teaching even more explicit: "He declared all foods clean" (7:19).

How is this Jesus, who decisively determines what "defiles" and what merely passes through, the same Jesus who discriminates against the Gentile woman? Perhaps there is something else at work in Jesus' encounter with the woman. Based on Jesus' teaching that defilement comes from within and not without, we need to observe not only what comes out of the woman's mouth, but also the mouths of the Pharisees and the scribes. In truth, Jesus is not only offensive to the woman; he is also offensive to the Pharisees and the scribes. Jesus is both theologically and culturally offensive. For the woman, the privilege of salvation is for the Jews first (cf. John 4:22). For the Pharisees and the scribes from Jerusalem, Jesus flagrantly and repeatedly disregards their religious regulations. In view of his Sabbath-breaking activity (Mark 2:23-3:6; Matt. 12:1-14, Luke 6:1-11; 13:10-17; John 5:1-18, 9:1-34), perhaps this dismissal of hand-cleaning ritual is minor by comparison. Nevertheless, the Pharisees and the scribes are offended by Jesus' disregard for their purity regulations and his severe criticism: "you invalidate the word of God for the sake of your tradition" (Matt. 15:6; Mark 7:8 says, "you leave the command of God"). Matthew explicitly notes: "Then the disciples came and said to him: 'Do you know that the Pharisees were offended when they heard this saying?'" (15:12). In contrast, the Gentile woman, faced with Jesus' offensive reference (i.e., "dogs"), presses further to receive the healing only Jesus can supply; as noted in Matthew, such persistence is surely driven by faith in Jesus' power to heal (Matt. 15:28). Both are "pressed" by Jesus' nonconformist, offensive behavior, but faith "comes out" of the Gentile, while the Jewish leaders are scandalized.

The Gentile woman doesn't simply serve as a foil for the Jerusalem Pharisees and scribes; she is also a contrast to the disciples. The disciples fail to understand Jesus' teaching on the triviality of dietary regulations as the means for determining purity (Matt. 15:15-16; Mark 7:17-18). The woman, however, immediately understands that while priority is given to the Jews, she as a Gentile can share in the messianic blessings, albeit only "crumbs." Her external "unclean" status is not a hindrance in pursuing and receiving the messianic blessings Jesus bestows. Jesus affirms the woman's interpretation of her standing in the Jew-Gentile dynamic and yields to her request (Matt. 15:28; Mark 7:29). The inclusion of this story in both Matthew and Mark does not serve as evidence that Jesus was racist or simply advancing the cultural norm. Rather, it serves as an illustration that "it is not what goes into a person that defiles, but what comes out of the person." Whereas neither the disciples nor the Pharisees and scribes seem to recall God's purpose for Israel to be "a light for the nations," Jesus fulfills Israel's calling in his interaction with this Gentile woman.

I the LORD called you [Israel] in righteousness; and I will take you by the hand and protect you and will give you as a covenant for the people and a light for the nations to open the eyes of the blind, to bring out prisoners from the dungeon, those who live in darkness from the prison. (Isa. 42:6–7)

While these two stories, along with many others, show Jesus' positive reception of the Gentiles, at no point are the Gentiles called to join the Twelve. In fact, after Jesus restores a certain man from a demon called "Legion" (Mark 5:9) the man "begs" Jesus "so that he might be with him" (5:18), but Jesus did not permit him. Instead he instructs the former demoniac to "go home to your family and tell them how much the Lord has done for you, and how he has had mercy on you" (5:19). Even more, during his earthly ministry, Jesus never explicitly instructed his disciples to receive Gentiles into their fellowship. For our purposes, the gospel stories of Gentile inclusion, while plentiful, do not necessarily provide reasons why the church should receive Gentiles into their midst. There are, however, two well-known parables that supply precisely what is needed: the parable of the prodigal son (Luke 15:11–32) and the parable of the good Samaritan (Luke 10:25–37). Their familiarity gives us immediate and easy access to the broad story line, but further examination will lead to discovery of new insight in these stories. Both parables illustrate that the claim to "know God" or to be a "disciple of Christ" requires a mind-set that looks beyond the cultural-social norm. Indeed, it requires a disposition that concedes God's desire, and his commands override all other protocol. Traditionally, neither parable has been linked with the issue of racial reconciliation.[2] But both are highly significant for this particular issue because these parables uniquely teach us *why* the church should receive the "other," the "foreigner," or even the "hated."

JEWS, GENTILES, AND SAMARITANS

Before we turn to the two parables, we need to address the issue of racial discrimination and enmity in the New Testament. This is

---

2. One might argue that the overtone of racial reconciliation is obvious in Luke 10:25–37. The parable, however, has often been perceived as simply a model of loving a neighbor, not as a counter-cultural statement in regard to racial relations. On this issue, see I. H. Marshall, *The Gospel of Luke: A Commentary on the Greek Text*, NIGTC (Grand Rapids: Eerdmans, 1978), 445.

necessary since some basic understanding of racial relations in the first century A.D. will be necessary to grasp the extraordinary message Jesus teaches his disciples through these parables. For example, the phrase "good Samaritan" was an oxymoron in Jesus' day. That a Samaritan could be called "good" would have been ludicrous. For a better grasp of the parable of the prodigal son, as well as increased understanding of Gentiles as those excluded from the covenant relationship, we need to clarify the relationship between Jews and Gentiles. As both Old and New Testaments teach, God's intention was never to exclude people from worshipping him. But as we can all testify, knowing God's laws and desires and living by his mandates are often two separate things.

Jews and Gentiles

The issue of racial reconciliation is prominent in the New Testament. Paul's letters (e.g., Galatians, Ephesians, and Romans) and Acts 10 and 15 demonstrate that racial reconciliation, particularly that of Jew-Gentile, was a controversial issue for the church in its early years. The Jew-Gentile reconciliation for the church in the New Testament was not so much a sociological issue as it was a *theological* issue.

The concern for racial reconciliation, while conspicuous, is distinct from the contemporary issue of racial reconciliation. These points of difference need to be understood before any attempt at application. The term "Gentile(s)" translates the Greek word *ethnos* and in the plural does not communicate "plurality of nations."[3] The term "is used non-sociologically to describe all the individuals who do not belong to the chosen people."[4] "Gentile(s)" signifies *all* nations apart from Israel, a singular identity as non-Jews. This distinction is based on Israel's identity as the "chosen nation," built on the covenant relationship with Yahweh (see chapter 2 for an explanation of "chosen people"). The parameters of this relationship with God (the Torah, circumcision, Sabbath observance, and dietary regulations) determine Israel's distinct identity from all other

---

3. G. Bertram, "Ethnos," TDNT 2.364–369, here 367.
4. Ibid.

nations. Consequently, the self-understanding of Israel in contrast to all other nations is first and foremost theologically formulated. Israel worships the one living God; all other nations do not. The estrangement between Jew and Gentile in the New Testament stems essentially from this theological point. In view of this, the following elements can be noted: (1) the discrimination against Gentiles is not grounded in skin color; and (2) the discrimination is not motivated by hatred of a particular ethnicity—it encompasses *all* outside of the covenant relationship. Any attempt to argue for superiority based on skin color or priority of ethnicity based on cultural reasons alone will find no correlation with the Jew-Gentile relations. Then, apart from Messianic Jews, all American Christians and all non-Christians, regardless of color, are Gentiles. But as the examination of the four passages will demonstrate, even this Jew-Gentile distinction, which was theologically motivated at the outset, becomes null and void in view of the Christ event.

But how does the exclusion of Gentiles evident in the New Testament correlate with God's clear purpose for Israel to be a testimony to the nations? According to the Old Testament prophets, Israel never fulfills her role as God's people (Isa. 1:1–31; Jer. 17:1–13; Ezek. 2:3–5). In her inability and refusal to worship Yahweh, Israel not only receives God's judgment of captivity but also cannot function in the capacity of a witness to all other nations (Isa 59:1–21; Ezek. 5:5–8). When Israel returns from captivity in the sixth century B.C., her commitment to avoid idolatry is firmly implanted in her identity. As the Roman Empire grows in power, and Hellenization (the influence of Greek culture) becomes pervasive, both invade the world of the Jews geographically and culturally. The resolve to maintain Israel's worship of God leads to a concentrated effort in retaining ritual purity through law observance.[5] By the first century A.D., the external political-social-economic-cultural threat of the wider secular world results in an intense concern to hold on to their unique identity as the people of God. Law observance was the convenient means to preserve Israel's identity, but it failed to lead Israel to a genuine

---

5. See J. C. VanderKam, *An Introduction to Early Judaism* (Grand Rapids: Eerdmans, 2001) for the history of Judaism in and around the first century A.D.

worship of God. The failure to genuinely worship God again results in the inability to serve as a testimony to the Gentiles. Once more, Gentile exclusion in the New Testament is theologically motivated, but ultimately it betrays a distorted understanding of God as Creator and Redeemer (cf. chapter 1) and God's desire for all peoples to worship him (cf. chapters 3 and 4).

Jews and Samaritans

The Jew-Samaritan relationship is somewhat different. The animosity between Jews and Samaritans goes back to about 538 B.C. when Zerubbabel returned with the first group of deportees. During this time the Samaritans considered Jerusalem/Judah to be their domain, and they did not welcome the returnees, especially when they wanted their former properties returned.[6] For the returnees, neither the Samaritans nor the peasants were religiously pure.[7] Again, the enmity between Jews and Samaritans is theologically based.

Yet the Samaritans were not as foreign to the Jews as were the Gentiles. In truth, the Samaritans shared with the Jews several core beliefs: worship of one God, rejection of idols, adherence to the Mosaic law, lineage from the patriarchs, and messianic expectation. In spite of similarities, the points of divergence were significant: the Samaritans chose Shechem and Mount Gerizim as the place of worship rather than Jerusalem and Mount Zion (see John 4:20); and the Samaritans viewed only the Pentateuch as authoritative (similar to Sadduccees). Through the years, the Jew-Samaritan relationship deteriorated. Everett Ferguson notes: "There was apparently a period of gradual drifting apart during which a number of antagonisms, economic and political advantages, as well as religious differences intensified feelings. The separation of Samaritans and Jews was more a

---

6. Samaritans were of mixed blood. Those left behind from the northern kingdom intermarried with the foreigners brought into the area by the Assyrians (2 Kings 17). The animosity between the Jews and the Samaritans is still strong during Jesus' time. See John 4 and Luke 10:29ff for Jesus' words and actions, which must have been controversial, if not offensive, to his Jewish audience.

7. H. T. Frank, *Discovering the Biblical World*, rev. ed. (New Jersey: Hammond, 1988), 141.

process than an event."[8] To be sure, Josephus, a Jewish historian in the first century, records the historical enmity:

> And when they [Samaritans] see the Jews in prosperity, they pretend that they are changed, and allied to them, and call them kinsmen, as though they were derived from Joseph, and had by that means an original alliance with them: but when they see them falling into a low condition, they say they are no way related to them, and that the Jews have no right to expect any kindness or marks of kindred from them, but they declare that they are sojourners, that come from other countries.[9]

Although Josephus provides a one-sided view (the Jewish perspective), the enmity between Jews and Samaritans was mutual and well-established by New Testament times. The Gospel of John states that Jesus' request for a drink from the Samaritan woman was a radical departure from the cultural norm: "For Jews do not associate with Samaritans" (4:9). Jesus' interaction with the Samaritan woman, and the Samaritans' confession that Jesus is "truly the Savior of the world" (4:42), cannot be appreciated apart from the historical antipathy between Jews and Samaritans. This long-standing racial enmity and discrimination comes to an end through Jesus Christ (see especially Acts 8:4–25).

THE PARABLE OF THE PRODIGAL SON

The age-old story of the prodigal son (Luke 15:11–32) has an important message for God's story of reconciliation. Most people familiar with the parable will recall the story. Familiarity, however, can cause us to overlook some significant factors. So, we will begin with some observations on the context of the parable; it's not just the parable itself, but the parable set within the context of the surrounding passages, that provides theological depth and substance.

---

8. E. Ferguson, *Backgrounds of Early Christianity*, 3rd ed. (Grand Rapids: Eerdmans, 2003), 534.
9. Josephus, *Ant.* 9.14.3.

The Same Story in Three

First, the parable of the prodigal son is naturally connected with the preceding two parables of the lost sheep (Luke 15:4-7) and the lost coin (Luke 15:8-10). All three parables contain three common elements:

- The lost object[10]

- Search for the lost object (in the third parable, this comes through the father's eager anticipation for his lost son in 15:20)

- Joy or celebration (individual and corporate) in recovering that which was lost[11]

Second, in all three parables, the theme of "lost object and joy in its recovery" is tied to God and sinners. In the parables of the lost sheep and the lost coin, the active search for the lost object and the individual and corporate joy in its recovery is directly interpreted within the framework of (1) sin and (2) joy in the repentance of a sinner. The lost object is equated with a sinner (15:7, 10); and the joy of the shepherd and the woman and the invitation for corporate celebration are paralleled with joy in the heavenly realm (15:7, 10). There is no recovery of the sinner without repentance; the joyous celebration is a direct response to repentance. But even further, as Joel Green notes, "references to responses 'in heaven' and 'in the presence of the angels of God' make clear that these parables are fundamentally about God,

---

10. The notion of "lost" is conveyed in all three parables by the Greek term *apollumi* (15:4 [twice], 6, 8, 9, 24, 32), which means "to ruin, destroy" or "lose."

11. Joy or rejoicing (together) at the recovery of what has been lost is denoted by *chairō/chara/synchairō* in 15:5-7 in the parable of the lost sheep. Similarly in the parable of the lost coin, "joy" and "rejoicing together" is communicated by the same words used in the previous parable—*chara/synchairō* in 15:9-10; and in the third parable, the sense of "rejoicing" is conveyed by *euphrainō* in 15:23-24, 29, 32, and here it carries the overtone of "feast" or "celebration." See J. B. Green, *The Gospel of Luke*, NICNT (Grand Rapids: Eerdmans, 1997), 572-73 for further insightful analysis of the parables.

that their aim is to lay bare the nature of the divine response to the recovery of the lost."[12] These parables, then, are not simply stories of "lost and found" but stories that communicate God's response to lost sinners: a search and rescue mission. These themes are sustained and further developed in the third parable of the prodigal son.

Third, the context (15:1-3) confirms that the theme of "lost and found" in all three parables is to be equated with God's desire to seek out and restore the sinner. *Because* the tax collectors and sinners were all gathering around to hear Jesus, the Pharisees and scribes grumbled, "This man welcomes sinners and eats with them" (vv. 1-2). The issue for the Pharisees and scribes was not "lost and found"; it was Jesus' reception and table fellowship with sinners. Jesus tells the series of parables to address this theological issue. This context will be meaningful later in our study of racial reconciliation, but for now we simply note that Jesus tells the parables in order to address the theological issue of receiving and eating with sinners.

Fourth, although Jesus teaches frequently through parables, it is rare that he repeats the parable in similar form three times. The threefold repetition of basically the same story in one setting indicates that the lessons within the "lost and found" stories are especially significant and merit our utmost attention. What other features in the final parable supplement and intensify this basic story? We turn to the parable of the prodigal son for answers. By examining Jesus' teaching, we will discover implications for ethnic inclusion in the church today.

God's Desire for Restoration of Severed Relations

As the story of the prodigal son unfolds with the previous two parables, the notion of "lost" is linked with "sin." Upon returning to his father, the prodigal son states, "Father, I have sinned against heaven and against you" (15:21). The father's description of the previous and current state of his son is phrased as follows: "he was lost and is found" (15:24). "For" (*hoti*), which stands at the beginning of 15:24, provides the *reason* for celebration—the recovery of what was lost; repentance of sin is the reason for celebration. The broken

---

12. Green, *Luke*, 573.

relationship described as "dead" (15:24) is made "alive again" not merely through the physical return, but through the penitent disposition of the son (15:18-19). Thus, the relationship between the father and the prodigal son is now repaired: the father, out of compassion (15:20), renews the prodigal's status as son (15:22-24). The father's compassion comes to full expression through his call for a joyous celebration: "Quickly bring out the best robe and put it on him and put a ring on his hand and sandals on his feet. And bring the fattened calf and kill it and let us eat and celebrate" (15:22-23 NASB). All three elements found in the previous two parables are also found here: lost object, search (desire) for the lost, and celebration at the recovery of the lost. If a theological interpretation is valid, the story of the father and the prodigal son ultimately reveals God's desire and compassionate love for the sinner.

Rejection of God's Desire for Restoration

In the third parable, however, a unique dimension of the story absent in the previous two parables is introduced; this element together with the other features noted will have significance for racial reconciliation. Namely, it is the response of the older son and the father's response to his complaint (15:25-32). First, the older son's response indicates the perception of himself as the *obedient* son. This is in fact true; he was in the field, presumably working (15:25).[13] Indeed his complaint is based on his faithfulness: "Look! All these years I've been slaving for you and never disobeyed your orders" (15:29). This faithfulness is never questioned by the father. In view of the audience for these parables—the grumbling Pharisees and scribes (15:2)—perhaps this portrait of the older son is critical in that it resembles them.

Second, the older son's anger toward his brother is, at least outwardly, contingent upon his own self-perception as the faithful son and the younger son as the unfaithful (15:29-30). This categorical distinction between the two is bluntly expressed in his separation

---

13. D. L. Bock, *Luke 9:51-24:53* BECNT 3B; (Grand Rapids: Baker, 1996), 1316.

from his brother: "But when *this son of yours*" (15:30). In effect, he denies the fraternal connection with his brother.

Third, his anger resides not merely in that he perceives himself as the faithful one, while his brother is unfaithful, but ultimately that the father treats the unfaithful with overwhelming mercy while his own faithfulness is seemingly under appreciated (15:29–30).[14] Thus, in light of what he has deemed unjust, the older brother refuses to participate in the celebration of the younger son's return and renewal even when the father entreats him to participate (15:28).

In response to the older son's grievances, the father, in a surprising manner, does not rebuke or reject the older son. He responds with continued love. "My son," the father said, "you are always with me, and everything I have is yours" (15:31). The father continues to explain in order to persuade the older son to rejoice with him in his brother's return. Two factors are significant in the father's explanation.

First, the term *edei* is translated "it was fitting" and usually conveys a sense of necessity. Thus it was necessary "to celebrate and be glad." D. L. Bock states it well: "It was morally right to rejoice, given the circumstances of the return. A resurrection of sorts has occurred. A dead brother is now alive. That which was lost has been found. Such circumstances should result in joy, not questions about fairness."[15] Regardless of the older son's objections, the father's perspective is entirely appropriate and resembles the heavenly celebration of the two preceding parables.

Second, the father does not allow the older son to forget his fraternal relations with his younger brother: "we had to celebrate and be glad, because this brother of yours was dead and is alive again; he was lost and is found" (15:32).

The Message of the Parable

The older brother's reaction to the return and festive reception of the prodigal provides the principal message of these parables. This is particularly valid in view of Jesus' immediate audience and its critique of his associations: "Now the tax collectors and 'sinners' were all

---

14. See Green, *Luke*, 585, for a good discussion of these issues.
15. See Bock, *Luke*, vol. 2, 1320.

gathering around to hear him. But the Pharisees and the teachers of the law muttered, 'This man welcomes sinners and eats with them'" (15:1-2). We can observe the following points.

First, the older brother has thoroughly misunderstood the father's heart with respect to the sinner or the "lost." As the threefold parables emphasize, God actively searches for and strongly desires the return of the lost. Further, the joy and the ensuing call to others to celebrate together at the recovery of the lost clearly portrays God's joy in the penitent sinner. This divine compassion is what the older son does not understand. And this misunderstanding of the father is remarkable given the older son's self-understanding with respect to the father; he believes that he is the "good son," the one who is faithful and obedient to the father. But was the older son's understanding of himself right? Is it truly faithfulness and obedience when the core concerns of God are misunderstood or dismissed?

Second, it is interesting that on the one hand the older son perceives himself to be far superior to his brother, precisely *because* he is obedient in his relationship to his father. As noted earlier, he bases his complaint to his father on his own virtue of faithfulness. On the other hand, he commits a great offense to his father by refusing to honor his father's decision to extend mercy to the younger son and celebrate. Indeed, as K. E. Bailey observes, it would have been customary for the older son to play the host at this banquet.[16] In his refusal, he insults the father.[17] It is also notable that the older son in his complaint to the father never addresses him as "father," which is another indication of insolence.[18] It appears that in spite of the older son's protestations of faithfulness to the father, in reality, his behavior betrays a severed filial relationship. One wonders if, ultimately, there is a difference between the severed relations of the older son and the father and that of the younger son and the father. These two points in the end raise this question: Is it possible to claim righteousness before God without recognizing and being in agreement with God's compassionate outreach for those "lost"? Put another way, is it not

---

16. K. E. Bailey, *Poet & Peasant* (Grand Rapids: Eerdmans, 1976), 194.
17. Ibid., 195.
18. Green, *Luke*, 585.

arrogance to reject table fellowship with "sinners" when clearly God has recovered them?

These questions are, in effect, questions concerning loyal discipleship. Is discipleship merely faithfulness with respect to the law, or does it also require a disposition consistent with God's love for and reception of the socially marginalized? Given the fact that the three parables concerning the "lost and found" fall immediately after a discourse on discipleship (14:25–35), this concern for receiving "sinners" within the context of table fellowship (15:2, 23) becomes a required, not a discretionary, feature of discipleship (see chapter 8 for further discussion on table fellowship).

Can Gentiles Be Defined as "Sinners"?

Don't be alarmed! We're not saying minorities are sinners! We need to remember from the previous section that "Gentile" means all non-Jewish people. It would be a mistake to equate "Gentile" with ethnic minorities. It does, however, refer to the majority of the ancient world population (all non-Jews) and the ethnic diversity of all peoples outside of the covenant relationship. "Gentile" also refers to this vast group of people formerly *excluded* from membership in the community of God. As we will see, the term "sinner" points to a person's exclusion from covenant relations with God and his people. In this way, "Gentile" can be seen in the same light as "sinners"; both are excluded from covenant relations.

Turning our attention back to Luke 15, we note that the context of the passage concerns the acceptance of "sinners and tax collectors" (15:1), but not necessarily that of Gentiles. Three factors might suggest a broader application of these parables. First, often in the New Testament, "sinners" and "Gentiles" are synonymous; thus, "Gentile" signifies "sinner."[19] But even if these terms are distinct from each other, the semantic overlap is too great to be ignored. "Sinners" were "perceived as forfeiting their relationship to God because of a lifestyle unfaithful to God's law."[20] And tax collectors with their abusive practices

---

19. Matt. 26:45; Mark 14:41; Acts 2:23; Gal. 2:15; Luke 6:32–36; Matt. 5:47. See K. H. Rengstorf, "Hamartolos," *TDNT* 1:317–35.
20. Bock, *Luke*, Vol. 2, 1298.

of extorting monies would have been included in the group marked as "sinners." Thus, those falling under the category of "sinner" would have been perceived as those excluded from the covenant relationship and most certainly from table fellowship with covenant members. Their theological exclusion from the covenant relationship renders them social outcasts.

Second, in the Gospel of Luke, the constituents of this "new community," centered on Jesus, are not only Jewish undesirables but often also non-Jews.[21] Bock rightly states, "This multiracial theme becomes prominent in Acts, but more important to the Gospel is the fact that the message goes out to those on the fringe of society."[22] Therefore, reaching out to Jewish social outcasts is the tip of a wider concern for all sinners, without regard for racial distinctions.

Third, the theological reason for the inclusion of "sinners" in Luke 15:11–32 is the same rationale Peter provides (Acts 15:9–11).[23] *Because* God has made no distinction between Jew and Gentile, the Jews' refusal to accept Gentiles' salvation apart from adherence to the law would be in effect "testing God" (Acts 15:10).[24] Thus, the proper response for either Peter or James is to accept what God has accepted (15:13–19). From here the concern turns to the nuts and bolts of table fellowship between Jew and Gentile (15:20–21)—it is not a question of *should* there be table fellowship, but *how* to implement table fellowship. Further, the same rationale leads Peter not only to share the gospel with Cornelius (Acts 10) but also to eat with them (Acts 11:3).[25] This reason is supplied as he answers charges from the

---

21. See Luke 3:4–6; 4:22–30; 7:1–10; 13:23–30; 14:16–24; 17:12–19; 20:15–16; 24:47.
22. D. L. Bock, "Luke," *Dictionary of Jesus and the Gospels*, eds. J. B. Green and S. McKnight (Downers Grove: InterVarsity, 1992), 506.
23. Acts 10 and 15 will be examined extensively in chapter 8.
24. Note the emphasis on God's choice (*eklegomai*) in 15:7 not only for Peter as the vessel, but for Gentiles to hear the gospel and believe. B. R. Gaventa, *Acts*, ANTC (Nashville: Abingdon Press, 2003), 215, astutely observes that *eklegomai* "to choose" is also used for the choosing of Israel and the disciples (Acts 1:2, 24; 13:7; Luke 6:13). See also D. L. Bock, *Acts*, BECNT (Grand Rapids: Baker, 2007), 499–500 for an insightful discussion on the importance of God's initiative.
25. The concern not only for divine impartiality in regard to salvation but also for table fellowship between Jew and Gentile becomes emphatic when Peter's vision of unclean animals, including the command to "kill and eat," is

circumcision party: "if God gave to them the same gift as He gave to us also after believing in the Lord Jesus Christ, who was I that I could stand in God's way?" (11:17 NASB). As the following verse indicates, this reason is sufficient to silence the opponents' objections (v. 18). The primary theological thrust in Acts 11 and 15, as well as in Luke 15—acceptance of "sinners" or "Gentiles"—lies in God's initiative in receiving the sinner/Gentile. The appropriate and only response of a disciple is the acceptance of and agreement with this divine initiative through table fellowship. If God has made it possible for people of all nations to be saved through Jesus Christ, is it possible for a genuine disciple of Christ to deny fellowship with brothers and sisters of different ethnicity?

THE PARABLE OF THE GOOD SAMARITAN

Again, this story is familiar to many Christians. The phrase "good Samaritan" is often used to describe someone who is financially generous or simply a good neighbor. But in the first century, the phrase "good Samaritan" would have been considered an oxymoron and certainly controversial. A general knowledge of this parable can easily bypass the profound theological message contained in the story. So we start once more with the context. This passage, similar to the parable of the prodigal son, is also set in the context of discipleship.

The Privilege of Discipleship: Listening to Jesus' Teaching

Just prior to the parable of the good Samaritan is a passage about the sending of the seventy-two and their report to Jesus on their evangelistic activity (Luke 10:1-20). Upon their return, the disciples give a positive report to Jesus: "Lord, even the demons are subject to us in your name" (10:17). Jesus affirms them and explains their experience as authority *given* to them: "I have given you authority to trample on snakes and scorpions and to overcome all the power

---

given three times. Accepting God's impartiality toward Gentiles will necessary mean acceptance of table fellowship with Gentiles.

of the enemy; nothing will harm you" (10:19). The disciples' experience of authority over demons is authority *given* to them by Jesus. This connects nicely with the disciples' description of this experience (10:17); it is in Jesus' name that they exercise authority over demons. According to Jesus, however, this is not the primary reason for rejoicing: "do not rejoice that the spirits submit to you, but rejoice that your names are written in heaven" (10:20). Outstanding as the authority over demons might be, it is not the dominant reason for rejoicing. Rather, this spiritual power is merely the by-product of something much greater: discipleship.

At this point, the careful reader will note that Jesus does not say "rejoice that you are my disciples," but "rejoice that your names are recorded in the heavens" (10:20). Yet aren't these two things one and the same? To have our name recorded in the heavens is to be a disciple. But why is discipleship greater than spiritual power over demons? Jesus provides the answer (10:21–24).

First, discipleship is not born out of self-will and self-determination but out of the Father's will. Jesus' prayer of gratitude to the Father expresses this: "I praise you, Father, Lord of heaven and earth, because you hid these things from the wise and the intelligent and revealed them to infants; indeed, Father, such was your good pleasure" (10:21). We are called to discipleship because it was the Father's will. The great value of discipleship is found not in human virtue but in God the Father's will.

Second, knowledge of the Father is possible only through the Son. Jesus says several things that are crucial for understanding the nature of discipleship. He begins with the declaration that his authority is an all-extensive authority given to him by the Father: "All things have been committed to me by my Father" (10:22). Jesus' authority is not partial but comprehensive, and ultimately it comes from the Father. Consequently, Jesus' call to discipleship, which falls under "all things," comes with nothing less than the absolute authority endorsed by God the Father.

Jesus goes on to say that knowledge of either the Father or the Son is limited to the two members of the Godhead: "no one knows who the Son is except the Father, and who the Father is except the Son." Phrased positively, only the Father knows the Son, and only the Son knows the Father. It appears to be an exclusive relationship in which only two (Father and Son) participate. This is important because in the final phrase of 10:22, the privilege of discipleship is emphasized. Those who are called to discipleship are able to participate in this seemingly exclusive relationship. Whereas "no one" knows the Father except the Son, the disciples of Jesus Christ are able to know the Father because Jesus enables it: "No one knows who the Son is except the Father, and no one knows who the Father is except the Son and those to whom the Son chooses to reveal him" (10:22). The privileged knowledge of the Father given only to the Son is now given *through* the Son to his disciples. Without a doubt this is a cause for rejoicing! To be sure, knowing the Father is better than having authority over demons.

Let's summarize what we have learned so far concerning the context of discipleship.

- Although the disciples' authority over evil spirits is authority given by Jesus, discipleship rather than spiritual power over demons is the primary reason for rejoicing.

- Discipleship is a direct consequence of the Father's will.

- Discipleship falls under the umbrella of Jesus' comprehensive authority endorsed by the Father.

- Although only the Son knows the Father, this knowledge of the Father is given to the disciples of Jesus Christ.

That discipleship is far greater than spiritual authority over demons is affirmed by Jesus (10:23-24). At this point, he speaks exclusively to his disciples: "And turning to the disciples he said privately." Jesus tells the disciples that their eyes are blessed because they see what the prophets and kings longed to see and hear but did not. What the disciples "see and hear" is privileged "sight and hearing" that was not granted even to the prophets and kings of old. That the disciples were of little social consequence, since they were certainly not prophets or kings, heightens the sense of honor and privilege. This links back to Jesus' thanksgiving: "I praise you, Father, Lord of heaven and earth, because you have hidden these things from the wise and learned, and revealed them to little children" (10:21). This revelation is nothing less than the knowledge of God the Father (10:22).

Why is this passage so important for the parable of the good Samaritan? The parable is part of this privilege given to the disciples; it is part of what the disciples get to "hear." The word "to hear" (akouō) often means "to pay attention" or "to heed" and it is often used in the context of Jesus' teaching. This is not merely background noise or "light" music that we listen to while multitasking. It requires careful attention to Jesus' teaching *and* practice of Jesus' teaching. The information that we've gained is important for understanding the parable, and we will return to these points as we explore the parable itself.

Love Your Neighbor! But Who Is My Neighbor?

The parable of the good Samaritan teaches an essential component of discipleship—to love our neighbor as we love ourselves. It does not, however, stand alone; it is followed by two other passages on discipleship: Luke 10:38–42 focuses on the importance of listening to Jesus' teaching, and 11:1–13 concentrates on the importance of persistent prayer. Discipleship requires not only diligence in prayer and careful attention to Jesus' teaching but also love for one's neighbor. So the entirety of Jesus' teaching in 10:25–11:13 falls under the privilege of discipleship to "see and hear." We cannot be disciples if we do not love and care for our neighbors!

Another dimension of discipleship surfaces in the story: what Jesus is about to teach through the parable is not new but consistent with the requirements of discipleship or "following God" in the Old Testament. The explicit mention of the law (10:26) within the framework of salvation (10:25 "eternal life") indicates that Jesus' teaching on loving one's neighbor is a necessary component of salvation. Further, the lawyer's citation of Deuteronomy 6:5 and Leviticus 19:18 in 10:27 as well as Jesus' affirmation of his answer in 10:28 indicates that Jesus' teaching in what follows is coherent with the

Old Testament's understanding of Israel's covenant relationship with God.[26]

The story begins with a lawyer who stood up and asked Jesus a question *in order to test him* (10:25). His question is simple: "What must I do to inherit eternal life?" (10:25). Jesus points to the law and asks the lawyer: "How do you read it?" (10:26). At first, the lawyer and Jesus are in agreement as to the requirements for eternal life: eternal life requires not only comprehensive love for God but also love for one's neighbor as oneself. Their agreement is short-lived, however, for the lawyer poses the question: "And who is my neighbor?" (10:29). At this point, Luke provides the motivation behind the question: self-justification. Precisely *why* the lawyer wanted to justify himself is unclear.[27] At minimum, the question seeks to delimit the command to love one's neighbor. The concern to identify who is *not* a neighbor is implicit in the question "Who is my neighbor?" This needs to be unpacked even further.

We can safely assume that the lawyer is not concerned with identifying which Jew is not his neighbor. That Jesus lifts up a Samaritan as the hero in the parable suggests that the lawyer's concern is to draw the line between Jews and non-Jews. Perhaps, for the lawyer, the command to love the neighbor applies only to Jews. Jesus' use of a Samaritan as the model suggests that the focus on the exemplary nature of the Samaritan at the expense of dismissing the social dimensions is insufficient. In other words, simply noting that extreme generosity defines what it means to love the neighbor is not enough. The lesson Jesus teaches here is radical: *extreme generosity transcends the social and ethnic boundaries.* N. T. Wright correctly observes that the passage is fraught with socially and theologically radical challenges: Israel's covenant boundaries are redefined.[28] If you recall, ethnic discrimination for Israel was never motivated simply on social concerns, but ultimately theological. But how is all this found in the parable?

In Jesus' parable of the three travelers from Jerusalem who

---

26. See Bock, *Luke*, vol. 2, 1024.
27. Bock, *Luke*, vol. 2, 1027 lists three possible reasons why the lawyer poses this question: 1) justification of past neglect; 2) correction of past remiss; and 3) justification in his status quo.
28. N. T. Wright, *Jesus and the Victory of God* (London: SPCK, 1996), 307.

encounter the unfortunate man, the one who fulfills the law by "loving his neighbor" is neither the priest nor the Levite but a Samaritan. Given the historical and mutual hatred between Jews and Samaritans,[29] Jesus' parable would surely have challenged the Jewish certainty of salvation based on ethnic pedigree.[30] If indeed the lawyer sought to justify himself by clarifying the boundaries for his own definition of "neighbor," then Jesus' protagonist, the Good Samaritan, subtly yet unmistakably discourages such efforts. In the parable, the one who fulfills the mandates of God's commandments is clearly, as the lawyer affirms (10:37), the "one who showed mercy on him." Thus, the Samaritan, rather than the priest or the Levite, is the one who stands to "inherit eternal life" (10:25-28). This inclusion of those considered to be excluded from salvation (Samaritans) is radical but consistent with Jesus' ministry.[31] Jesus calls for a discipleship that is radical, active, and spiritually motivated. A passive attitude toward care for hurting humanity describes the religious bigot not the follower of Jesus.

Love Your Neighbor! To What Extent?

This parable operates on yet another level, not simply that of inclusion of the socially and theologically marginalized. The entire passage is centered on the second part of the mandate of a covenant relationship. The command to "love one's neighbor as oneself" is defined in the fullest sense. The distinction between the lawyer and Jesus sharpens precisely at this point. Whereas the lawyer seeks to delimit this command, and thereby communicates a minimalistic mind-set, Jesus defines the same command in the fullest sense. The Samaritan is set apart from the previous two travelers in that he "has compassion." The verb "to have" and the noun "compassion" are often used by Luke to describe divine compassion.[32] This compassion is expressed not merely through staying on the same side of the road

---

29. See above, pp. 149-50.
30. See also John the Baptist's critique of the similar attitude in Matt. 3:7-10 and Luke 3:7-14.
31. See above, pp. 142-6.
32. See Luke 1:76-78; 7:13; 15:20.

(cf. 10:31–32) but also through personal attendance to the wounds, bearing the wounded on his own animal, and sacrificing out of great cost to himself (10:34–35). The Samaritan's disposition of extreme generosity stands in contrast not only to the priest and the Levite, but more significantly to the lawyer who seeks to fulfill only the minimum. The minimalistic mind-set, clearly rejected by Jesus, is perhaps motivated by social discrimination operative in the first century. The fulfillment of God's mandates for a covenant relationship or salvation requires a comprehensive disposition that penetrates through social barriers and stigma of the day. Especially important for us is that the ethnic identity of the wounded man may be purposely undisclosed: the Samaritan's compassion is not dependent on the ethnicity of the wounded man.[33]

The final element of this story is practical application. The word repeated throughout is *poieō* which means "to do." The lawyer begins with the question, "Teacher, what must I *do* to inherit eternal life?" (10:25). Jesus replies to the lawyer: "You have answered right; *do* this, and you will live" (10:28). To Jesus' question, "Which of these three do you think was a neighbor to the man who fell among the robbers?" the lawyer answers: "The one who did mercy on him" (10:37). Jesus' final words complete the exhortations toward exercise of mercy: "Go and *do* likewise" (10:37). The parable emphasizes not mere knowledge of what is required in the covenant relationship with God but the *practice* of God's commandments. As the priest and the Levite in the story demonstrate, knowledge of God's mandates does not insure its practice. Just as the lawyer "knew" the law, we assume that both the priest and the Levite also were aware of the command "love your neighbor as yourself" yet did not practice it. Obedience to God's decrees is necessary for eternal life. Further, it is not just any neighborly love that is commended but the expansive

---

33. Neither the priest nor the Levite is motivated by the ethnic identity of the wounded man. Their lack of compassion has to do with selfish concerns, a moral flaw that becomes stark in view of their status as those who are considered especially pious and zealous for the things of God and his people. This moral flaw/lack of compassion is even worse if they came upon the wounded man after worshiping in Jerusalem (they are on the road from Jerusalem to Jericho, 10:30). See Green, *Luke*, 430–31.

love demonstrated by the Samaritan, who simultaneously breaks through historical social hostility and risks personal loss of time, resources, and money.

Jesus' teaching raises some provocative questions on the issue of racial reconciliation and the Christian faith. Is it possible to be Christ's disciple and not fulfill the twin commands to love God wholly and to love our neighbor as we do our self? This double mandate is difficult for most believers even without the element of breaking social boundaries. While it might be relatively easy to love God, it is another matter to love our neighbor in the same way we love ourselves. This parable suggests that those who are "saved" regardless of ethnicity will live out both commands. Perhaps we can invert this: If love for our neighbor is the litmus test for salvation, would the test prove positive for salvation? John expresses the very same concern:

> Everyone born of God does not practice sin, for God's seed abides in him, and he is not able to keep on sinning because he has been born of God. By the children of God and the children of the devil are evident: whoever does not practice righteousness is not of God, nor is the one who does not love his brother. (1 John 3:9–10)

Let's move on to the crucial point of this parable. How often do we interpret the command to love our neighbors along the lines of Jesus' interpretation? Do we have the mind-set that seeks to accomplish this in the uttermost sense, or do we too often mirror the lawyer's minimalistic attitude? As demonstrated by the Samaritan, loving a neighbor requires personal investment of time, energy, and money; being a "good Samaritan" is far more than lending a cup of sugar to a neighbor (cf. James 2:14–17). As the Samaritan also demonstrates, love for a neighbor exceeds ethnic boundaries. It's one thing to exercise extreme love for a neighbor who falls within my own ethnic category, but it is an entirely different matter to extend this extreme love to those who are not like me. Jesus says this: "And if you do good to those who do good to you, what is the benefit to you? Even sinners do the same" (Luke 6:33).

As an Asian, can I (Park) love in the spirit of the Good Samaritan my black, white, or Hispanic neighbors? How often do I see another person fallen on hard times and cross the road to avoid contact and responsibility? How many of our churches have moved into "clean and safe" neighborhoods to avoid the responsibility to love the unfortunate and wounded in the ghetto? In modern times, racism can be effectively carried out by economics. While certainly whites are found in the ghettos, poor neighborhoods are predominantly populated by non-white ethnic groups. The Christian church has been commendable in its consistent support of homeless ministries; yet does it exemplify loving our neighbors as Jesus has defined it here? Is the need of the "other fallen on the road" only that of clothes, food, and temporary housing? What about medical or legal care? What about education? What about personal friendship? Given the treasure of various gifts available in the well-established church, is it not possible to provide voluntary services (medical, legal, education) to those in economically depressed communities?

Conclusions

This familiar yet highly challenging parable provides a theological reason for racial reconciliation. The direct command to love our neighbors as ourselves, as interpreted by Jesus, requires not only compassion akin to God's compassion but an all-inclusive position with respect to ethnic boundaries. Namely, the disciple of Christ loves the other fully regardless of race. But given the examination of the Old Testament in chapters 1 through 4, it is clear that Jesus' teaching reflects God's desire for all nations to worship him. His people are called to reflect the same desire in their treatment of neighbors within and without the covenant community. That God's people practiced exclusion on multiple levels (sinners and Gentiles) only affirms their misunderstanding of their covenant relationship and validates all the more their need of a Savior.

Further, if we tie the lessons of this parable back to what we learned about discipleship (10:17–24), this complete and ethnically inclusive compassion for our neighbors is not simply a requirement for discipleship. In obedient practice of this radical love, the disciple of Christ affirms that indeed what has been "seen and heard" through Jesus' teaching is the very privilege that was denied to the prophets and kings of old. It is God incarnate who speaks now directly to the disciples who will herald the fulfillment of God's commands. In opening up our compassion for the "foreigner" we show that God the Father has truly been revealed to us. For it is not possible "to know" God's compassionate love for the sinner as exemplified on the cross and not practice the same compassion for the unfortunate, the wounded, and the "foreigner" as demonstrated by the Samaritan. Can the outside world tell that we "know" God through our practice of God's compassion and openness to receive all peoples as "neighbors"?

THOUGHT PROVOKERS

1. How often and in what ways do we mirror the older son's attitude in the parable of the prodigal son?

2. How should Jesus' continual fellowship with sinners affect our understanding of church? Who is included and excluded?

3. If the parable of the prodigal son teaches that there is no genuine discipleship when we fail to understand God's desire to seek out the lost, what features of our church practice need reform?

4. Who are the "Samaritans" for you or your church?

5. What are some of the reasons we practice the minimalistic mindset of the lawyer when it comes to loving our neighbors?

6. What are the implications for you and your church of loving a neighbor as Jesus defined it in the parable of the good Samaritan?

7. If loving our neighbors is a critical factor in our discipleship, and if loving our neighbors self-sacrificially serves as the litmus test for our discipleship, does the test prove positive for you and your church?

Chapter 6

Stories of Peace and Worship

APART FROM JESUS, PAUL is the strongest advocate for ethnic inclusion in the New Testament. He explicitly and repeatedly articulates throughout his letters that in Christ Gentile exclusion is invalid (Rom. 2:1–7:6; Gal. 3:1–5:15; Eph. 2–3; Phil. 3:2–11; Col. 2:16–23). We recall Paul's famous words to the Galatians: "There is neither Jew nor Greek, there is neither slave nor free, there is neither male nor female. For all of you are one in Christ Jesus" (3:28). Paul's understanding of freedom in this verse relates to freedom from ethnic, gender, and social discrimination with respect to salvation. It is not the kind of freedom guaranteed to U.S. citizens by the nation's Constitution.

But our examination requires another dimension. The portrait of the end times as described in the book of Revelation is not only relevant but critical. In today's church culture, the average Christian might receive a diet of sermons from either the gospels or Paul's letters, but rarely from Revelation. A sermon on doom and destruction of the world does not sit well with those who want to hear about "health and wealth" and "eternal bliss" in the afterlife.

Regardless of what might be in vogue in Christian culture, Revelation is part of the New Testament canon and, therefore, provides a critical perspective for Christian living in the present. Revelation is relevant now. In supplying a picture of what is still to come, Revelation teaches Christians not only *what* to anticipate but *how* we ought to live as we strive toward that end. The letters to the seven churches in Revelation 2:1–3:22 illustrate this; the time of judgment is coming, and judgment falls first on the churches (see also

1 Peter 4:17). Those who claim to know Jesus Christ are admonished to live in accordance with that claim.

But Revelation is more than just doom and judgment. Revelation contains the most poignant worship scenes in all of Scripture (5:9–10; 7:9–17; 21:24, 26; and 15:3–4). In the midst of what sounds like a cosmic, universal collapse, God is worshipped by all of creation; these scenes evoke awe and holy fear akin to what Isaiah experienced in his vision of the holy God (Isa. 6:1–7). It is precisely in these worship scenes that we find references to the multiethnic character of those who worship God (i.e., the church). Apart from the fact that this portrait of a racially diverse church provides us with motivation to strive toward this end-time vision, there is further significance to the presence of a multiethnic church in the context of worship. Can the Triune God, the Creator, the Savior, and the Judge of all things be worshipped by anything less than "all peoples"? Ethnic diversity and reconciliation in the church is not simply about mixing up skin colors; in Revelation it is ultimately tied to the character of God and the worship due him.

ONE NEW MAN IN CHRIST: A HOUSE WITHOUT WALLS

Can we say, in this modern age, that racial enmity has been effectively resolved nationally and globally? This is to ask whether or not we as the human race have determined the root cause of and solution to racism. Atrocities such as the slave trade in North America and the Holocaust in Germany had their beginning in socioeconomic factors (tobacco/cotton and living space respectively). Yet socioeconomic factors alone do not explain the isolation of one particular ethnic group (Africans, or black-skinned people, and people of Jewish descent) for persecution and oppression in either case. To be sure, racial intolerance justified by socioeconomic factors is a common recipe for oppression and bloodshed around the world: Japan's domination of Korea in World War II, genocide of Native Americans from the sixteenth through nineteenth centuries, genocide in Rwanda in 1994 and in Bosnia in 1995, and the continual and reciprocal carnage between Israel and Palestine. As this list verifies, racism is not particular to one race or country.

In the 1970s, as a Korean growing up in the western suburbs of Chicago, a predominantly white Anglo-Saxon Protestant neighborhood, I (Park) faced an onslaught of racist comments on a daily basis. Being ignored and segregated to the front of the bus (in high school in the 1970s, the back seats were "cooler") was preferable to attention in the form of ridicule and harassment. But one day, as a white boy spewed out his racist comments to me, my usual practice of silent endurance came to a halt and I called him "white trash." The boy was shocked into silence. When he found his voice, he said, "You can't be racist, you're not white!" What the boy did not realize was that while I was not aggressively vocal in my racism, I had through the years of living in the United States steadily grown in anger and bitterness against whites. No one race or country has a monopoly on racism. Indeed, I wasn't called "Chink" or "Slanty-eyes" by whites only but also by blacks and Hispanics (see my testimony in the conclusion).

More often than not, we are like the lawyer in the parable of the good Samaritan: it is infinitely easier and more natural to love and embrace what is socially, culturally, politically, economically, and theologically familiar. This innate trait in all humanity explains in part racial antipathy. But what is the solution? Should we agree with the columnist Lance Morrow that the solution to racism is a matter of looking beyond color and judging each person according to character? In his *Time* magazine article "The Cure for Racism,"[1] Morrow critiques strategies such as "affirmative action, quotas and punitive political correctness" as also guilty of racism. Affirmative action simply affirms that African Americans are inherently inferior. So even the policies placed on behalf of minorities are founded upon and perpetuate racism. Morrow concludes that the only solution is to follow Martin Luther King's proposal: "The content of one's character, not the color of one's skin, is the sole decent American criterion." Recalling my school bus incident, the boy's racist comments were indeed based on my color and race, but my own prejudice against whites was formed by their racist behavior. The *lack* of character is precisely the building block for prejudice, racial profiling,

1. Lance Morrow, "The Cure for Racism," *Time* (Dec. 5, 1994). http://www.time.com/time/magazine/article/0,9171,981945,00.html.

and stereotypes. And given that racism is universal, the problem is systemic. Judging by character is not a fail-safe solution, since so many regardless of color and ethnic origin demonstrate moral failure especially in this postmodern age of relativism. Is there a solution?

Paul provides one of the most explicit theological treatises on reconciliation of Jews and Gentiles (see Eph. 2:11–22). Given that Jews together with Gentiles constitute the entire world in the first century, Paul's understanding of racial reconciliation encompasses *all* peoples. The death and resurrection of Jesus Christ fundamentally changed racial relations. So much so that Jesus, a Jewish rabbi who primarily ministered to the Jews within the limited geography of Judea, was able to command his Jewish disciples "to make disciples of all nations." This Jewish Messiah is now also the Messiah for the Gentiles (all nations). Paul, in particular, underscores the significance of the Christ event for Jew-Gentile relations. For Paul, there is a "once for all" solution to the historic and incessant racial enmity—the cross of Jesus Christ.

Life Before and After the Cross

Paul's letter to the Ephesians is addressed to Gentile Christians: "Therefore remember that at one time you were Gentiles in the flesh" (2:11), and he describes salvation through contrasts: life prior to salvation and the life of salvation (see table).

EPHESIANS 2:1-10		EPHESIANS 2:11-21	
INDIVIDUAL APPLICATION		**CORPORATE APPLICATION**	
Prior to Salvation	**Prior to Salvation**	**Prior to Salvation**	**Salvation**
dead in trespasses and sins (v. 1)	made alive together with Christ (v. 5)	Gentiles in the flesh (v. 11)	drawn near in the blood of Christ (v. 13)

Prior to Salvation	Prior to Salvation	Prior to Salvation	Salvation
walked in trespasses and sins (vv. 1–2)	raised us up with him (v. 6)	called uncircumcision (v. 11)	Christ made both one (v. 14)
following the course of this world (v. 2)	made us sit with him in the heavenly places in Christ Jesus (v. 6)	separated from Christ (v. 12)	the dividing wall of hostility has broken down (v. 14)
following the prince of the power of the air now at work in the sons of disobedience (v. 2)	in the coming ages God will show the immeasurable riches of his grace (v. 7)	alienated from the commonwealth of Israel (v. 12)	the law of commandments and ordinances are abolished (v. 15)
following the passions of flesh (v. 3)	saved by grace through faith (v. 8)	strangers to the covenants of promise (v. 12)	there is peace, no more hostility (vv. 15–16)
following the desires of body and mind (v. 3)	grace is gift of God (v. 8)	having no hope (v. 12)	both have access in one Spirit to the Father (v. 18)
by nature children of wrath (v. 3)	created for good works (v. 10)	without God in the world (v. 12)	not strangers but fellow citizens with saints and members of the household of God (v. 19)

The table above shows that Paul draws this contrast between life prior to salvation and the life of salvation consistently and emphatically. Why is this important, and what does Paul seek to accomplish through this contrast?

It is difficult to appreciate salvation in Christ without remembering precisely what he saved us *from*. We live in an age when the sense of entitlement is pervasive. Television commercials tell me that beautiful and famous Hollywood starlets use certain products because they're "worth it," and I should, of course, also use the products because I'm equally "worth it." While these examples come from a secular world with the explicit intent to sell their products, does the same mind-set of entitlement bleed into the church? Paul makes it clear that while the benefits of salvation are truly extravagant, they are by no means what we deserve. But they are explicitly and exclusively the work of God alone: "For by grace you have been saved through faith. And this is not your own doing, it is the gift of God. Not from works so that no one should boast" (2:8–9). God saves us not because we're worth it and not because God owes us, but in spite of the fact that we "were dead in trespasses and sins" (2:1). Remembering that we in no way *deserve* salvation allows us to fully appreciate God's grace and to live appropriately, not boastfully, in humility and faithfulness (cf. Rom. 2:1–3:31).

The necessity to live faithfully in God's saving grace is precisely what Paul seeks to underscore through his contrasts. If indeed God "has blessed us in Christ with every spiritual blessing in the heavens," (Eph. 1:3 ESV) then God also "chose us in him before the foundation of the world *that we should be holy and blameless before him*" (v. 4). Paul brings this to light through the double set of contrasts. He describes in detail life prior to salvation in contrast to the life of salvation (2:1–10). The underlying logic is this: if we are saved then we no longer live according to the pattern of life prior to salvation. We do not "walk" in trespasses and sin (2:1–2), we do not follow the course of this world (2:2), we do not follow the prince of the power of the air by being disobedient (2:2), and we do not live according to the passions of our flesh nor the desires of body and mind (2:3) *because we are no longer children of wrath*. "Saved by grace" means that such a lifestyle no longer describes us. Instead, we are "created in Christ Jesus for good works, which God prepared before hand, so that we might walk in them" (2:10).

The same logic can be found in 2:11–22. Whereas the contrast of pre-salvation and post-salvation status is directed toward each individual in 2:1–10, in the following passage the same contrast is framed corporately. Paul identifies his readers collectively as "you Gentiles" (2:11), in other words, the "uncircumcised." Paul then unpacks the significance of what it means to be a Gentile: (1) separated from Christ; (2) alienated from the citizenship of Israel; (3) foreigners or strangers to the covenant of promise; (4) having no hope; and (5) without God in the world (2:12). Each describes the condition of Gentiles prior to salvation. But now, in Christ Jesus each disadvantage is reversed: (1) alienation turns into proximity (2:13); (2) there is peace in place of enmity (2:14); (3) there is unity rather than separation and disunity (2:14); (4) the reason for separation and hostility (the law of commandments and ordinances) is now destroyed (2:15); and (5) strangers and sojourners become citizens and members of the household of God (2:19). Just as the description of life prior to salvation became null and void for those saved in Christ (2:1–10), the life of alienation and separation becomes equally invalid (2:11–22). Alienation, separation, and enmity between races describe the condition *prior to* salvation, not the life of salvation. Going back to Ephesians 1:3–4, if Christians are truly "saved by grace," and if Christians are the recipients of "every spiritual blessing in the heavens" so that we might be "holy and blameless before him (i.e., God)," then the Christian life should not and cannot fall under the description of life prior to salvation.

Not Enmity, but Peace

Beyond this broad overview of Ephesians 2 are some key elements we need to attend to. First, there is only one source of resolution for racial enmity—the death of Jesus Christ on the cross. Paul's description of the Gentiles' condition (2:11–12) dramatically shifts in the next phrase (v. 13). The phrase "but now" combined with "far" and "near"[2] place the work of Christ, specifically the cross ("by the blood of Christ"), as the decisive event that transforms the predicament

---

2. See E. Best, *A Critical and Exegetical Commentary on Ephesians,* ICC (Edinburgh: T & T Clark, 1998), 244–45. The terms "far" and "near" are most likely borrowed from Isa. 57:19.

of alienation to reconciliation. Christ is the primary agent for this transformation,[3] and this shift from alienation to reconciliation is identified as "peace." Many have noted that the theme of peace is dominant in 2:14-17. The term "peace" occurs four times in verses 14 and 15 and twice in verse 17. Paul states that Christ is "our peace" (2:14).[4] Some might interpret the notion of Jesus as "our peace" in an individual or emotive sense, but the phrase points to something more than "personal emotional stability." The context of the entire passage (2:11-22) is corporate and not individual. Further, the term "peace" does not occur in any corporate sense but with specific reference to racial relations (i.e., Jews and Gentiles). Christ is "our peace" with respect to racial relations.

Second, *how* precisely does Christ become "our peace" in interracial relations? Peace is the consequence of Christ's work on the cross. As such, it is not the result of mere human effort, but of the Son of God, Jesus Christ. This peace is neither superficial nor temporary, as 2:14-15 demonstrate, because Christ decisively addresses the core theological issue of enmity between Jew and Gentile. Christ is "our peace" because he (1) "made both one" (v. 14); (2) destroyed the dividing wall that separates, the hostility (v. 14); and (3) abolished the law of commandments (v. 15).[5] All three actions effectively refer to the cross event mentioned in 2:13: peace between Jews and Gentiles (i.e., all races) was accomplished two thousand years ago.[6] Each of these three phrases requires further elaboration.

The phrase "made both one" and the other two phrases refer not to God-human relationships but to the distinct groups of Jews and Gentiles. Through the work of Christ on the cross these two groups become one, and the previous distinctions that separated the two are no longer in effect, as the following two phrases demonstrate.[7] The second phrase "destroyed the dividing wall that separates, the

---

3. Christ is the subject of the verbs and participles in Eph. 2:14-18.
4. The personal pronoun "he" (*autos*) stands at the beginning of 2:14 and is emphatic.
5. All three actions are conveyed by aorist participles.
6. See H. W. Hoehner, *Ephesians: An Exegetical Commentary* (Grand Rapids: Baker, 2002), 368.
7. The last two phrases explicate the first.

hostility"[8] is most likely a metaphorical reference to the Torah and not the wall separating the court of Gentiles from the court of the Jews in the Jerusalem temple.[9] P. T. O'Brien appropriately notes: "The real barrier was, in fact, the Mosaic law itself with its detailed holiness code. . . . It separated Jews from Gentiles both religiously and sociologically, and caused deep-seated hostility."[10] Here, it is explicit that the separation between Jew and Gentile is primarily theological. The law as a "fence" provided protection for Israel from pagan influences of her neighbors. Although the intention of the law was to preserve Israel's unique identity as God's people and not to create ethnic strife, the law also engendered hostility between Jew and Gentile. Through the cross ("in his flesh"), this fundamental division described as "hostility" has been destroyed. The third phrase "abolished the law of commandments" is parallel to the preceding phrase. The verb *katargeō* means "to make ineffective, or powerless, nullify." The entirety of the law as the means of a covenant relationship with God has been nullified through the cross; the separation, or the hostility, between Jew and Gentile is destroyed.

Here, three points can be highlighted. First, it is clear that the enmity between Jew and Gentile is first and foremost theologically based. This means that discrimination and alienation existed not simply due to skin color or cultural/ethnic differences. Enmity was based on the fact that Gentiles were *not* the people of God. But through the cross, the Gentiles are God's people: "I will call those who are not my people, my people and the one who was not beloved, I will call beloved" (Rom. 9:25, citing Hos. 2:23). Peter expresses the same: "But once you were not people [of God] but now you are God's people, once you had not received mercy but now you have received mercy" (1 Peter 2:10). If this critical reason (exclusion from the covenant relationship with God) is now abolished in the cross, is there any justification for racial discrimination

---

8. The genitive *phragmou* ("of the fence") is a genitive of apposition. Thus, the phrase *mesotoichon tou phragmou* is translated "the dividing wall which/that separates."

9. Hoehner's argument against a reference to the Jerusalem temple is persuasive. See Hoehner, *Ephesians*, 369.

10. P. T. O'Brien, *The Letter to the Ephesians*, PNTC (Grand Rapids: Eerdmans, 1999), 196.

based purely on skin color or ethnicity? Second, racial reconciliation accomplished at the cross through Jesus Christ is the fulfillment of God's desire for all peoples to worship him (cf. chapter 6). As Paul states (Rom. 9:25), reconciliation of races now made possible through the cross brings to reality God's welcome of all peoples reflected in the Old Testament. Third, if racial enmity for all races (Jew and Gentile) was effectively destroyed at the cross, why do we still live in racial tension and practice discrimination and separation? Is the cross no longer effective? Is the work of the cross somehow incomplete? This is a significant issue, and we will return to this at the end of our examination of Ephesians 2:11–22. But for now, we simply note that for Christians who confess the atoning effects of the cross, the issue of racial reconciliation is not merely sociological but ultimately theological, as Paul portrays (Eph. 2:11–22). In other words, it's not sufficient to relegate racial reconciliation as either the work of the theologically liberal or the secular realm; it is, according to Paul, the work of the cross and, therefore, the concern of the church.

Growing Pains

The final element we need to consider in this passage is the purpose of Christ's work on the cross for racial relations. Specifically, what is the end goal of the cross? The obvious answer to this question is atonement. Atonement, however, is not simply individualistic ("atonement for my sins") but has a corporate dimension too. In Paul's letter to the Ephesians (2:15), he indicates that the purpose of the cross was reconciliation between Jew and Gentile. The clause at the end of 2:15, translated "so that," governs verses 14–15 and provides the purpose of all three actions examined above: "so that he might create in himself the two into one new man, thus making peace." Somewhat surprising is the primacy of the horizontal reconciliation (Jew-Gentile) rather than the vertical (God-human); this reversal emphasizes the significance of racial reconciliation all the more.[11] Further, this peace is not applied in the universal sense but is specifically tied to Christ, as indicated by

---

11. Ibid., 195; Hoehner, *Ephesians*, 383.

the phrase "in him." It is *in Christ* that the two divisions become one "new" man; thus, old division markers no longer apply in Christ.

Both Jew and Gentile, now one in Christ (2:16), are reconciled to God through the cross. And by the cross, Christ "put to death the hostility in him." Here, as H. W. Hoehner observes, "hostility" does not refer to racial relations but to God-human relations; and "in him" links back to "the cross" in the preceding phrase.[12] Reconciliation on the horizontal dimension (between humanity) is not independent of the vertical dimension (between God and humanity); both are intrinsic to the other. Both Jew and Gentile are reconciled to God in the same manner—by the work of Christ on the cross. Further, it is not one race reconciled to God, nor many races separately, but both in "one body" are reconciled *together* to God.

The following verse reiterates the claim made in 2:14: "And coming he preached peace." The issue of *when* precisely Jesus preached peace to both Jews and Gentiles is much debated. The bulk of Jesus' earthly ministry was directed to the Jews.[13] Most scholars perceive Paul's statement as a reference to the effects of the resurrection. Peace is accomplished on the cross and proclaimed to both Jews and Gentiles by the Holy Spirit working in his apostles.[14] For our purposes, the primary factor in this verse is that proclamation of peace in both dimensions (vertical and horizontal) is inevitably tied to the gospel message. This message of peace stems from Jesus and is carried out by the Holy Spirit. All three members of the Trinity are mentioned and linked with this message of comprehensive reconciliation. The entire Godhead is actively invested in reconciliation, not merely on the vertical plane but also the horizontal.

The result of this proclamation of "peace" is specified in 2:18: "so that through him we both have access in one Spirit to the

---

12. Hoehner, *Ephesians*, 383–84. The change of context in 2:16 justifies this interpretation.
13. See Matt. 10:5–6 and 15:24–27. These passages may be perceived as evidence that Jesus' intention was never to preach salvation to the Gentiles. If so, all passages that speak of Gentile inclusion, including the Great Commission (Matt. 28:18–20; Mark 16:15; Luke 24:46–47; Acts 1:8), pose a dilemma. The limitation evident in Matt. 10:5–6 and 15:24–27 is to be interpreted as a temporal limitation that is lifted after the resurrection.
14. Hoehner, *Ephesians*, 385.

Father." A few elements need mention. First, the word *amphoteroi*, meaning "both" in conjunction with *duo* ("two"), has been used consistently throughout 2:14–18: "having made the *both* one" (2:14); "might create in himself the *two* into one new humanity" (2:15); "might reconcile them *both* into one body" (2:16); and "we *both* have the access in one Spirit" (2:18). Notice that there is transition from "both"/"two" to "one" in each case. And in 2:18, the phrase "both have access" does not refer to the two individually but to the two together as one: "we both *together* have access."[15] Second, just as reconciliation takes place "in one body" (2:16), access to the Father occurs "in one Spirit."

The words "so then," which stand at the beginning of 2:19, draw the logical conclusion from what has been relayed in 2:11–18. The result of Christ's reconciling work is the transformation of the Gentiles' status from that of "foreigners" and "aliens" to that of "fellow citizens"[16] with the saints or those redeemed and to that of "members of the household" of God. This transformation effected by the cross moves from separation and enmity to reconciliation and peace. This sense of unity is appropriately communicated not only as "fellow citizens" but most effectively through the phrase "members of the household of God." It signifies the kind of ties that exist within a family unit.

In the concluding verses of 20–22, the metaphor of building is emphasized and connects well with the notion of "household of God" (2:19). Throughout the verses, four words are created on the base meaning of *oikos* ("house" or "household"): "having been built" (*epoikodomēthentes*) 2:20; "the whole building" (*oikodomē*) 2:21; "you are being built" (*synoikodomeisthe*) 2:22; and "dwelling place" (*katoikētērion*) 2:22. This new community of both Jews and Gentiles is shaped by the teachings of the apostles and prophets and built on the cornerstone of Jesus Christ (2:20). Since this new community is created by Jesus Christ himself, it is only logical that this community is established on the person and work of Jesus Christ and the teachings of the apostles and prophets concerning Jesus Christ.

---

15. Ibid., 388.
16. The word "fellow citizen" (*sympolitai*) is used only here in the NT; it is a compound of the word *politēs* meaning "citizen" with the preposition *syn* meaning "with." The preposition emphasizes unity and togetherness.

Further, this new community is a structure that is "being joined or fitted together" (2:21). "Structure" is immediately preceded by an adjective (without a definite article) *pasa*, which means "all, whole, entire." Thus, not one structure or merely a few, but the *entire* structure is in view. The word *harmologeō* with the prefix *syn* means "to join or pile together," and in the context of first-century construction activity, the absence of mortar required each stone to be cut and tailored to fit with another off-site and brought to the site to be made into a building (cf. 1 Kings 6:7). *Synharmologeō* is immediately followed by *auxei,* which means "to grow" and appears in the present tense. Together the words *synharmologeō* and *auxei* form the notion that the process of being "fitted together" is consistent with the process of growth. Further, growth is continual (present tense conveys continual action).

The end goal of this on-going growth is to become "a holy temple in the Lord." The final verse reiterates growth and corporateness with the goal of becoming a "dwelling place of God" directly addressed to the Gentile audience ("you"). These verses indicate that development of a "holy temple or dwelling place of God" does not isolate a single nation but requires both Jews and Gentiles. The unity of the two is part and parcel of this building process. And finally, these verses, especially 2:21, communicate the necessary ingredient in the construction of this building: being fitted together. Each stone in the entire structure, being cut and tailored to fit the other indicates that, while reconciliation is effectively accomplished with the cross event, the process of growing into a "dwelling place of God" requires continual adjustment to and accommodation of each other. "Being cut and tailored to fit the other" implies a certain level of discomfort and pain.

In discussing racial reconciliation with many Christian leaders, the most frequent reason for not pursuing racial integration is that the differences in culture and collective worship practices are "too uncomfortable" to overcome. How does the fact that "discomfort" is normative in the process of being "built" as one temple affect this common hindrance against racial reconciliation? Inconvenience, discomfort, vexations and hardship are all natural and ongoing features of growing and being built together as one temple.

186 | *Chapter 6*

In conclusion, Ephesians 2:11-22 provides indisputable evidence that genuine racial reconciliation is found in the church. First, racial reconciliation is directly tied with the identity of Jesus Christ as peace for his people and the agent who accomplishes reconciliation. To recognize his identity as Lord and Savior necessitates recognition of his role as the ultimate reconciler for all of humanity on both vertical and horizontal dimensions. It is entirely impossible to attribute racial enmity, ethnic discrimination, or a separatist mindset to Jesus Christ.

Second, it is also clear that racial reconciliation is ultimately tied to the salvation event of the cross. Ethnic peace is the result of the work on the cross. Thus, if we are to claim salvation in the name of Jesus Christ and by his work on the cross, it is impossible to stand against racial reconciliation.

Third, the church as the living body of Christ is multiethnic. There is no support for the perception that the church is exclusively composed of one ethnic people or of one color. The result of the work on the cross is specifically the formation of all humanity, side by side, being fitted together as one holy temple before God. This point is highly significant for drawing up not only the church's position on racial reconciliation, but more importantly for developing its identity as a thoroughly multiethnic body.

Fourth, it should also be clear from the previous three points that this reconciliation effected by the cross surpasses any secular notion of peace, good will, and tolerance. Racial enmity, like all sin, is conquered only through the blood of Jesus Christ, and the ensuing peace is profound and sincere.

Fifth, racial reconciliation is directly linked to the cross event. Thus, the work of reconciliation was effectively accomplished two thousand years ago. The blood of Christ conquers the timeworn and deeply embedded history of enmity and alienation. The church as the redeemed by Christ accomplishes genuine racial peace by recognizing that all reasons for racial enmity have already been destroyed through the cross. And finally, God's consistent desire for whole-hearted worship (Jer. 32:38-41) and his purpose for Israel to be a testimony of salvation for all nations (Isa. 49:6) comes to fulfillment in the cross of Jesus Christ. Where the law could not produce its intended purpose

of genuine worship nor racial reconciliation, Jesus Christ as the fulfillment of the law effects both for his people through the cross.

A SYMPHONY OF PRAISE: MULTIETHNIC WORSHIP

Recently in U.S. politics, something many believed to be impossible happened. On January 20, 2009, Barack Hussein Obama II
was inaugurated as the forty-fourth president of the United States of
America. He is the first African American to hold this office. Given
the historical precedence of slavery and civil rights riots in the 1960s
and 1970s in America, the election of Obama is nothing less than
phenomenal. Further, to date, no person of African descent has been
nominated and elected as the leading political figure of a European
nation. America has indeed come far and is leading the way for many
Western nations with respect to racial equality. To add even more
diversity to the American political arena, Judge Sonia Sotomayor was
confirmed as Associate Justice of the U.S. Supreme Court in August,
2009. She is the first Latina to serve on the U.S. Supreme Court.
Yet while these appointments are significant, others have also paved
the way. Under the Bush administration, Colin Powell was the first
African American to be appointed as Secretary of State, and his suc-
cessor, Condoleezza Rice, was the first African American woman to
serve in this position. Is this genesis of diversity in the leadership of
American politics akin to the diversity we can anticipate in the second
coming of Christ? Perhaps two black men, one black woman, and one
Latina woman doesn't truly convey the full sense of ethnic diversity.

I (Park) once attended a conference in Long Beach, California,
where I encountered the type of "diversity" that is normative for
major American cities. I found blacks, Hispanics, whites, and Asians
all walking the streets under a perfect blue Southern California sky. Is
this a better portrait of what awaits the church in the New Jerusalem?
Is ethnic diversity the picture of perfection? While ethnic diversity may be virtuous on several grounds, multiplicity of races alone
doesn't fully express the treasures that await the church in the Second
Coming. The end times (eschatology) as revealed in Revelation is not
simply about adding color on a white canvas but unity of races held

together by the saving work of Jesus Christ on the cross and the worship of the Triune God. Without a doubt, racial diversity is a critical theological factor, but not a virtue in and of itself.

Multiethnic Worship: God's Perfect Sovereignty

There are four texts in Revelation (5:9–10; 7:9–17; 21:24, 26 and 15:3–4) that deal with worship of God in various contexts. Yet all four describe the worship of God with the same factor: multiethnic worship. All four passages provide an end-time perspective on the Christian faith, vis-à-vis worldly powers and the all-important sovereignty of God. These passages show that the church is multiethnic. The theology that surfaces from these texts emphasizes elements already explored and provide further nuance to the theology behind racial reconciliation.

The first two passages (5:9–10 and 7:9–17) use the same language to describe the multiethnic worship of God: "from every tribe and language and people and nation" in 5:9 and "from every nation, from all tribes and peoples and languages" in 7:9. While the order is not the same, in each case the entirety of the human race is conveyed through the reiteration of the words for "tribe," "language," "people," and "nation." This phrase for all of humanity is repeated in Revelation in three other passages in different order: 11:9; 13:7; and 14:6. Two other passages that convey the comprehensive sense of "all nations" are in 10:11 and 17:15. In 10:11, "many kings" replaces "tribe," and in 17:15 "multitudes" replaces "tribe." Thus, in all seven instances the entirety of the human race is expressed through four nouns with small variations. In all seven, note that the order is not the same. Given the apostle John's use of numbers as symbols in Revelation, the numbers four and seven are highly significant.[17] Number four, as in the four directions of the compass, represents the world, and seven conveys completeness. Hence, these references are comprehensive, and all the nations are in view. As the examination of these seven texts will reveal, not all references are in a worship

---

17. See R. Bauckham, *The Climax of Prophecy: Studies on the Book of Revelation* (Edinburgh: T & T Clark, 1993), 29–37.

setting; but for our purposes, the two passages (5:9–10 and 7:9–17) are found in the context of worship.

The revelation of divine judgment of the world and persevering but suffering saints begins with a scene of the heavenly throne room (4:1). This scene continues until the opening of the first seal (6:1). Two groups of worshippers are identified: four living creatures and the twenty-four elders (Rev. 4). Before we probe the significance of their worship, let's identify these two groups. There are many proposals for the identity of the "living creatures" and the "twenty-four elders," but the best proposal comes from G. K. Beale. The four living creatures, he says, are "heavenly representatives of all animate life throughout creation."[18] Likewise, the elders are "probably heavenly representatives of God's people. The four creatures represent general creation and the elders the elect of God's special creation."[19] The worship offered by the four living creatures and the twenty-four elders represents comprehensive worship of God.

Two songs of worship are offered by these groups to the Lord God. The first comes from the living creatures. Their song "Holy, holy, holy is the Lord God Almighty" is reminiscent of Isaiah 6:3 and indicates that the one worshipped is none other than the God of the Old Testament. The creatures' worship of God highlights not only God's holiness but also his eternal existence: "who was and is and is to come" (4:8). God is the God of time, and all aspects of time (past, present, and future) are under his sovereignty.[20] The second song is offered by the twenty-four elders who worship simultaneously with the creatures (4:9–10). Their song highlights God's worthiness to receive glory and honor and power based on God's identity as the Creator and Sustainer of all creation: "Worthy are you, our Lord and God, to receive glory and honor and power, for you created all things and by your will they existed and were created" (4:11). Thus far the worship songs offered to God in the heavenly throne room focus on God's holiness, sovereignty over

18. G. K. Beale, *The Book of Revelation: A Commentary on the Greek Text*, NIGTC (Grand Rapids: Eerdmans, 1999), 322.
19. Ibid., 322.
20. G. R. Osborne, *Revelation*, BECNT (Grand Rapids: Baker Academic, 2002), 237.

time, and worthiness of worship based on God's unique identity as the Creator and Sustainer of life.

Our first passage is the third song in this sequence and comes immediately after the one "worthy to open the scroll and break its seals" (5:2) is identified as the Lamb (5:6). The close connection of the description "as though it had been slain" with "Lamb" coupled with the previous description ("the Lion of the tribe of Judah, the Root of David") (5:5) points to Christ. Thus, only Christ is worthy to break the seven seals, which represent God's judgment.[21] In response to the fact that there is one who is worthy to open the scroll and break the seals, both the living creatures and the twenty-four elders worship the Lamb (5:8) and sing another song (5:9–10). This song begins in similar fashion to the second song by proclaiming worthiness to receive worship, but the reasons for worthiness are different from the previous two songs. Here, Christ is praised as worthy for his ability to take the scroll and break its seals due to his unique qualifications: "for you were slain, and by your blood you ransomed people for God" (5:9). Christ is worthy to inaugurate God's holy judgment because of his identity as the Redeemer. This redemption is further clarified in the phrase "from every tribe and language and people and nation" (5:9). Christ's redemption is comprehensive and available to all nations, all ethnic groups, and all races.

Further, Christ's redemption makes all nations a kingdom of priests to God, and they will reign on earth (5:10). To narrow the ethnic dimension of God's people to one or few is to diminish the all-extensive range of Christ's redeeming work and, thereby, his worthiness. Hence, the multiethnic aspect of those redeemed plays a critical role in the worship of Christ by the living creatures and the twenty-four elders. Finally, the worship of Christ based on his redemptive role is reiterated in the fourth song: "Worthy is the Lamb who was slain, to receive power and wealth and wisdom and might and honor and glory and blessing" (5:12). This song is sung not only by the four living creatures and the twenty-four elders but also by "the voice of many angels, numbering myriads of myriads and thousands of

---

21. The seven seals along with seven trumpets and seven bowls represent God's judgment on the world.

thousands." The word "myriad" is the highest number in the Greco-Roman world, and the phrase in 5:12 increases it exponentially: "ten thousand times ten thousand and a thousand times a thousand."[22] The entire celestial body worships Christ as the Redeemer of all people.

But the worship scene does not end here. It continues with a description of the entire universe ("heaven, earth, under the earth and sea," in corporate worship singing the final song: "To him who sits on the throne and to the Lamb be blessing and honor and glory and might forever and ever!"(5:13). The final song is offered by all created beings in every dimension of the universe. The object of worship is not only Christ but also God, who received worship in the first two songs.[23]

In conclusion, the worship offered by multiethnic people is theologically significant; it contributes to the portrait of God's and Christ's all-encompassing worthiness and all-extensive work of redemption. These divine attributes command worship not only from a partial group, whether earthly or heavenly, but indeed from the entire universe. The reason behind a multiethnic worship lies primarily in God's worthiness of character and Christ's perfect work of redemption made available to all of humanity. Multiethnic worship is a factor in God's and Christ's worthiness to receive worship from the entire creation.

If, indeed, a multiethnic worship signifies God's all-encompassing sovereignty over all nations and his all-extensive work of redemption, what does a worship limited to one or a few races indicate? Even within a one-race congregation such as Korean-American churches, if there is wholehearted devotion to God, the worship is rich and truly satisfies the soul. If that worship is multiethnic, would it not be exponentially more glorious?

Recently, a white student told me (Park) of his experience in this type of worship. His church rents space to a Chinese congregation. This leasing arrangement led to an opportunity to hold a common service. While the sermon was preached in English, they worshipped

22. Osborne, *Revelation*, 262.
23. Note the similarities in the phrases "to receive glory and honor and power" in 4:11 and "be blessing and honor and glory and might" in 5:13.

together by singing hymns that were familiar to both cultures; the whites sang in English and the Chinese sang in Chinese. According to the student, it was one of the richest worship experiences he had encountered as a Christian because it gave him a glimpse of what the church will be in the end of times. This worship had only two racial groups; how much more fulfilling would worship be with a multiethnic group? How powerful would the gospel message be in such a setting? Jesus Christ has made us one through the redeeming work of the cross! We lift our voices together to worship the one true living God!

Multiethnic Worship: God's Consummate Redemption

The second passage (7:9–17), as noted above, uses a similar formula (5:9) where the same key words "tribe," "language," people," and "nation" appear in different order. This passage comes immediately after the sealing of 144,000[24] (7:1–8), but prior to the opening of the seventh seal (8:1–5). The scene is set before the throne (7:9), and here again, the context is worship (7:10–12). As in 5:9, the multiethnic group participates in worship along with the angels, elders, and living creatures (7:11–12). However, in this passage, the focus is on the "great multitude" rather than the elders or the living creatures; their identity stands at the forefront of this passage and receives further attention (7:13–17). The "great multitude" is described as countless and "from every nation, from all tribes and peoples and languages" (7:9). This multiethnic group stands before "the throne and the Lamb, clothed in white robes with palm branches in their hands" (7:9). "White robes" have already been mentioned. They are promised to those who overcome (3:4–5) and are given to martyrs (6:11). G. R. Osborne notes that the white robes signify victory and purity. Victory is set in the context of the Roman victory procession where the conquering generals were clothed in white.[25] The robes are made white (i.e., pure) through their martyrdom or sacrifice: "made them white in the blood of the Lamb" (7:14). In other words, they

---

24. The number 144,000 equals 12 x 12 x 1000 and conveys completeness.
25. Osborne, *Revelation*, 319.

remained pure in their faith and devotion to God to the point of death. This links well with the white robes in 3:4–5 and 6:11; purity is defined as faithfulness even to death, and faithfulness is equated with victory. Another element should be noted. The phrase "in the blood of the Lamb" indicates that they are made pure by the salvific sacrifice of Jesus Christ (i.e., they are those saved). Here and throughout Revelation, the notion of salvation is faith that remains steadfast and overcomes (2:7, 11, 17, 25–29, 3:5, 12, 21). Thus, this multiethnic group is one that is bonded in the blood of Christ; they are not merely saved but have "overcome."[26] Christ is the common bond for all. The redeeming blood of Christ unites all peoples, and once united they are commanded "to overcome" and obey even at the cost of death.

The elder describes the outcome of this multiethnic group wearing white robes (7:15–17). First, their reward is the privilege of being in the presence of God and serving him continually in his temple (7:15). They are protected by God's very presence. The word *skēnoō* means "to dwell" and conveys the Old Testament notion of "tent" or "tabernacle" where God's presence is the key feature (cf. John 1:14).[27] Thus, God's presence covers them and conveys protection and comfort, two elements that are further elaborated (7:15–17). Second, all forms of suffering are removed: they neither hunger nor thirst, and neither the sun nor scorching heat will harm them (7:16). Third, in place of suffering, Christ himself will be their shepherd and guide them to provision of life and removal of all sorrow (7:16). This is similar to the description of life in the New Jerusalem. God dwells with his people in the New Jerusalem: "Behold, the dwelling place of God is with humankind. He will dwell with them, and they will be his people, and God himself will be with them as their God" (21:3). God removes sorrow and suffering: "He will wipe away every tear from their eyes, and death shall be no more, neither shall there be mourning nor crying nor pain anymore"(21:4). And God provides life: "Then the angel showed me the river of the water of life" (22:1). The similarities in both passages may indicate that what is foreshadowed here (7:9–17)

---

26. See Rev. 12:11.
27. L. Morris, *Revelation*, rev. ed., TNTC (Grand Rapids: Eerdmans, 1987), 115.

is the presence of the multiethnic people of God not only in the heavenly throne room, but ultimately in the New Jerusalem.

This link between the multiethnic people of God described in 7:9-17 and the New Jerusalem in 21:1-22:5 is supported by 21:24 and 26. All nations and kings of the earth benefit from the light shining in the city (21:24). The light is not the luminary planets but the glory of God himself and Christ, who is the lamp (21:23). Thus the glory of God is that which benefits all peoples. Further, all nations will walk by that light, and the kings of the earth will "bring their glory into it" (21:24). The word *peripateō* means "to walk" and is often used to indicate discipleship. Thus, this verse speaks of the conversion of all nations and not merely one or a few in the New Jerusalem. The second part of this verse draws on the imagery of the military conquest procession (Isa. 60:1-5). The phrase "the riches of the nations be brought to you" in Isaiah 60:5 has been changed to "the kings of the earth will bring their glory into it." The change from "riches" to "glory" signifies that the context of military conquest is modified to one of worship.[28] It is not material wealth but the kings themselves that are brought into the city of God. Perhaps the notion of conquest should not be completely eliminated from this text. The earthly kings' submission to God in bringing their own glory into the city signifies divine victory: they no longer worship either themselves or the beast but surrender their glory to God in the act of worship. The portrait of all nations surrendering their glory is repeated for emphasis: "They will bring glory and honor of the nations" (21:26). In conclusion, "the kings of the earth" and "the nations" together convey the presence of a multiethnic people in the New Jerusalem. Here, L. Morris's comments are insightful: "John does not envisage the salvation of a tiny handful and the destruction of the vast majority of mankind. He sees God as bringing 'the Gentiles' into his holy city. God's purpose for mankind will not be frustrated."[29]

The presence of all nations and their worship of God *is* the final consummation of God's passion for all peoples in the Old Testament. God as Creator and Redeemer is the Almighty God who accomplishes

---

28. Beale, *Revelation*, 1095.
29. Morris, *Revelation*, 247.

his purpose for his creation. In Revelation we see the psalmist's words come to fulfillment:

> There is none like you among the gods, O Lord, nor are there any works like yours. All the nations you have made shall come and worship before you, O Lord, and shall glorify your name. For you are great and perform wondrous deeds; you alone are God. (Ps. 86:8–10)

Multiethnic Worship: God's Righteous Judgment

Our final passage, Revelation 15:3–4, falls immediately before the pouring out of the seven bowls, which represent the wrath of God in the form of plagues (16:1). The worship is offered by "those who had conquered the beast and its image and the number of its name" (15:2). These "conquerors" are those who conquered by dying. Osborne states: "Even as the beast 'conquers' the saints by killing them (11:7; 13:7), he is being 'conquered by' the saints (12:11) and the Lamb (17:14). Their death is their final victory!"[30] Their victory song praises God for his attributes; and these attributes command the worship of all nations. First, God is praised for the greatness of his actions. The following phrase calls God "the Almighty," which conveys God's omnipotence and power. He is worshipped for his sovereignty and omnipotence. Second, God's ways are declared to be "just and true." So again, God's deeds are praised. This declaration of God's ways as just and true is followed by another name for God: "The King of the nations!" This title parallels the preceding one: "The Lord God the Almighty!" With the second title a new theme is introduced: "there is movement from sovereign judgment here to salvific promise in verse 4b."[31] Indeed, the phrase "all nations will come and worship you" foreshadows the multiethnic worship described in 21:24 and 26. But here, perhaps, the concept of God's sovereignty and omnipotence needs to be accounted for along with God's "just and true" ways. God's righteous

---

30. Osborne, *Revelation*, 563.
31. Ibid., 565.

judgment is unquestionable and universal; thus it is applicable not only to one nation but to all nations. God's universal ability to judge in righteousness, beyond any doubt and challenge, is the foundation for the sequence of end-time judgments for all nations, which began with the first seal opened (6:1). In view of this sovereignty, power, and judgment, the song asks: "Who will not fear you, Lord, and glorify your name?" (15:4a).

This question is followed by three explanatory clauses that provide the reasons why everyone should fear and glorify God's name: (1) God is exclusively holy; (2) all nations will come and worship God; and (3) God's righteous acts have been revealed. The term "righteous acts/deeds" conveys a sense of judgment; thus, it is "God's righteous acts of judgment." Scholars are divided on this issue. Some propose that, given the context of worship in the preceding phrase, the term should be interpreted in a positive sense, that is, "righteous acts in salvation."[32] But the divine attributes praised here (15:3-4) are repeated in the context of judgment: "And I heard the altar saying: Yes Lord, God Almighty, true and just are your judgments!" (16:7). In both passages, similar terms appear: "Lord, God Almighty," "true," and "just." Indeed, these verses using the same words appear in the same sequence in both passages; "just and true" immediately follow the title "Lord, God Almighty." The terms "just and true" are reversed in 16:7. While 15:3 applies these words to "your ways," they apply specifically to "your judgments" in 16:7. These parallels possibly argue for the sense of divine judgment in both passages where the portrait of slain saints immediately precedes both these verses (15:2; 16:6). We offer this resolution: Divine sovereignty in salvation is not antithetical to divine sovereignty in judgment. It is nonsensical to maintain that God is an omnipotent God who saves but does not judge the unrighteous. Regarding the suffering and perishing saints, their faithfulness to the God who saves is vindicated by the same God. This is the point the apostle John seeks to communicate to Christians who are tempted to compromise in view of clear and present persecution: endure and overcome *because* God who offers salvation to the entire world is the same God who

---

32. Ibid., 568.

judges the entire world. The multiethnic context here is consistent with the other passages in Revelation examined above. To diminish the multiethnic context to one or a few nations is to diminish the omnipotence and the sovereignty of God. All nations are called to bow before him and worship him based on his omnipotence and sovereignty to save and judge all nations.

To close our examination of Revelation, we want to highlight several points. First, the comprehensive notion of "all nations" serves as a critical factor in the depiction of God's sovereignty, omnipotence, and worthiness. The multiethnic context accurately highlights God's universal sovereignty in salvation and judgment. Thus, the inclination to favor or exclude one race ultimately betrays a belief in a less-than-sovereign God. Second, given the fact that the multiethnic group appears repeatedly in the context of worship, it is clear that worship of God requires a multiethnic people. This presents an insightful critique to the statement: "Sunday morning is the most segregated hour in America." All four passages in Revelation offer a theological rationale for multiethnic worship. Even if segregation occurs in the secular world, the church should be the one place where multiethnic groups can worship together as one body. Third, in the passages examined above, the multiethnic church not only shares the common element of worship but also stands together as a corporate group suffering for the name of Christ. The bonds that hold this multiethnic group together is their faith in Christ, the command to persevere, and the willingness to suffer even death in their faithfulness. Thus, solidarity for this multiethnic group is not due to the virtues of diversity, but to Christ. They are all participants of faith in Christ, and their suffering for the same faith joins them together as one comprehensive group before God.

Perhaps the best way to conclude this chapter is a testimony. I (Park) attend a mid-size congregation in Birmingham, Alabama. Most of the members are elderly. Most are white and have spent most of their lives either in Alabama or the South. We have a few families with young children. We have a few black members and one Korean (me), a Yankee to boot. Out of the many churches I visited in Birmingham, I feel at home in this church. The reason for this sense of belonging is not that the church is ethnically diverse. Indeed, I jokingly tell my colleagues at Beeson that simply by *being* in Birmingham I am practicing racial reconciliation. In my present context, either at work or church, I am surrounded by whites and blacks; I am one of the few Asians in Birmingham. This congregation has come to be my family, in spite of the fact that I am quite different from everyone in the church. I am the only Asian, and I am one of the few single females in my forties without children. I feel at home in this church regardless of these differences because we share a common bond in Jesus Christ. These people, so different from me in various ways, worship him wholeheartedly and are willing to suffer for the name of Jesus Christ. They are humble and modest, and they delight in learning Scripture. This bond of love for Christ alone effectively ties me to this congregation and provides me with the intimacy, the true sense of fellowship and "belonging," that should characterize the people of God. This is possible only through Christ. And in Christ, it is not just I who accepts the "other," but they in turn receive and care for me as one of their own. No common language or culture can provide this profound sense of unity. But Christ can! Enmity, alienation, and separation have been resolved in the cross. All that is left for me to do is worship him who has provided such rich diversity in my new "family" in Birmingham—an impossibility apart from Christ. And together we sing:

> Holy, holy, holy, is the Lord God Almighty,
> Who was and is and is to come!
> Worthy are you, our Lord and God,
> To receive glory and honor and power,
> For you created all things,
> And by your will they existed and were created.
> Worthy are you to take the scroll
> And to open its seals,
> For you were slain, and by your blood you ransomed people
>   for God
> From every tribe and language and people and nation,
> And you have made them a kingdom and priests to our God,
> And they shall reign on the earth!
> Amen.

THOUGHT PROVOKERS

1. If the "good news" as preached by Jesus is not exclusively limited to one race, what needs to change in your daily life and your local church in order to effectively proclaim the gospel to all races?

2. If we limit God as only God of one particular race, how does this affect God's sovereignty, redemption, and judgment?

3. If racial reconciliation is effectively provided by the cross, what image in Ephesians 2:11-22 implies integration?

4. What are some of the obstacles in pursuing racial reconciliation and integration in your church? How can these obstacles be addressed?

5. How does Paul's claim that racial enmity has been destroyed at the cross affect, for example, the historical antipathy between blacks and whites, Japanese and Koreans, or Jews and Germans? What are some of the reasons for holding on to historical atrocities with respect to racial relations?

6. How important are repentance and forgiveness individually and corporately within the body of Christ?

7. How does the end-time portrait of multiethnic worship in Revelation motivate us toward diversity?

8. Do you or your church find common ethnicity to be a stronger bond than the redemption of the cross? What kind of kinship and intimacy can result in suffering together on behalf of the gospel, regardless of ethnicity?

Chapter 7

The Proclamation of the Church

FROM THE PREVIOUS CHAPTERS, some may conclude: "Yes, I see that God's desire and intent all along has been reconciliation among all his people regardless of race. But does it *really* need to be preached from the pulpit on Sunday morning? Isn't this just turning the pulpit into a soap box for social justice? And does 'proclaiming' mean just preaching, or does it also include practicing racial reconciliation throughout the week?"

Some might think that preaching racial reconciliation is too radical and verges on being activist. This leads to another question: In cases where this message is countercultural, how much should the Christian risk in proclaiming this truth? Should I risk losing a job for the sake of the testimony that Jesus Christ reconciles all races? Should I risk social ostracism and gossip against my reputation? What about the safety of my family? Does witnessing for Christ and his reconciling work mean suffering on this level? How proactive should the church be in proclaiming racial reconciliation in the message of Jesus Christ?

Three New Testament passages address these concerns: Ephesians 3:1–13, Revelation 16:1–17, and Revelation 17:1–18:24 indicate that the church has a vital role in the proclamation of racial reconciliation and the opposition to the acts of tyranny and cruelty against people.

PREACHING RECONCILIATION

If indeed Jesus Christ reconciled all races through his work on the cross, then how, and to what extent, do we communicate this message?

Reconciled to Both Humanity and God

Since Ephesians 3:1–13 immediately follows 2:11–22, it will be useful to recall the main point of our examination from chapter 6. And the main point is this: Humanity is reconciled only by the cross. *Reconciliation* is understood by most Christians as reconciliation between God and humanity. While this is certainly right, *reconciliation* in Ephesians 2:11–22, especially in verses 13–15, is primarily among humans: Jews and Gentiles. Not until verse 16 does Paul mention reconciliation with God: "and might reconcile both in one body to God through the cross, killing the hostility in him." A simple diagram can clarify this two-dimensional reconciliation:

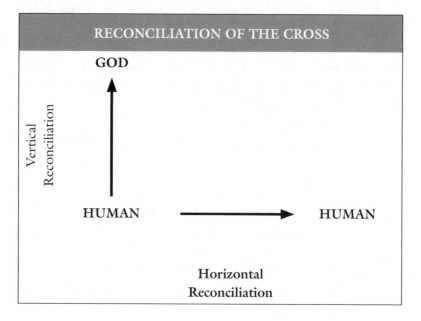

Paul says that the cross brings about reconciliation not only with God, but also with other races (Eph. 2:11–16). It is impossible to say that we have been reconciled with God and at the same time to live without reconciliation with other races and vice versa. Reconciliation in both directions has already taken place in the cross, and one is naturally tied to the other. This may be understood through simple equations:

Reconciliation with God	=	Reconciliation with All Races
No Reconciliation with God	=	No Reconciliation with All Races

These equations show that where there is reconciliation with God; there is also reconciliation between races. But the opposite is also true: when there is no reconciliation with God, there is also no reconciliation between races. That reconciliation on both ends is connected to each other is very important; it is the vital point of Ephesians 2:11-21.

So, once again, we want to show how both aspects of reconciliation are linked together, but this time negatively.

No Reconciliation with God	≠	Reconciliation with All Races
No Reconciliation with All Races	≠	Reconciliation with God

These equations show that when there is no reconciliation on either side of the equation; there is no reconciliation on the opposite side. This highlights two important points: (1) there is no reconciliation with God without reconciliation with races; and (2) there is no reconciliation with races without reconciliation with God. The two points are tied together.

Last, if reconciliation with both God and humanity ultimately comes from the cross, then one equation is excluded:

Reconciliation with All Races	≠	Reconciliation with God

Reconciliation with humanity does not necessarily lead to reconciliation with God. In fact, without the cross, there can be no authentic reconciliation with other races. Genuine racial reconciliation exhibits self-sacrificing love and fosters enduring community. This is possible only if there is reconciliation with God.

The Gospel Message: Spiritual but Not Social?

Pause here and consider this statement: "The cross reconciles humanity not only with God but also with other races." Isn't it clear that the cross, which is central to the gospel of Jesus Christ, naturally speaks to social concerns? Yet some Christians divide the social concerns from those that are spiritual. Throughout the Old Testament, God calls people of all races to worship him. Israel's election aims toward testimony to the nations about God's goodness and grace (see chapters 3 and 4). Consistently, God sits in judgment over Israel's failure to live in righteousness and justice. God is blunt in his judgment:

> Did not your father eat and drink and do justice and righteousness? Then it was well with him. He judged the cause of the poor and needy; then it was well. Is not this to know me? Declares the Lord. But you have eyes and heart only for your dishonest gain, for shedding innocent blood, and for practicing oppression and violence. (Jer. 22:15b–17 ESV)

Paul defines the gospel of Jesus Christ as not just spiritual but also social. Paul says that the gospel of Jesus Christ speaks not only of reconciliation between God and humanity (theological or spiritual) but also of reconciliation between races (social) (Eph. 2:11–21). The cross has an impact on both spiritual and social concerns.

Now then, we return to the question we asked at the beginning: If the gospel of Jesus Christ is defined this way in Ephesians 2, does this mean that Christians should proclaim this truth on Sunday morning as well as other days of the week? The answer to this question can be found in Ephesians 3:1–13.

The Model of Proclamation: Paul's Testimony

In his letter to the Ephesians, Paul provides what we might call a miniature testimony (3:1–13). He doesn't describe how he was converted from Judaism to Christianity (this can be found in Acts 8:1–3, 9:1–31, and briefly in Philippians 3:4–11). Instead, he describes how (the manner), why (the cause), and for what purpose (the result) he was appointed to "preach to the Gentiles" (3:8). All three elements of Paul's calling as an apostle to the Gentiles (manner, cause, and result) are linked together with the reconciling message of the gospel of Jesus Christ.

Let's begin with the question of "how." Paul says, "Of this gospel I was made a servant according to God's gift of grace which was given to me by the working of his power. To me, the least of all saints, this grace was given, to preach to the Gentiles the unsearchable riches of Christ" (Eph. 3:7–8). One of the first things to notice is Paul's humility. In fact, it's difficult to ignore. Paul understands his calling to preach to the Gentiles as something that God has given to him. Further, Paul sees this calling as "God's gift of grace." This is a wonderful phrase that boldly underlines the element of grace. If preaching to the Gentiles is a gift, then Paul's understanding of his calling is that it is *neither burdensome nor even a duty*, but a *privilege*. This gift does not come from humans but from God: it is a *divine* gift. Paul goes even further, saying that this divine gift is also a gift of *grace*. This calling to preach to the Gentiles is not based on merit but entirely on God's grace. Just as salvation by faith in Jesus Christ is understood as God's grace or mercy to sinful humanity, Paul understands his calling to preach to the Gentiles as God's mercy to him.

Paul's humility doesn't end with how he understands his calling. He also calls himself a "servant" (3:7). This word *diakonos* is sometimes translated as "minister," but "servant" is more accurate in describing the lowly and humble aspect of leadership in ministry. In the next verse (3:8), Paul calls himself "the least of all the saints." The word *elachistoteros,* translated "least," means "lesser, inferior, the most insignificant," or "less than the least." Paul understands his calling to preach to the Gentiles as something that he does not deserve; it is God's gift of grace.

The second point, tied closely to this notion of God's gift of grace, is the strong emphasis on God's initiative. Paul says three times that it (i.e., grace) "has been given" (Eph.3:1–11):

- God's gift of grace "was given to me" (3:7)

- "*To me*, the least of all saints, *this grace was given* to preach to the Gentiles" (3:8)

- "surely you have heard of the administration of God's grace *which was given* to me on your behalf" (3:2)

It makes sense that God's gift of grace is one that is *given*. But in this simple phrase ("it was given") lies an important theological point. The calling to preach to the Gentiles is not something that Paul chooses to endorse or to enact simply because he thinks it is a good idea. This calling is not Paul's idea; it comes directly from God. Paul does not pick and choose any message he wants to preach but submits his life and his work to what God has given to him.

Paul preaches to the Gentiles precisely because God has given him this task. If the calling is *divinely given*, then it also makes sense that there is accountability before God for the faithfulness to this calling: "surely you have heard of *the administration of God's grace which was given to me* on your behalf" (3:2). The word *oikonomia*, meaning "administration," can be translated also as "responsibility" or "stewardship," highlighting the idea of accountability or faithfulness. If the calling to preach to the Gentiles is a gracious, God-given gift, then faithfulness to that calling is necessary. This element of accountability fits well with Paul's humility in identifying himself as a "servant" and "least of all saints" (3:8).

Paul's attitude toward this divine calling to the Gentiles is exemplary and stands in contrast to other models in Scripture. For instance, Jonah in the Old Testament did not respond with eagerness but with resistance to God's calling for him to preach to Nineveh (Jonah 1:1-3). Even after his change of heart, Jonah remains a reluctant participant in God's plan of mercy to Nineveh. Jonah is "exceedingly displeased," not because Nineveh rejects his preaching for repentance but because they do repent, and God has mercy on them (4:1-2). Jonah's initial rejection of God's calling, and his displeasure after Nineveh's repentance, comes from his view that God's mercy and compassion should not extend beyond Israel. Jonah's allegiance to Israel overrides God's calling to preach to those outside of Israel. Another negative example is Peter in the New Testament. Peter is persuaded that God accepts both Jew and Gentile: "In truth, I understand that God is not one who shows favoritism, but in every nation, the one who fears him and does what is right is acceptable to him" (Acts 10:34-35). Peter's insight is the result of a threefold vision in Joppa (10:9-16) and the divinely arranged meeting with Cornelius (10:17-33). Peter communicates these events and justifies his table fellowship with Gentiles to the apostles and other brothers in Jerusalem (11:1-18) with these words: "If then God gave the same gift to them as he gave to us when we believed in the Lord Jesus Christ, who was I that I could prevent God?" (11:17). But Peter's strong conviction that God equally receives Jews and Gentiles is challenged when he withdraws from table fellowship in fear of criticism from the "circumcision party" (Gal. 2:12). Paul criticizes this behavior as being inconsistent with the truth of the gospel (2:14). Although Peter believes that God saves both Jews and Gentiles, he does not always behave in accordance with this truth for fear of social censure. In view of both Jonah and Peter, Paul's ready response of humility and consistent obedience to God's calling is commendable.

So, how does Paul understand his calling to preach to the Gentiles? So far, we have learned that Paul is humble. And his humility is demonstrated in the following manner:

- He understands that he is a servant and he is undeserving of God's calling.

- He understands that his calling is God's gift of grace.

- He understands that his calling is given to him by God.

- He understands that he needs to be faithful to God's gift.

Why Proclaim Racial Reconciliation?

Up to this point, we have examined Paul's understanding of his calling to preach to the Gentiles. Now we turn to the question of "why," the motivating reason behind his apostleship. Some might ask: "Didn't we just learn that Paul preaches to the Gentiles because God calls him to do so?" Yes, Paul preaches to the Gentiles because God has called him to that task. But we want to explore whether or not Paul's call to preach to the Gentiles is based on his individual experience. Without question, Paul has a dramatic conversion experience on the way to Damascus (Acts 9:1-19). However, is this the reason Paul provides (Eph. 3:1–13)? In particular, we want to discover if Paul's reason for preaching is solely based on experience. If so, then the calling to preach to the Gentiles might be valid only for him or those with similar experience, but not valid for all Christians. Nowhere in Ephesians 3:1–13, however, does Paul recount his Damascus road experience. Is there another reason behind Paul's apostleship to the Gentiles?

Paul's understanding of his calling to preach to the Gentiles is not based on experience but rather on the gospel of Jesus Christ. Paul says: "For this reason I, Paul, a prisoner for Christ Jesus on behalf of you Gentiles . . ." (3:1). The three words "for this reason" provide the "why," or reason, for his imprisonment ("prisoner") and his apostleship to the Gentiles ("on behalf of you Gentiles"). The phrase "for this reason" points backward to all he has just stated (2:11–21). We know from our examination of this passage that Paul defines the gospel of Jesus Christ as the message of reconciliation for both Jew and Gentile with respect to one another and with respect to God. If reconciliation is made possible through the cross, it means that now unity is possible for all races. It is because of this gospel that Paul endures imprisonment and preaches to the Gentiles.

Evidence that Paul understands his calling based on the truth of the gospel doesn't end with the words "for this reason." Paul's calling as a steward of God's grace (3:2) is directly linked with the "mystery of Christ," which was made known to him through revelation (3:3). What is this mystery of Christ? He supplies the answer: "This mystery is that the Gentiles are co-heirs, members of the same body, and co-participants of the promise in Christ Jesus through the gospel" (3:6). So, "mystery of Christ" is not secret knowledge known only to the elite. This mystery is revealed not only to Paul but also to "his holy apostles and prophets by the Spirit" (3:5). This mystery is what Paul has just described (2:11–21), just as he plainly states (3:6). But it doesn't end here. Paul goes on to say that this is the gospel that he is called to preach to the Gentiles (3:8). So what is the mystery of Christ? It is that now all races are not only reconciled but also integrated in Christ. There are three adjectives that communicate both reconciliation and integration in 3:6: "co-heirs" (*synklēronoma*); "members of the same body" (*syssōma*); and "co-participants" (*symmetocha*). All three words are relatively rare and share the common prefix *syn* ("with"), which has the meaning of corporateness or togetherness. This connects nicely with *sympolitai*, meaning "fellow citizen" (Eph. 2:19). Reconciliation naturally leads to integration. All three words highlight unity between Jews and Gentiles, in other words, unity of all races. This unity is made possible only through the gospel of Jesus Christ. This gospel motivates Paul to preach to the Gentiles.

Why does Paul say that this mystery was "not revealed to the people [sons of men] in other generations"? (3:5). Some may say, "Wait a minute. Haven't we seen in previous chapters that God has always desired both Jews and Gentiles?" Some may also point out the words of Isaiah: "It is too light a thing that you should be my servant to raise up the tribes of Jacob and to restore the preserved of Israel; I will make you *a light for the nations*, that my salvation may extend to the end of the earth" (49:6). And some may cite Zechariah: "*Many peoples and strong nations shall come to seek the Lord of hosts* in Jerusalem and to plead for the favor of the Lord. Thus says the Lord of hosts: In those days ten men from the nations of every language shall seize the robe of a Jew, saying, 'Let us go with you, for we have heard that God is with you'" (8:22–23).

Is Paul misinformed or wrong? There is another explanation. As shown in chapters 1 through 4, God desires all nations to worship him. Both Isaiah (49:6) and Zechariah (8:22–23) state that God explicitly reveals this desire to Israel. What is not clear, however, is whether or not Israel fully *understood* God's desire revealed in these passages. According to Paul this insight could be realized only after the death and resurrection of Jesus Christ by the working of the Holy Spirit (Eph. 3:5). Why was it so difficult for Israel to recognize that God desires all nations to worship him together when it is explicitly written? Perhaps the answer can be discovered with another question: Why have Christians not actively pursued racial reconciliation and integration when God's desire for ethnic inclusion among his people is clear not only in the Old Testament but also in the New Testament? Can it be that we are even more guilty than Israel? Paul clearly states that this "mystery of Christ" has now been revealed and is actively preached (3:1-11). Asking why modern-day Christians have not pursued racial reconciliation changes our perspective on Israel's failure to understand God's desire. Perhaps a challenge can be made at this point. Will Christians today follow wayward Israel and remain deaf and blind to God's consistent desire for racial reconciliation? Should we live as if God has not revealed this mystery to his apostles and prophets through the power of the Holy Spirit? Or will we follow Paul and preach racial reconciliation and integration *because* the gospel of Jesus Christ demands it?

Let's summarize what we've learned so far. What are the reasons behind Paul's calling to the Gentiles?

- Paul is an apostle to the Gentiles because of the gospel of Jesus Christ.

- Paul preaches racial unity because the gospel of Jesus Christ declares racial reconciliation and integration.

- To preach racial unity is to affirm God's revelation in the gospel of Jesus Christ to his apostles and prophets through the Holy Spirit.

Revealing God's Manifold Wisdom

Finally, we come to our last question: What does Paul seek to accomplish (result) through his calling? Drawing from some of the points we have already made, we can phrase the question this way: What must Paul do with this gospel of Jesus Christ in order to be faithful to God's gift of grace or stewardship given to him? Here it might be best to begin with a simple question: What should Christians do with the gospel message? The answer every Christian learns is: Tell everyone about the gospel of Jesus Christ all the time! This is precisely what Paul does with the gospel truth that in Christ there is racial reconciliation and integration. Paul says that he is called "to preach to the Gentiles" (Eph. 3:8). The word *euangelizō* is translated "to preach," which means "to spread the good news." The English word "evangelism" is derived from this word. So we can say that it means "to proclaim the good news of racial reconciliation and integration either through preaching or evangelism." This answers one of the questions we asked at the beginning of this chapter. We should preach racial unity in the cross from the pulpit and also evangelize or spread the good news of racial unity the other six days of the week.

This leads us to the next question: "To whom does Paul proclaim this good news?" The answer is found in the same verse (3:8): "to the Gentiles." What does this mean for modern-day Christians? It means that Paul preaches and evangelizes that there is now reconciliation and integration for all peoples in Christ—to people who were formerly excluded. It means that we also preach to all ethnic groups that have formerly been excluded. The Asian Christians should proclaim to the Hispanic Christians: "We are now reconciled and united in Christ Jesus!" The white Christians should proclaim to the black Christians: "There is now no enmity between races in Christ Jesus!" The Indian Christians should proclaim to the Hispanic Christians: "Because of the cross of Jesus Christ we are members of the same body!"[1]

Some might say: "Hold on! This sounds like each race is proclaiming to all other races the message of reconciliation and integration!" This is precisely right! And this is exactly what Paul seeks to accomplish: "and to bring to light for everyone what is the plan of the mystery hidden for all ages in God who created all things" (3:9). The message of racial reconciliation and integration is for everyone. And the responsibility to proclaim this message is laid upon *all* Christians, regardless of race. If every Christian is called to be a steward of this message of reconciliation and integration, it essentially means that the church is called to this stewardship. This brings us back to what Paul says:

> To me, the least of all saints, this grace was given, to preach to the Gentiles the unsearchable riches of Christ and to bring to light for everyone the plan of the mystery hidden for ages in God who created all things, so that the manifold wisdom of

---

1. One ethnic group of Christians proclaiming to another ethnic group of believers reflects the contemporary problem of segregation in the church. This does not exclude, for example, the need for Asian Christians to simply proclaim the gospel to Hispanics, blacks, etc.

God might be made known now through the church to the
rulers and authorities in heaven. (Eph. 3:8-10)

Paul doesn't preach just to the Gentiles, but to all. And through
his preaching he makes it clear that he also sees the church involved
in the process of proclamation. It means that Paul sees all Christians
involved in this proclamation of racial unity achieved through the
cross, individually (everyone) and corporately (the church). It is not
enough that each individual Christian proclaims racial reconciliation
and integration, but that the church as a corporate body also participates in this proclamation.

This means that the church as a spiritual entity on earth is not
known to the secular world only for its proclamation of racial unity
but also for its *practices* of reconciliation and integration for all races.
It means that in the church, people of all color and ethnicity will find
something more than superficial toleration; they will find peace and
unity as "members of the same body," which can come only from
the reconciliation of the cross. It means that the church cuts right
to the core issues of racial enmity and discrimination because racial
anger and hatred have already been put to death through Jesus Christ
on the cross. The church preaches this message of racial unity in the
midst of political, social, and economic trends that create, foster, and
perpetuate racial hatred.

We come to our last point. What does Paul intend to accomplish through his faithfulness to God's calling? Is it Paul's objective
to simply have all the races get along? Racial unity is not Paul's ultimate objective. Some might object: "Wasn't this the whole point
of this chapter and even the book?" Racial reconciliation, in and
of itself, is not Paul's ultimate goal. Paul's final aim is God's glory
(see chapter 4). Specifically, he says: "so that the manifold wisdom
of God might be made known now through the church to the
rulers and authorities in heaven" (Eph. 3:10). The words "so that"
indicate what Paul hopes to accomplish (result) through his proclamation. The result is not simply the church's participation in the
same proclamation but God's glory. To be more exact, Paul wants
God's manifold wisdom to be revealed to the rulers and authorities
in heaven. But what does the phrase "God's manifold wisdom"

mean? What does it refer to specifically? This phrase refers to what Paul has already said:

> To me, the least of all saints, this grace was given to preach to the Gentiles the unsearchable riches of Christ and to shed light to all what is the plan of the mystery which was hidden for eternity in God who created all things, *so that now* God's manifold wisdom might be revealed to the rulers and the authorities in the heavens through the church. (Eph. 3:8–9)

For clarity, we need to see how verses 8 and 9 connect with verse 10. First, the phrase "God's manifold wisdom" links back to "the unsearchable riches of Christ." What precisely is being preached to the Gentiles? Paul says it is "the unsearchable riches of Christ," which means that the riches in Christ are so profound that it is unfathomable. Then again, what is this profound richness in Christ? It points back to 3:6: the Gentiles are now reconciled and integrated with the Jews. To proclaim racial unity is to proclaim the unsearchable riches of Christ. This in turn reveals God's manifold wisdom. Second, Paul also links this plan of racial unity (mystery) to God the Creator. This plan for racial unity comes not from any human ideal or ingenuity but from the Creator of all life. This divine plan is the one that God accomplished in Christ Jesus (3:11). So, proclaiming the unity of all peoples reveals God's manifold wisdom. And God's wisdom in all its richness and diversity is revealed not only to Gentiles, or individuals, but to all aspects of creation *through the church.*

This wonderful gift of grace (3:8) is given to the church because it is called to be the vehicle for God's glory. This brings us to this essential question: *How* does the church become the vehicle for God's glory? By proclaiming and preaching that through Jesus Christ all races are now reconciled and integrated.

As we come to a close, we return to the beginning of our examination of Paul's testimony (3:1–13). If the church is called to preach racial unity as Paul is called to preach reconciliation, how will we respond to this calling? Will we, like Paul, respond with humility and receive this calling as "God's gift of grace," or will we respond with stubborn rejection and grumbling like Jonah? Turning a blind eye or a deaf ear to this calling will not eliminate the stewardship of preaching racial rec-onciliation placed before all Christians (cf. Isa. 42:18–19; 43:8). If we do not faithfully respond as Paul responds, how will God's manifold wisdom be made known to all? If we do not preach racial reconcilia-tion and integration, is the church still the instrument of God's glory? Paul's faithfulness in proclaiming God's provision of salvation to all nations is not simply coherence to the gospel message of Jesus Christ but to the entirety of the Old Testament. As Creator, God created all humans, and as Redeemer, he offers salvation to all humans (cf. chapter 1). In spite of Israel's failure to live in righteousness before God and to lead other nations to God, God the Redeemer provides a way for all nations to worship him. Jesus Christ as the Jewish Messiah succeeds where Israel failed on both accounts. Through Jesus Christ, God's manifold wisdom is revealed. How can we not make this known to all by living in peace and unity with all races?

THE LAST STAND—THE FINAL WITNESS AGAINST OPPRESSION

A Lesson from Buenos Aires

In 1997, I (Park) visited Buenos Aires, Argentina, to participate in a revival in Argentine churches. In Buenos Aires there weren't as many skyscrapers as we might find in North American cities, but there were a few in the center of the city. The portrait of the city was marred, however, by one building that was half built. It would be natural to assume that the building was in the process of completion except that black soot covered the top of it, making it appear to have been de-serted for some time. I asked one of the Argentines what happened to that building. He answered that it was incomplete and abandoned because they ran out of money. They didn't have money to complete it, and they didn't have money to tear it down, so it remained at the center of the city, a constant reminder of poor civic planning.

The Cost of Discipleship

This incident reminded me of Jesus' words concerning the cost of discipleship.

If anyone comes to me and does not hate their own father and mother and wife and children and brothers and sisters, and further, even his own life, he is not able to be my disciple. Whoever does not carry his own cross and comes to me, is not able to be my disciple. For which of you desiring to build a tower does not first sit down and count the cost, whether he has enough to complete it? Otherwise, after laying down his foundation and he is not able to complete it, all who see it begin to mock him, saying "This man began to build and was not able to finish." (Luke 14:25–30)

It is one thing to read Ephesians 2–3 and begin to see that the gospel of Jesus Christ is a message of racial reconciliation. And seeing Paul's commitment to preach racial unity to everyone, we can agree that all Christians should be committed to proclaiming racial reconciliation. It is, however, an entirely different thing to actively engage in proclaiming this message of reconciliation and integration. How do we move from knowledge to action?

Jesus' words tell us that discipleship requires a total renouncement in the areas most important to us: family and our own lives (Luke 14:25–30). Indeed, this radical commitment to God is nothing new, but one that begins in the Old Testament. The model of Abraham's willingness to sacrifice his only son, Isaac, out of obedience to God sets the precedence for all who claim to be children of faith (Gen. 22:1–19; Rom. 4:16). Commitment to Jesus and his gospel precedes all other concerns. This total devotion to Christ is demonstrated through "carrying [our] own cross." Jesus' illustration of the man who wasn't able to complete his building explains this commitment process (cf. Matt. 19:16–29; Mark 10:17–31; Luke 18:18–30). We must begin by taking Jesus' advice to first sit down and count the cost of discipleship.

What is the risk involved in a radical commitment to Jesus Christ and commitment to the reconciling message of his gospel? Jesus tells us that we must be willing to "renounce all" for Christ (Luke 14:35). This is what it means to "carry our own cross" (14:27). We see a practical example when Paul says that he is a prisoner for the sake of the reconciling message of Jesus Christ (Eph. 3:1). So then, before we begin to proclaim racial unity of the gospel, we need to understand beyond dispute that this may mean risking our jobs, criticism, rejection from others, and suffering for ourselves as well as our families.

Resistance Against All Forms of Oppression

The risk of difficulties is not the only concern to consider. If we preach racial reconciliation and integration, this will lead us into political and economic issues. If we preach racial unity we will also speak against political and economic injustice, which causes us to engage larger and more complex issues.

In the summer of 2008, the immigration issue heightened and received much attention in the news. Immigrants from south of the U.S. border not only were gaining entry into the United States but also offering labor services at a much lower rate than the norm. The immigrants' concern wasn't so much for health and retirement benefits but for food and shelter. There are two sides to this story. On the one hand, the national economy benefits from immigration. On the other hand, the immediate consequence of these low-cost labor services is the loss of jobs for many Americans already struggling economically. The vocal and written protests called the government to place stricter measures on immigration and border watch. In the midst of all this, racial discrimination increasingly became a sensitive issue. This incident shows that the racial issue bleeds into politics and economics. So the Christian position for racial reconciliation will necessarily mean a comprehensive position against all forms of injustice. This sounds a bit too radical, doesn't it? Some may think that this is biblically unjustified and ask: "Is there any support that Christians should take such a drastic and all-encompassing stand against social, political, and economic injustice?" The two passages we have selected from Revelation supply this support.

In Revelation, John's critique of Rome has implications for racial reconciliation. Revelation describes an end-time (eschatological) battle not only between God's people and those who oppose God but also wickedness and the effects of human depravity in comprehensive terms. Thus, God's judgment is extensively directed to human acts of atrocity, natural disasters, and Satan himself embodied in human culture: all forms of wickedness are called to account. Racial discrimination or enmity is but one form of wickedness under social, political, and economic oppression. In Revelation all of humanity is separated into two groups: those who worship God and those who rebel against God. Ethnic distinctions do not form the dividing line in this cosmic battle.[2] Yet at the same time, Revelation speaks against the oppression of all people groups motivated by greed for money and power. Two passages in particular highlight God's condemnation of this oppression.

The Four Horsemen: God's Judgment Against Oppression

The first six seals that are opened release various forms of oppression and wickedness (6:1-17). These seals are the first in the sequence of judgments that will later lead to the seven trumpets (8:6-21; 11:15-19) and seven bowls (16:1-21). These judgments include not only human deeds of atrocity but also natural catastrophes. There are three elements we want to highlight in the opening of these seals: (1) political, social, and economic oppressions are interconnected; (2) God's sovereignty in judgment; and (3) Christian witness against oppression.

When the first four seals are opened, they bring forth four horsemen. The first three horsemen release both military and economic oppression upon humanity. The first horseman comes and releases war: "And its rider had a bow, and a crown was given to him and he came out conquering and to conquer" (16:2). The words "bow" and "crown" suggest military power. This is confirmed by the phrase "conquering and to conquer." It is unlikely that the rider on the white horse represents Christ. Rather, the rider is the agent of destruction and signals war and human depravity associated with war. The Roman Empire was founded chiefly on the conquest of other nations. Although war may aim toward the gain of land and resources, ultimately it must conquer people in order to meet these objectives. So, oppression of people in the form of war is in view here.

The second horseman (6:4) is an extension of the first horseman—he removes peace from humanity and brings slaughter: "Its rider was permitted (given) to take peace from the earth, so

---

2. See Rev. 6:15; 11:9, 18; 13:7-8; 14:8; 17:15; 18:3, 23; and 20:8.

that people should slaughter one another, and he was given a great sword." Again, the Roman Empire conquered other nations with relentless force, all in the name of peace (*pax Romana*); this passage unmasks the truth behind such conquering forces. In spite of the Roman Empire's claim that it brought "peace," peace is not attained by slaughter; bloodshed indicates absence of peace. The word *sphazō*, "to slay," means not simply "to kill" but "to slaughter." Cruelty and brutality are in view. The spirit of slaughter affects all of humanity. This is indicated by the reflexive pronoun "one another" and the phrase "from the earth."

Whereas the first two horsemen bring war and bloodshed to humanity, the third horseman (6:6) releases economic oppression: "A quart of wheat for a denarius, and three quarts of barley for a denarius, and do not harm the oil and wine." Military oppression goes hand in hand with economic oppression. A denarius, the wage for an entire day's work, can buy only a quart of wheat or three quarts of barley.[3] A quart of wheat is the portion for one person per day; and three quarts of barley, the portion for a small family.[4] If the entire day's wage is required for meager portions of food, the situation described is that of famine. There is another telling feature: while the basic staples of wheat and barley are scarce, the luxury items of oil and wine are not harmed. This is a picture of economic depression where the poor are the most affected, while the rich continue in their opulent lifestyle. This judgment of economic depression echoes the concerns of the Old Testament prophets such as Amos when one of God's judgments on Israel is due to economic oppression and injustice.[5] The description of the end-time judgment brings together both military (political) and economic oppression. Both have an effect on the social level. The powerful slaughter the weak and the poor who suffer, while the rich continue in luxury.

Our second point deals with God's role in the midst of these judgments. The judgments released by the opening of the first four seals and the four horsemen are given to them from God. The phrase "it was given" (*edothē*) occurs with the first horseman (6:2). The same phrase

---

3. A quart equates to 1½ to 2 pints.
4. Osborne, *Revelation*, 280.
5. See Amos 2:6–7; 4:1–3; 5:11–15.

is used in 6:4 with the second horseman: "[it] was given," or "[it] was permitted" (*edothē*). The same phrase is also found in 6:8 for the fourth horseman. The phrase "it was given" is missing for the third horseman, but the reference to the voice "in the midst of the four living creatures" points to divine authorization. It is important to ask why these horrific events are pictured as events from God. God permits evil not because he is lacking in the ability to judge, not because he is impotent in the face of evil, and most certainly not because he endorses evil. God permits evil until the final end so that his judgment is perfectly justified and righteous. The call to prophesy to the nations (10:11; 11:3) as well as the call for these nations to repent (14:6–7) indicates that God stays his final judgment and continues to extend mercy to the unrighteous. This does not mean that oppression and slaughter affected by these horsemen are to be endorsed. Yet it was vital for Christians who suffered under these oppressive forces to remember that God is sovereign even in these circumstances. G. K. Beale notes:

> Rev. 6:1–8 is intended to show that Christ rules over such an apparently chaotic world and that suffering does not occur indiscriminately or by chance. This section reveals, in fact, that destructive events are brought about by Christ for both redemptive and judicial purposes. It is Christ sitting on his throne who controls all the trials and persecutions of the church.[6]

This leads us to our final point. What does all this mean for Christians? Precisely *how* should Christians respond to political, economic, and social oppression? The answer is found with the fifth seal. The fifth seal marks a change from the previous four seals. Here, John sees the martyred souls of those who remained faithful to God. Indeed, he specifically states that these souls under the altar are those that were slain *on account of* the word of God and *on account of* the witness they maintained (Rev. 6:9). Again, the word "slain" is the same word used in 6:4, meaning "to slaughter." These martyred souls are not victims of chance. Rather, they are martyred *because* of their

---

6. G. K. Beale, *The Book of Revelation*, NIGTC (Grand Rapids: Eerdmans, 1999), 370.

commitment to the word of God and to maintaining that witness. This suggests that their witness, either passively or actively, stood against the political, social, and economic oppression described in the preceding verses (6:2–8). This picture of Christian commitment against all forms of oppression is daunting and sobering.

"Come Out of Her, My People!"

That Christians are to stand in complete opposition to political, social, and economic oppression becomes even more vivid in Revelation 17:1–18:24. The three aspects we explored in Revelation 6:1–17 will also be examined here. First, the condemnation of the great prostitute and the beast she rides (17:3) is a comprehensive judgment against all forms of oppression. The image of the great prostitute (Rev. 17) must be seen together with the beast rising from the sea (13:1). The portrait of the woman on the beast (17:3) confirms that they are to be interpreted together. The beast (Rev. 13) represents Rome in its military might, and the woman is its counterpart and represents the corrupting influences of Rome.[7] Rome's power was first and foremost built on the conquest of other nations. As its military power grows, its economic, social, religious, and political influences also increase. The rhetorical question in 13:4 provides a good indication of its seemingly invincible power: "Who is like the beast, and who can fight against it?"

The Sins of the Great Prostitute

Many interpreters understand the woman's sins as *theological* sins. But her sins spread beyond the theological into social and economic dimensions. First, Rome's power was not only in its military domination and political sophistication. As its influence grew, it proclaimed and cultivated emperor worship, and Rome itself became an idol through the worship of the goddess Roma. Acceptance of Roman rule also meant acceptance of its idolatrous religion. The idolatrous

---

7. R. Bauckham, *The Climax of Prophecy: Studies on the Book of Revelation* (Edinburgh: T & T Clark, 1993), 343.

nature of Rome is clearly described in 13:14–15: "it deceives those who dwell on earth, telling them to make an image for the beast that was wounded by the sword and yet lived. And it was allowed to give breath to the image of the beast, so that the image of the beast might even speak and might cause those who would not worship the image of the beast to be slain."[8] Christians who exclusively worship the living God posed a threat to Rome and stood in direct opposition to Rome. So then, is the great prostitute guilty only of theological sins—namely, idolatry? According to Revelation 17–18, there is more to her sins.

The woman is called the "Great Prostitute" (17:1–18) because she seduces others to participate in her immorality: "Come, I will show you the judgment of the Great Prostitute who is seated on many waters, with whom the kings of the earth have committed sexual immorality, and with the wine of whose sexual immorality the dwellers on earth have become drunk" (17:1–2). It would be easy to assume that "sexual immorality" refers to both actual and religious adultery. But in Revelation 18 her "sexual immorality" is inseparably linked with her sins of "luxury," which includes trade and commerce. The description of the woman (17:4) conveys an extravagant lifestyle; the items of purple, scarlet, gold, jewels, and pearls are all items of luxury.[9] This picture of exorbitant wealth is continuously connected to the description of the woman throughout Revelation 18, spells out in detail God's judgment on her sins. The woman's sexual immorality is tied to how the merchants have grown rich through her luxury (18:3); likewise, her sin of glorifying herself and living in opulence receives divine judgment described as "torment and mourning" (18:7). Kings and merchants who committed sexual immorality and shared her wealthy lifestyle bemoan her fall because her downfall signifies their own economic loss and the subsequent loss of power (18:9–18). "And the merchants of the earth weep and mourn for her, since no one buys their cargo anymore" (18:11). We can conclude that the woman's sins are much more than actual and religious adultery. Rather, her adultery is bound to the sins of economic oppression that underwrite her extravagant living.

---

8. See Osborne, *Revelation*, 514–15.
9. See Bauckham, *Climax*, 350–371.

Economics and Slavery

At this point an objection can be raised: Surely economic wealth in and of itself is not evil? We can answer this with three points. First, economic wealth as depicted in Revelation 18 is condemned by God's righteous judgment. Second, her economic wealth is tied to her adultery: she relishes and takes pride in her wealth (18:7), and her confidence in wealth leads her to believe she is invincible (18:7). And third, the most significant point is that her economic wealth is gained at the expense of other people; her wealth is accrued through oppression of various people groups. This is most explicitly noted in 18:12-13 where the cargo lost in divine judgment is listed item by item. It begins with items only the rich can afford: precious metal (gold, silver), jewels (pearls), fine cloth, and the accompanying dyes, expensive wood and ivory, precious metal and stone for furnishings (bronze, iron, marble), precious spices (cinnamon, spice, incense, myrrh, frankincense), luxury food items (wine, oil, fine flour, wheat), livestock (cattle, sheep, horses), and vehicles of transportation (chariots). With the exception of wheat, all the items are commodities for the wealthy. This alone tells us that Rome's trade does not provide for the common people but specifically caters to the rich at the expense of others. Indeed, given the population of nearly a million people in Rome, the burden of feeding citizens of Rome (80,000 tons annually) meant suffering for the rest in the empire.[10] But oppression is underscored by the final item on this list: slaves. The final phrase unambiguously indicates that "living bodies, that is, human souls" refers to slaves shipped as merchandise along with other items. Human beings serve as a chattel for the elite of Roman society. One scholar makes this observation:

Romans imported incredible numbers of slaves (estimated at 10 million, or close to 20 percent of the population of the Roman Empire), and the rich based their status somewhat on how many slaves they owned. Slaves were obtained through war, debt, parents selling their children for money, kidnapping,

---

10. Osborne, *Revelation*, 649. See also his exposition on the entire list in 648-50 as well as Bauckham, *Climax*, 338-83.

as punishment for criminals, or unwanted children exposed to the elements and left to die (common in the ancient world). While in the first century B.C., war produced the greatest numbers of slaves, during the Pax Romana, the others were the primary sources. Asia Minor was a primary source of wheat and slaves for Rome, heightening the sense of the list emphasized items that reflected not only the Romans' lust for consumer goods but also their consequent exploitation and plundering of the other nations in the empire.[11]

It is impossible to view the economic wealth of Rome described in Revelation 18 as innocent and noble; it is fundamentally intertwined with indiscriminate exploitation and oppression of other people groups. The Romans perceived themselves as superior and all those they conquered were considered inferior. According to B. Isaac, the success of the Roman Empire rested precisely on its ability to subjugate others: "what is seen in our days as a remarkable success of the Roman Empire, namely its integration of subject peoples, is represented by at least some of the important Roman authors as a process which reduces those peoples from fierce and free humans to degenerate slaves."[12] Domination and coercion of people go hand in hand with the military and economic power of Rome. And God in all his righteousness, justice, holiness, and sovereignty stands against all that Rome represents in Revelation 18. The exploitation of people is but one element of her many sins. At this point, another objection can be raised: Is exploitation of people or slavery always linked with racial issues? We need only to remember American history: slavery fueled racial discrimination, and the current issue of racial enmity between blacks and whites is the consequence of the practice of slavery in the past.

Lest You Take Part in Her Sins

Now we turn to the issue of God's sovereignty. Revelation 17 and 18 indicate that God judges the economic, political, and social

---

11. Osborne, *Revelation*, 650.
12. B. Isaac, *The Invention of Racism in Classical Antiquity* (Princeton: Princeton University Press, 2004), 193.

sins as represented by Rome. The description of the downfall of the Great Prostitute (18:1–24) also tells us that God's final judgment is comprehensive. If economic, political, and social oppression receives God's full and final judgment, then it should also be clear that Christians stand entirely opposed to such tyranny.

This leads us to the final point. What should a Christian do in the midst of all these oppressions? Christians are called to a lifestyle that is radically different from the lifestyle of the Great Prostitute. God's people are commanded to separate themselves from the Great Prostitute: "Come out of her, my people, lest you take part in her sins, lest you share in her plagues" (18:4). The command "to come out" is a call to separate from all that the Great Prostitute represents. The meaning of separation comes through the verb "to share" (*synkoinōnēsēte*) plus the negation (*mē*);[13] the same verb is used in Philippians 4:14 to convey ideas of "sharing" or "co-participation." To remain and participate in her sins is to share in the coming judgment of her sins. Those who testify against her are slaughtered (*sphazō*) (Rev. 6:9–11; 18:24). This is the same word used in 6:4 and 6:9. The description in 18:24 indicates that Christians have suffered and died because of their testimony against the unjust practices of Rome. The song of praise in heaven that follows the downfall of the Great Prostitute confirms this: "Hallelujah! Salvation and glory and power belong to our God for his judgments are true and just; for he has judged the Great Prostitute who corrupted the earth with her immorality, *and has avenged on her the blood of his servants*" (19:1–2).

These Christians are slaughtered because they stand against the various forms of tyranny represented by the Great Prostitute. The final stand of Christianity, as described in Revelation, resists economic, political, and social oppression at the risk of death. If Revelation describes the final battle between God's people and all those who oppose God, then it also seems clear that this is our future. Are we ready to make the last stand against all forms of oppression?

This brings us to our final question: Is racial discrimination a separate issue from those addressed here in Revelation 18? In Revelation

---

13. See also Eph. 5:11 and the noun "co-participation" (*synkoinōnos*) in Rom. 11:17; 1 Cor. 9:23; Phil. 1:7, and Rev. 1:9.

18, the exploitation of people groups is indiscriminate. Yet it is not difficult to link greed for money, power, and land with persecution of various people groups. We need only to recall the catalytic reasons behind historical atrocities such as the Holocaust (living space) and slavery in America (tobacco and cotton trade) to recognize the inevitable link between ambition for money, power, and land with racial discrimination and the ensuing consequence of racial enmity. To stand against racial discrimination and the various oppressive strategies invented to slake the thirst for power, money, and resources is the final Christian proclamation as depicted in Revelation. And this proclamation, as amply indicated throughout Revelation, does not gain victory by aggression but through self-sacrifice. It is a proclamation based on a conviction that risks even death.

Conclusion

The proclamation of the gospel is necessarily the proclamation of racial reconciliation. As indicated by Ephesians 3:1–13, they form one coherent gospel message. This has certain implications for the modern-day church, which too often has ignored the subject of racial reconciliation as the agenda of the liberal or relegated the message as a footnote to the overall concerns of the gospel. Further, it is also clear from Ephesians 3:1–13 that the burden to preach racial reconciliation falls to the church and not to the secular world precisely because reconciliation stems from the cross. The proclamation of the church is preached to all of humanity and all of creation. This unique posture against all oppression and enmity emerges poignantly in Revelation as the believers make a final stand. They stand even in the face of death, against a regime that systematically subjugates various people groups for the sake of its own comfort and greed. The proclamation of racial reconciliation is preached selflessly to the end because the message is coherent with God's character. This commitment to the gospel and the message of racial reconciliation endures the censure and persecution from the wider secular culture.

The level of risk for this type of commitment is high and reminds us once again of Jesus' words: "Whoever does not carry his own cross and comes to me, is not able to be my disciple" (Luke 14:27).

Throughout the New Testament the call to discipleship is simultaneously a call to stand against various forms of oppression. James speaks out explicitly against those who show partiality to the rich and dishonor the poor (James 2:1-13). For James, concern for the poor is tied to God's compassion for the poor and the weak (2:5) and the command to love one's neighbor (2:8). Later, James condemns the rich for their self-indulgent lifestyle and oppression of others (5:1-6). Similarly the apostle John exhorts believers to love others with a self-sacrificing love: "By this we know love, that he laid down his life on our behalf and we ought to lay down our lives on behalf of the brothers [and sisters]. But if anyone has the goods of the world and sees his brother [or sister] in need and shuts his compassion from him, how does the love of God remain in him?" (1 John 3:16-17). And Paul devotes a long section on financial generosity to encourage the Corinthians to aid the Jerusalem believers suffering from financial difficulty (2 Cor. 8-9). This concern for the poor and the oppressed is central to the messianic blessings Jesus claims in fulfillment of Isaiah 61:1-2: "The Spirit of the Lord is upon me, because he has anointed me to bring good news to the poor, to proclaim to the captives liberty and recovery of sight to the blind, to send out those oppressed in liberty, to proclaim the year of the Lord's favor" (Luke 4:18-19). Are the messianic blessings of Jesus Christ, the Messiah, still in effect today? If so, can Christians afford to turn a blind eye to oppression in the world? The concern for the poor and the oppressed as reflected in the teachings of Paul, James, and Jesus is not different from God's message in the Old Testament. God stands consistently against all forms of oppression and rebukes those who participate in oppression. God's judgment is laid upon Israel because of her oppressive lifestyle:

> For three transgressions of Israel, and for four, I will not cancel its punishment, because they sell the innocent for silver, and the needy for a pair of sandals—they trample the head of the poor into the dust of the earth and turn aside the weak from the road. (Amos 2:6-7)

Isaiah echoes similar concerns:

Woe to those who proclaim wicked decrees and write oppression, to turn aside the weak from justice and to rob the poor of my people of equal treatment, that widows may be their spoil, and the fatherless their prey. What will you do on the day of punishment, in the devastation that will come from far away? (Isa. 10:1-3; cf. also Ezek. 22:1-12)

God grieves that his people "do not judge with justice the cause of the fatherless, that they may prosper, and they do not defend the rights of the needy" (Jer. 5:28). And he asks: "Shall I not punish them for these things?" (Jer. 5:29). The call for the people of God to stand against oppression is consistently conveyed through both Old and New Testaments.

THOUGHT PROVOKERS

1. How often do you or your church proclaim racial reconciliation through preaching?

2. What is the difference between adopting a multiethnic position based on secular notions of political correctness or basic human virtue and adopting a multiethnic position based on the theology of Ephesians 3:1-13 and Revelation 6:1-17; 17:1-18:24?

3. In view of the gospel, how important is it for you or your church to lay aside the historical and current enmity of races? Identify some practical steps you or your church can take to resolve racial enmity.

4. In view of Ephesians 3:10, do you or your church aim to make God's wisdom and sovereignty known to everyone by advocating racial reconciliation? Does the burden to proclaim fall only to white Christians? Or are all races called to proclaim racial reconciliation?

5. Do you or your church speak against economic, social, and

political oppression in the proclamation of the gospel? If the answer is negative, why not?

6. Since God opposes all forms of oppression, how should you or your church respond to the political and economic oppression in the world?

7. Identify some areas of oppression you or your church can address. What are some of the risks you or your church will undertake in order to obey the command to separate from oppressive social and political practices?

Chapter 8

One Salvation, One Fellowship

IT'S ONE THING TO know that God desires all races to worship him, that his son Jesus Christ makes this possible at the cross, and that we are, regardless of race, one body of Christ. But it is a different matter entirely to implement this. Each church will be different. Some churches may have the benefit of being located in racially diverse communities of major cities. For these churches, reaching out to the "other" might be a matter of extending their outreach by a couple of blocks. The inner-city black church can take a few steps toward the Hispanic or Asian community within the same perimeter. However, this solution is not an option for churches located in predominantly white suburbs. Churches that cannot rely on the natural multiethnic context of an inner city will need to reach further. For these suburban churches, the effort to reach ethnically diverse communities requires crossing another social barrier: economics, which can be even more difficult to cross than ethnicity.

When I (Park) was in Aberdeen, Scotland, for my doctoral work, I visited a Korean church. That particular Sunday was the celebration of Korean Harvest, much like Thanksgiving in the United States. There was a table full of Korean cuisine. Since there were no Korean restaurants or Korean grocers in Aberdeen, this was a rare treat for me! As we gave thanks and ate, two young men walked into the fellowship hall. It was clear by their appearance that the two men, one black and one white, were homeless; they had the look of shabbiness and dirt that hadn't been washed off in weeks. They came into the feasting group of Koreans and asked for food. We had plenty to spare, and food was given to them. They sat in the same large room, but at an empty table. Not ten minutes passed when one of the deacons came up to the pastor and requested that these two men be removed to a separate smaller room. The reason for his request? "They are ruining my appetite," he said. My appetite also was ruined—but by the deacon, not the transients. I wondered how often the Pharisees' and the scribes' appetites were ruined by Jesus' unclean hands and his routine association with those labeled "dirty." Although the racial barrier was certainly a factor for this deacon, the economic barrier was the more critical component in his request to deny fellowship.

Can the rich or even the moderately rich church reach out to the poor and receive them as brothers or sisters in Christ? Some may contend that racial discrimination is not the same as economic discrimination. Indeed, it is not. There are many Korean immigrants who send their children to Ivy League schools, own grand homes in the suburbs, and shun other Koreans classified as "low" so that they are no longer defined as the same by association. This scenario is not particular to Koreans; it is equally true for blacks, Hispanics, and whites. Economic discrimination isn't necessarily racial discrimination. But you don't need a sociologist to see that economically poor areas are predominantly populated by minorities; reaching out to different ethnic groups will necessitate a willingness to invite the poor into our midst. Can we have table fellowship with the socially marginalized in spite of vast social differences based on the proclamation that we are joined together as one family by the blood of Christ (cf. 1 Cor. 11:17–22; James 2:1–13, 5:1–6)?

Yet simply overcoming racial and economic boundaries is not the only concern for the church striving to live out the reconciling message of the gospel for all races. There are practical matters that waylay the desire for a racially integrated congregation. Language is the simplest barrier to overcome: provide translation. If missionaries can develop intimate ties in spite of their cultural and linguistic limitations, surely the same can occur in the United States; it requires a mutual willingness to learn the other culture and adopt creative solutions to bridge the language barrier. It's not a matter of giftedness (cf. Rom. 12:3–8;

Eph. 4:8–12); the mandate to disciple all nations (Matt. 28:19) applies to all Christians. Most American Christians don't even have to leave the country to fulfill the Great Commission. The United States is such a melting pot that any number of cities offers some ethnic diversity. For example, even in Birmingham, Alabama, a moderate-sized city, there is a steady growth of Hispanic and Asian communities—it's not just black and white!

But the most common reason for segregation in the church is not lingering historic prejudices or even language barriers; it is worship style. When I (Park) worked in Minnesota, I had an opportunity to visit a unique church in downtown Minneapolis called Bethlehem Baptist led by John Piper. This Scripture-centered church welcomed various ethnic groups from within the multiethnic context of the inner city and the nearby university. What was interesting to me, however, was not the mix of color in the congregation but the variety in worship styles. On some Sundays, worship was a combination of hymns and praise music; other Sundays, it was a combination of African-style music and hymns. The worship style was constantly in flux, yet the non-negotiable factor of genuine, heartfelt worship of God was present each Sunday. Regardless of race and color, all stood in the presence of God. Apart from this common desire to worship God, another primary component was present: people of all ethnic origins gathered with the collective desire to hear the word of God.

How do we negotiate the differences in worship styles? The key to genuine worship is not a particular style; rather, it is a life of faith—exemplified through sacrifice and centered on Scripture—that yields true worship. Given Christ's reconciling work on the cross, Jews and Gentiles living together is *non-negotiable*.

Regardless of possible solutions, there may still be resistance to the two primary issues addressed: table fellowship and worship. We've already explored why multiethnic table fellowship and worship are coherent to the Christian faith (chapter 5). Here we direct our attention to two particular matters: (1) the experience and solution of the early church with similar issues; and (2) why the practice of table fellowship and collective worship are integral to the unity of the body of Christ.

THE STORY OF RECONCILIATION AND TABLE FELLOWSHIP FOR THE EARLY CHURCH

Solomon once said, "There is nothing new under the sun" (Eccl. 1:9). The difficulty the contemporary church encounters in living out the implications of racial reconciliation is nothing new; the New Testament provides ample evidence of the same struggle. Although Jesus, prior to his ascension, commanded his disciples to make disciples of all nations (Matt. 28:19; Mark 16:15; Luke 24:47; Acts 1:8), it took some time for the disciples to unpack the practical significance of this command. If they were to make disciples of all nations, the existing barriers against fellowship with Gentiles could not be sustained. It would require a radical recalibration of preexisting ideology and custom; notions and attitudes (concepts) against Gentiles would have to be redefined along with praxis (the outworking of concepts). This was precisely what Peter had to learn (Acts 10) before he could effectively witness to Cornelius and his household.

Conversion of Cornelius: Acts 10

Acts is not simply a collection of "what the apostles did" in the aftermath of Christ's death, resurrection, and ascension but a story about how the gospel of Jesus Christ advanced beyond the boundaries of Judea and Judaism. From this perspective, much of Acts 1–7 is centered in Jerusalem and Judea, and not until the stoning of Stephen (7:54–61) and subsequent persecution (8:1–3) does the gospel cross over the boundaries of Judea and Judaism. Immediately after the observation that "all were scattered throughout the regions of Judea and Samaria, except the apostles" (Acts 8:1), Luke records Philip's evangelistic efforts in Samaria (8:4–25). Notice Luke's introduction to this report: "Consequently, those scattered went about preaching the word" (Acts 8:4). Evangelism to those outside the boundaries of Judea and Judaism (i.e., non-Jews or Gentiles) takes place as a consequence of persecution.[1] The historic enmity does not

---

1. F. F. Bruce, ed., *The Book of the Acts*, (Grand Rapids: Eerdmans, 1988), 163.

hinder Philip or the apostles in receiving former enemies into their fellowship (8:14–17). After the story of evangelism to Samaritans, Luke proceeds to the conversion of the Ethiopian eunuch (8:26–40). This Ethiopian is a Gentile who worships the God of Israel. He was on the road from Jerusalem to Gaza (8:26); he came to Jerusalem to worship (8:27) and was on his journey back home. The fact that he undertakes a long journey to worship in Jerusalem and reads Scripture (8:28) indicates that he is a pious man. It is uncertain whether or not the pilgrimage proves that he was a proselyte to Judaism. Deuteronomy 23:1 and Leviticus 21:20 prohibit eunuchs from becoming full members of Israel. It is unlikely that the Ethiopian was a proselyte, that is, "a Gentile who fully accepted the Jewish religion by undergoing circumcision."[2] Gentiles were permitted entry to the outer court of the Jerusalem temple.[3] The conversion of the Ethiopian serves as a precursor to the conversion of Cornelius (Acts 10:1–48).[4] Cornelius is similar to the Ethiopian in his piety: "a devout man and one who fears God with all his household, giving alms generously to the people and praying continuously to God" (Acts 10:2). Again, it is most likely that Cornelius was not a proselyte to Judaism but a Gentile worshipper of Israel's God.[5] Luke distinguishes between proselytes (cf. Acts 2:11, 6:5, 13:43) and "God-fearers" (cf. Acts 13:16, 26) or "devout men" (cf. Acts 17:4, 17, 18:7).

As the church is persecuted and scattered, conversion of those excluded from Judaism progresses from the Samaritans to the Ethiopian and finally to Cornelius. But these conversion stories are not merely about "those outside of Judaism"; there is also a progression of a different type. In spite of the historical hatred between Jews and Samaritans and the fact that Jews considered the Samaritans as Gentiles (cf. Matt. 10:5; John 4:9), they were akin to the Jews in faith and by heritage.[6] According to F. F. Bruce, Philip most likely built on

---

2. I. H. Marshall, *Acts*, TNTC (Grand Rapids: Eerdmans, 1980), 183.
3. See B. R. Gaventa, *Acts*, ANTC (Nashville: Abingdon Press, 2003), 142; and Marshall, *Acts*, 160.
4. See Gaventa, *Acts*, 140: "The Ethiopian is proleptic of all those who will be reached for God through the witness to the gospel."
5. D. L. Bock, *Acts*, BECNT (Grand Rapids: Baker, 2007), 386.
6. See chapter 5 for Samaritans.

the common hope of a deliverer.[7] Thus, the story in Acts begins with the less radical barrier. Then it progresses to the Ethiopian who is a Gentile, but this story does not introduce the concept of fellowship; Philip is spirited away immediately after the conversion of the eunuch (Acts 8:39-40). The story of Cornelius is framed in similar circumstances to that of the Ethiopian (both men are pious Gentiles, and both conversions are divinely initiated), but it introduces two significant factors: (1) evangelism of the Gentiles is now divinely appointed to an apostle (Peter); and (2) the element of table fellowship is introduced through Peter's vision (Acts 10:9-16) and by his prolonged visitation with Cornelius (10:48). Gentile inclusion becomes a sanctioned activity of the early church as the mediators of the gospel shift from Philip to Peter. While Philip was a Hellenist (6:1, 3)[8] and one of the seven deacons (6:5), he was not an apostle. Peter's apostolic authority legitimizes the inclusion of Gentiles. Bruce rightly observes: "The range of the apostolic message has been steadily broadened. Already it has begun to cross the barrier which separated Jews from Gentiles; now the time has come for that barrier to be crossed authoritatively by an apostle."[9] Indeed, this apostolic endorsement is critical not only for receiving Gentiles as those equally saved but also for table fellowship, the natural outcome of being equally saved. B. R. Gaventa makes a similar assessment: "Including Gentiles means receiving them, entering their homes, and accepting hospitality—even meals—in those homes."[10] Table fellowship with Gentiles was the critical issue that the early church needed to address if witness to the Gentiles was to continue.

The phrase "table fellowship" means sharing a meal within the context of a household—it conveys intimate relations of a family.[11] As such, it was a powerful means by which the early church

---

7. Bruce, *Acts*, 164. See also John 4:25.
8. "Hellenist" (*hellēnistēs*) is a rare term. In Luke it refers to Greeks (14:1; 18:4; 19:10; 20:21). But here, the context suggests that Philip is a Greek-speaking Jewish Christian. See Marshall, *Acts*, 125-26.
9. Bruce, *Acts*, 201.
10. Gaventa, *Acts*, 172.
11. D. W. Pao, "Family and Table-Fellowship in the Writings of Luke" in *This Side of Heaven: Race, Ethnicity, and Christian Faith*, ed. R. J. Priest and A. L. Nieves (Oxford: Oxford University Press, 2007), 186.

redefined family as allegiance to Christ. Although the shared meal (Acts 27:33-38) is most likely similar to the Lord's Supper (this is debated), the shared meal or breaking of bread in Acts usually refers to the act of eating together (Acts 2:42, 20:7, 11, 24:35). In spite of this plain sense, table fellowship indicates a profound theology—it redefines kindred relations and practices inclusion of those formerly excluded.

The importance of table fellowship is underscored several ways in Acts 10. First, the lengthy and detailed description of Cornelius's conversion (48 verses), in comparison with the two previous conversion accounts (Acts 8:4-8, 25, 26-40), indicates that the issues raised within the passage are significant. Second, Peter's vision of common or unclean animals and the divine command to "kill and eat" as well as the statement "What God has cleansed, do not call common" (Acts 10:15), are repeated three times (10:16); the threefold repetition suggests that the need for Peter to change his perspective on what is clean and unclean is neither a secondary nor peripheral concern but central. Third, the issue of table fellowship between Jew and Gentile does not end with the conversion of Cornelius, but table fellowship (11:1-18) is the chief matter raised for discussion in Jerusalem (Acts 15). The news of Gentile conversion is heard throughout Judea (11:1), and the circumcision party criticizes Peter in Jerusalem: "You went to uncircumcised men and ate with them" (11:3). In response, Peter relates the entire event—his vision, divine command, and conversion of Cornelius and his household (11:4-17). Peter concludes his story with a provocative question, "If then God gave to them the same gift as he gave to us when we believed in the Lord Jesus Christ, who was I that I could hinder God?" (11:17). And all objections are silenced (11:18). While Peter has not directly answered their objection to eating with Gentiles, the clear evidence that "God also gave to the Gentiles repentance that leads to life" (11:18) does answer this objection. If God also calls Gentiles to salvation on equal terms with the Jews, then table fellowship with the converted Gentiles is part and parcel of salvation. There is no distinction that would hinder table fellowship. Based on these three observations, it is evident that table fellowship between Jews and Gentiles was a substantial matter within the context of evangelism to the Gentiles.

Today's readers may have difficulty understanding why table fellowship was such a significant concern for the early church. People today are more likely motivated to abstain from sharing a meal with another for purely sociological reasons. Economic or social distinctions, as well as personality clashes, usually serve as reasons for exclusion in table fellowship. Yet sharing a meal still facilitates social identity—we eat with those with whom we identify. When I worked at a small college in Minnesota, I observed this on a daily basis. Nearly every day, during lunch in the cafeteria, the small group of Asian (Hmong) students on campus ate together, separate from the wider white student body. This was not a case of discrimination or exclusionary practice adopted by white or Hmong students; it was a matter of eating together with people who form a common identity. If eating together signifies common identity, then Peter's table fellowship with Cornelius indicates a common identity no longer based on ethnicity, history, or culture but exclusively on Christ.[12]

Yet table fellowship was not simply a sociological issue for Jews in ancient times, but ultimately a matter of retaining their religious purity and national identity as the people of God. Peter's strong resistance to the command to "kill and eat" (10:13–14) stems from the dietary regulations in Leviticus 11 and Deuteronomy 14. For Israel, not all living creatures were permitted for eating; Israel, called to be holy as the people of God, were confined to strict dietary guidelines. To eat what was marked "unclean," or even to touch an unclean animal, rendered Israelites ritually unclean:

> By these [animals] you will become unclean: whoever touches their carcasses will be unclean until evening. Whoever carries these carcasses must wash their clothes and will be unclean until evening. Every animal which divides the hoof but is not split-footed or does not chew the cud is unclean for you. Whoever touches them will be unclean. (Lev. 11:24–26)

So Peter's resistance to the Spirit's command reflects a historical tradition in the Old Testament. This tradition of distinguishing

---

12. Ibid., 181–193.

between "clean" and "unclean" is a core component of Israel's identity as the people of God, called to be separate from all other peoples. On the one hand, it reinforces their distinct identity; on the other hand, it strongly discourages any syncretistic tendency. Both work together to reinforce their covenant relationship with God.

In Acts 10, it becomes clear that the threefold vision is not simply about food but ultimately Gentile inclusion and table fellowship. Although Peter is "perplexed" about the vision (10:17), based on the Spirit's directive to "go with them [men sent by Cornelius] without hesitation, for I have sent them" (10:20), Peter correlates his vision with Gentile inclusion. He states: "You yourselves know how unlawful it is for a Jewish man to associate with or to visit anyone of another nation, but God has shown me to call no man common or unclean" (10:28). Since a Gentile is no longer considered "unclean" by God, Peter has no hesitation about prolonging his visit, which would require table fellowship.

While Leviticus 11 describes in clear terms the dietary guidelines, there is no explicit command prohibiting interaction with foreigners. As we learned in chapter 3, Israelites were explicitly commanded to show hospitality to sojourners (presumably non-Israelites). Further, we learned in chapter 4 that the refusal to show hospitality to a traveler had an adverse effect on the reputation of the host. So how are we to understand Peter's statement that "it is unlawful for a Jew to associate with Gentiles"? The custom of receiving sojourners or showing hospitality to travelers assumes that the outsider is welcomed into an Israelite household. The visitor would conform to the dietary regulations of the Jewish host. The context for Peter in Acts 10 is reversed: he has no control of the food preparations. Further, while Jew-Gentile interaction is not explicitly forbidden in the Old Testament, the natural consequence of the dietary regulations was Jewish exclusion from Gentiles.[13] Gentiles did not practice Jewish dietary rules and were usually tainted with idol worship; therefore, they were considered ritually unclean. While some interaction was permissible, prolonged visitation and table fellowship would most certainly render the Jew as "unclean."

---

13. See P. F. Esler, *Community and Gospel in Luke–Acts: The Social and Political Motivations of Lucan Theology* (Cambridge: Cambridge University Press, 1987), 73–86.

In the case of Cornelius, who presumably adopted Jewish monotheism (10:1), it is not idolatry but food that makes him "unclean."
Peter's interpretation of his vision contains a profound implication for
the identity of God's people; it becomes drastically altered to include
those formerly "unclean." Salvation is no longer exclusive to the Jews
but extended to all nations. And table fellowship is a critical component in the formation of the people of God, composed not only of
Jewish believers, but now together with Gentiles.

Jerusalem Council: Acts 15

As the gospel spreads beyond the borders of Judea through the
evangelistic activities of Paul and Barnabas (Acts 13:1–14:28), the
more conservative Jewish believers are uncomfortable with salvation
apart from the law. They come to Antioch and teach: "Unless you
are circumcised according to the custom of Moses, you cannot be
saved" (15:1). This creates "no small dissension and debate" for Paul
and Barnabas (15:2). Ultimately, the debate is submitted before the
apostles and elders in Jerusalem. During this debate, Peter relates
his experience with Cornelius and evaluates the demand for Gentile
converts to submit to the law as incongruous to salvation by grace:
"Now then why are you testing God by placing a yoke on the neck of
the disciples which neither our fathers nor we were able to bear? But
through the grace of the Lord Jesus Christ we believe we are saved,
just as they are" (15:10–11). After further testimony from Paul and
Barnabas (15:12–13), James delivers the final verdict. James interprets
Peter's experience with the Gentiles as coherent to the prophecy of
Amos 9:11–12 (Acts 15:16–17). The critical point of the prophecy
is that the restoration of David's tent will necessarily encompass "all
the Gentiles who are called by my name" (Acts 15:17 citing Amos
9:12). Thus, inclusion of the Gentiles is divinely ordained and is the
fulfillment of Old Testament prophecies. James concludes that law
observance should not be required for the Gentiles (Acts 15:19).

James lists several concerns: abstinence from pollution by idols,
sexual immorality, food strangled, and food not completely drained
of blood (Acts 15:20). Although it may not be immediately apparent,
these four concerns all have a common thread related to the issue of

idolatry. The first prohibition most likely addresses pollution associated with idols and idolatrous rituals. A similar sense of "pollution" or "defilement" is recorded in Daniel 1:8 with respect to food: "But Daniel resolved that he would not defile himself with the king's food or with the wine that he drank." Daniel's rejection of the king's food and wine doesn't necessarily reflect dietary regulations (clean vs. unclean) since wine is also mentioned. Most likely, Daniel exercises restraint to avoid defilement of idolatry. But precisely how did food come to be associated with idolatry? When God renews his covenant with Israel (Exod. 34), he explains that he will drive out various peoples (Amorites, Canaanites, Hittites, Perizzites, Hivites, and Jebusites; see 34:11) from the Promised Land to protect Israel from adopting pagan idolatry:

> Be careful not to make a covenant with the inhabitants of the land in which you are going, lest it become a snare in your midst. Rather, you shall tear down their altars and break their pillars and cut down their Asherim polls for you shall not worship any other god, for the LORD, whose name is Jealous, is a jealous God, lest you make a covenant with the inhabitants of the land, for when they prostitute after their gods and sacrifice to their gods and invite you, you eat of their sacrifice, and you take their daughters for your sons, and their daughters prostitute after their gods and make your sons prostitute after their gods. (Exod. 34:12–16)

In this passage, eating with pagan neighbors is linked to eating food sacrificed to their gods. The same connection appears in Numbers 25 when Israel falls into the trap of idolatry by participating in her neighbor's practice of idolatry. "While Israel lived in Shittim, the people began to prostitute with the Moabite women. The women invited the people to the sacrifices of their gods, and the people ate and worshiped down to their gods. So Israel joined themselves to Baal of Peor, and the anger of the LORD burned against Israel" (Num. 25:1–3).

Both passages help us understand Daniel's care in avoiding the king's food and wine. Food and wine of the non-Israelites were most likely associated with their idolatry. This association is explicit:

After Belshazzar tasted the wine, he commanded that the vessels of gold and of silver that Nebuchadnezzar his father had taken out of the temple in Jerusalem be brought so that the king and his lords, his wives, and his concubines might drink from them. Then they brought the golden vessels that had been removed from the temple, the house of God in Jerusalem, then the king and his lords, his wives, and his concubines drank from them. They drank the wine and praised the gods of gold, silver, bronze, iron, wood, and stone. (Dan. 5:2–4)

Belshazzar's profane use of the golden vessels from God's house in praise of idols brings divine judgment upon his kingdom (Dan. 5:24–28) and his death (5:30):

And you his son, Beshazzar, have not humbled your heart, though you knew all this, but you have exalted yourself against the Lord of heaven, and the vessels of his house were brought before you, and you and your lords, your wives, and your concubines drink wine from them. You praised the gods of silver and gold, bronze, iron, wood, and stone, which do not see or hear or know, but you have not honored the God in whose hand is your breath and all your ways. (Dan 5:22–23)

These Old Testament passages explain why Jewish people avoided pagan food. Pagan food is associated with pagan idolatry. The question remains: Was food also associated with idolatry in New Testament times? The notion that deities required sacrifice of food and drink was not only common in Old Testament times but also in the first century A.D.[14] It would have been difficult for Christians in the first century to avoid foods with idolatrous association.[15] Food sacrificed to idols would be found not only at religious ceremonies but at nearly all social functions (e.g., weddings, funerals), including social events for labor guilds (work-related associations), and in the market place where idol

14. E. Ferguson, *Backgrounds of Early Christianity*, 3rd ed. (Grand Rapids: Eerdmans, 2003), 170.
15. A. T. Cheung, "Idol Food in Corinth: Jewish Background and Pauline Legacy," JSOTSup 176 (Sheffield: Sheffield Academic Press, 1999): 27–38.

food was sold regularly.[16] So James's advice against eating food associated with idolatry reveals not only Old Testament concerns but also common knowledge of pagan idolatrous rituals in Gentile culture.

While sexual immorality can cover all forms of indiscriminate sexual behavior (e.g., Rom. 1:18-32; 1 Cor. 5:1; 7:2) in both the Old and New Testaments, sexual immorality is often linked with idolatry. In passages such as Hosea 5:3-4, Ezekiel 16:15-46, Jeremiah 3:1-10, and Revelation 2:14, 20, sexual immorality is frequently a metaphor for idolatry. This means that from God's perspective, idolatry, or the act of worshipping anything other than the one true God, is as despicable as sexual immorality. However, in Exodus 34:12-16 and Numbers 25:1-3, cited above, sexual immorality is not a metaphorical reference but actual deeds; sexual immorality goes hand in hand with idolatry. God specifies unlawful sexual behavior for Israel (Lev. 18:6-23) so that Israel may be different from her neighbors in their sexual ethics. These prohibitions against sexual immorality are directly tied to God's identity "I am the LORD your God" at the beginning of this passage (18:2) and at the end (18:30). The repetition of the phrase forms an *inclusio*, a literary device that serves as bookends for the entire section on sexual morality. Thus the identity of God ultimately provides the reason for sexual ethics. The practice of sexual immorality is not simply a matter of adopting the identity of non-Israelites, but a matter of denying God's identity and character. The knowledge of God as their God requires conformity to God's holy character: "Speak to all the congregation of the people of Israel and say to them, 'You shall be holy, for I the Lord your God am holy'" (Lev. 19:2). Sexual immorality betrays a lack of knowing this holy God, in other words, idolatry.

Returning to James's stipulations for Gentile Christians, the last two constraints regarding the treatment of animals are most likely linked together. The context is again in all likelihood idolatry or idolatrous rituals where animals are sacrificed by strangulation and

---

16. Pliny, a governor of Bithynia-Pontus writes to Trajan in 112 A.D. concerning the trials against Christians. In this letter he mentions the sale of idol food as a general and a long-standing procedure. See A. N. Sherwin-White, ed., *Fifty Letters of Pliny* (Oxford: Oxford University Press, 1969), 68-70, 171-78.

the blood is not drained.[17] Identical concern is found in Leviticus 17:10-16, which strongly prohibits eating blood. Ezekiel 33:25 also links eating blood with idolatry: "You eat meat with its blood and lift up your eyes to your idols and shed blood. Shall you then possess the land?"

So, while three of the four items James lists deal with food, all four are linked with idolatry. James' concern is to encourage Gentile Christians to distance themselves from their former context of idolatry. But the following verse (Acts 15:21) is a bit puzzling: "For from ancient times Moses has those who proclaim him in every city, for he is read every Sabbath in the synagogues." Although it is clear that Acts 15:21 provides the reason behind the four restrictions, the precise logic between prohibitions for the Gentiles and the presence of Jews in every city is not self-evident. For B. R. Gaventa, the mention of Jews and their weekly reading of Moses is a reminder to the Gentile Christians that prohibition against idolatry is fundamental and common knowledge.[18] D. L. Bock, however, is more specific. He perceives a missionary element in Acts 15:21: the Gentile Christians should be sensitive to Jewish concerns.[19] Perhaps the two are not mutually exclusive; while salvation by the grace of the Lord Jesus (Acts 15:11) renders circumcision unnecessary, it still mandates rejection of idolatry (1 Cor. 10:14; Gal. 5:19-20; Col. 3:5; 1 Pet. 4:3). While Gentile Christians are not bound to law observance, they still need to exercise sensitivity to Jewish practices. But these Jewish practices become an issue only if fellowship between Jews and Gentiles is in view. Jewish Christians would have found it difficult to fellowship with Gentile Christians who did not observe dietary regulations. Although all consent that both Jew and Gentile are saved by grace, the historical tradition of law observance as part of covenant requirement is not easily laid aside—the Gentiles are called to exercise sensitivity to their Jewish brothers and sisters so that common meals with Jews may be possible.[20] Then, James's concern is not with respect to *how* the Gentiles are saved, but how both Jews and Gentiles can

---

17. Bock, *Acts*, 506.
18. Gaventa, *Acts*, 224.
19. Bock, *Acts*, 507.
20. I. H. Marshall, *Acts*, 31.

hold common table fellowship.[21] The question of whether or not they should have table fellowship is not raised; it is assumed that there should be table fellowship between Jews and Gentiles based on the fact that all are now saved in the same manner—by grace. Indeed, Acts 2:42–47 mentions breaking bread daily as a core component of the fellowship of believers. Given this common assumption, the logistics of how both can hold table fellowship is a negotiable matter under discussion in Acts 15.

Freedom and Responsibility of the Gospel

In the early church, opinions on dietary regulations were diverse. For Paul, regulations concerning food and drink along with law observance and circumcision are no longer valid in view of the cross (see Col. 2:16–23; Gal. 2:15–21). Paul proclaims freedom from the law, yet he maintains the need for sensitivity to both Jews and Gentiles who might struggle with their conscience, especially with respect to dietary regulations. Paul addresses this particular issue to the church in Rome (Rom. 14:1–12), which most likely has a mixed congregation (both Jewish and Gentile believers):

> Welcome the one weak in faith, but not to quarrel over opinions. One person believes he may eat anything, while the weak person eats only vegetables. Let not the one who eats despise the one who does not eat, and let not the one who does not eat judge the one who eats, for God has welcomed him (Rom. 14:1–3).

The one weak in faith in this instance is most likely a Jew. Paul gives advice to the Corinthians on the same issue of food offered to idols (1 Cor. 8:1–13). Here, however, the one weak in faith is most likely a Gentile formerly associated with idolatry:

> Therefore, concerning eating of food offered to idols, we know that no idol has real existence and that no God exists except

---

21. Bruce, *Acts*, 295–96.

one. For if indeed there are so-called gods whether in heaven or on earth, then there are many gods and many lords. But for us there is one God, the Father, from whom all things come and we exist for him, and one Lord, Jesus Christ, through whom are all things and through whom we exist. But this knowledge is not in all. Some, until now, have been accustomed to an idol that they eat food as really offered to an idol; and their conscience, being weak, is defiled. (1 Cor. 8:4–7)

For Paul, the matter at hand is not "to eat or not to eat," but to not grieve the other: "For if by the food you eat, your brother is grieved, you no longer walk according to love. By what you eat, do not destroy the one for whom Christ died" (Rom. 14:15). This is basically the same logic used by James in his list of dietary prohibitions (Acts 15:20). Since law-observing Jews can be found in every city (15:21), James anticipates fellowship between Jews and newly recruited Gentiles everywhere and preempts possible conflict in their table fellowship.

In light of the influx of Gentiles into the Christian faith, the early church made informed decisions based on careful deliberation and examination of Scripture. First, all affirmed the inclusion of Gentiles as the work of God and the fulfillment of Scripture. Second, if there is no distinction between Jew and Gentile with respect to salvation, common table fellowship for both is assumed. Third, within this newly created body of believers, concession to the "other" is the operative norm. The verdict rendered at the Jerusalem Council and Paul's proclamation of a law-free gospel were not ordinary but ground-breaking developments. Law observance was central to the covenant relationship between God and Israel (Exod. 19:1–9; 34:10–28; Deut. 4:40). The affirmation of the apostles that all are now saved by grace required reassessment of their tradition and renewed insight into God's redeeming acts throughout their history. Dietary regulations, as part of law observance, were central to Israel's distinction from all other nations and thoroughly ingrained in their identity as God's people. These traditions were not simply cultural or sociological but ultimately tied to Israel's singular identity as the people of God. The reconsideration of these traditions through the lens of Christ is a radical reworking of their understanding of salvation, the people of God, and fellowship among the people of God.

In spite of the temporal distance and certain cultural and sociological differences, the early church provides us with an example to follow with respect to reconciliation for all ethnic groups. First, the early church's dependence on Scripture as the ultimate guide with respect to Gentile inclusion is a tradition contemporary churches need to resurrect. This volume is written in hopes of encouraging all churches to carefully examine Scripture on this important topic of openness to people of diverse ethnicity. Second, although our examination of critical passages (e.g., Eph. 2:11–21 and Rev. 5:9–10; 7:9–17; 15:3–4; and 21:24, 26) indicates that reconciliation of all peoples naturally implies integration, it is also evident that not all New Testament churches were integrated. For instance, the Jerusalem church, given its location, was, in all likelihood, mostly comprised of Jewish Christians. And churches located in Gentile regions, such as Corinth or Philippi, were populated mainly by Gentile Christians, while the church in Rome seems to have had both Jews and Gentiles due to the sizeable presence of Jews in Rome. Location is a reality that determines how much integration can occur in individual churches. Yet the lesson that the early church provides for contemporary churches is this: While integration might not always be possible due to location, we must be willing to receive those of all races in corporate worship and fellowship.

THE SERVANT ETHICS OF A RECONCILED COMMUNITY

As Acts 15 testifies, the early church seeks to work out possible obstacles to common fellowship between Jews and Gentiles. This interest for the "other" is not the innovation of the early church but the product of Jesus' teaching to his disciples and his self-sacrifice on the cross. For the church confessing "Jesus Christ is Lord," there can be no other mind-set than that of a servant. Is servanthood the core principle of today's church in the United States? Or have we adopted values foreign to the gospel as the norm for the church? As I was speaking to one pastor concerning the difficulties Christians experience in "living together," he relayed to me that the women in his congregation were in dissension over whether or not they should have covered dishes (sometimes called "potluck") during corporate fellowship. These women had such strong emotions on this issue that the conflict was nearly irreconcilable. While most of us might consider the dissension over covered dishes minor, we can all share examples of church life devoid of the self-sacrificing attitude of Christ. How often do we hear the complaint: "The church just doesn't meet my needs!" or "My gifts are not sufficiently recognized!"?

For a long time prior to the mid-1990s, there was a certain stereotype (no longer applicable due to diverse employment opportunities for second and third generations) concerning Asian immigrants in the United States: "The Chinese come and build dry cleaners; the Japanese build restaurants; and the Koreans build churches." In a paper presented to *American Academy of Religion* (AAR) in 2006, Chul Tim Chang cited the following figures: By 1967, there were 35 Korean churches in the United States; by 1970, 100 churches; the number doubled by 1973. By 1991, there were 2,515 churches, and in 2001, there were 3,375 Korean churches across the United States.[22] Yet numerical growth of some Korean-American churches was not due to evangelism but division. Dispute over various issues leads to an exodus—it's easier to build another church than to concede to the "other" and practice humility. The inability to work out differences and practice mutual submission is not particular to the Korean church. It is systemic, affecting many churches across America regardless of color. It is common to encounter those who profess "Jesus Christ is Lord" and simultaneously exhibit a disposition of entitlement and rights and a drive to shore up power rather than serve others in humility. Yet this self-promotion was never understood as the characteristic mark of a Christian either by the apostles or Jesus our Lord. Jesus Christ, throughout his earthly ministry and on the cross, demonstrates utter selflessness and humility. Throughout the early church, as described in the

---

22. Chul Tim Chang, "Korean Ethnic Church Growth Phenomenon in the United States," (paper presented at *AAR* in Claremont, CA, March 12, 2006).

New Testament, apostles taught the principle Jesus demonstrated as the axiom of love necessary for the church. It is the same mind-set that is necessary for racial reconciliation within the church. Three passages in particular (Eph. 4–5; Phil. 2:1–11; and John 13:1–20) teach us that the church created by the reconciling work of the cross lives according to the countercultural and counterintuitive principle of serving others.

The Paradigm of Christ's Self-Sacrifice: Ephesians 4–5

Our examination of Ephesians 2:11–22, especially verse 21 (see chapter 6), revealed that the process of being built together as a holy temple requires being mutually shaped "to fit" one another. This notion of being tailored for one another implies some level of discomfort for all in the community; this mutual shaping is part of becoming a holy temple of God. Each member of the new community reconciled to God and to one another assumes responsibility for embracing ethics consistent with Jesus Christ, the founder of the community. In his letter to the Ephesians, Paul describes in detail the ethics necessary for unity within the body.

For our purposes, we focus on Ephesians 4–5. The words "therefore I urge you" (4:1) indicate that the following exhortations are likely based on the arguments for unity provided in the preceding two chapters.[23] Thus, Paul exhorts his readers to certain character traits that are coherent to their calling in Christ: "I . . . urge you to walk in a manner worthy of the calling to which you have been called" (4:1). The characteristics of humility, gentleness, patience, and enduring one another in love are those appropriate to and worthy of our calling in the gospel of Jesus Christ; these traits are consistent with salvation. Further, these traits are also tied to the "effort or struggle to hold onto the unity of the spirit in the bond of peace" (4:3). While Paul says that Jesus brings about peace and unity through the cross (2:14), maintaining this peace and unity in the community requires active

---

23. Some argue that "therefore" refers only to the immediately preceding section of 3:14–21. However, this view is too narrow. See Hoehner, *Ephesians*, 502.

effort. The burden for maintaining peace and unity is not laid upon specific individuals. *All* are called to participate.

Paul anchors the attitude and conduct necessary for unity and peace to unity within the Godhead: one Spirit (4:4), one Lord (4:5), and one God and Father (4:6). Just as there is unity and peace within the Godhead, there is unity within salvation that is the work of the Godhead ("called to one hope" 4:4; "one faith" and "one baptism" 4:5). Thus, the previous exhortation to unity (4:1–3) is tied to the unity within the Godhead. Indeed, Paul will continue to link the indispensable ethics for the community of God with the attributes of the Godhead throughout his letter. He exhorts the Ephesians to put aside bitterness, wrath, anger, clamor, slander, and malice and to adopt kindness, tenderheartedness, and forgiveness in view of Christ's forgiveness for us (4:31–32). Christ's forgiveness for humanity demonstrated on the cross serves as the ultimate rationale for the virtues of kindness, tenderheartedness, and forgiveness of one another.

Paul continues to link believers and two members of the Godhead (God and Christ): "Therefore be imitators of God, as beloved children. And walk in love, as Christ loved us and gave himself up for us, a fragrant offering and sacrifice to God" (Eph. 5:1–2). This verse builds upon the exhortations of 4:1 and 4:17. The identity of believers as "beloved children" is important; the entreaty is secured on the fact that we are the recipients of God's love. This love is further specified as Christ's self-sacrifice (5:2). This serves as the foundation for the call "to walk in love." Thus, the command to love is specifically anchored to the cross[24] and precludes all other notions of love. "Love" is not a humanitarian notion, capricious emotions, or superficial pleasantries; it is concrete behavior as demonstrated on the cross. This type of love cannot be demonstrated to others without the realization that it was first demonstrated to us. If Christ's self-sacrificing love for us also served as a pleasing sacrifice to God, our Christ-like love has not only other believers in view, but God. Mutual, self-sacrificing love within the community is a pleasing sacrifice to God.

---

24. The verbs "loved" (*ēgapēsen*) and "gave himself up" (*parēdōken*) both point to the cross.

Humility of Christ: Philippians 2:6–11

The connection between believers' ethics and the character of God as revealed through Christ on the cross occurs not only in Ephesians but also in Philippians 2:1–11 and John 13:1–20. In both of these passages, the self-sacrificing love of Christ is linked to the concept of unity within the body of believers. Paul encourages the Philippians to be of the "same mind, having the same love, united in spirit, having the same mindset" (2:2). This instruction to unity is based on the grounds of salvation (2:1) highlighted by a series of conditional clauses:

- *if* there is any encouragement in Christ

- *if* there is any comfort of love

- *if* there is any fellowship of the spirit

- *if* there is any compassion and mercy

These conditional statements can be summarized as one fundamental question: "Are you saved?" The anticipated answer is the affirmative: "Yes!" Based on the affirmation of salvation, Paul instructs the Philippians to be united (2:2). In this postmodern age when many Christians believe there is liberty to choose any attitude based on personal preference, Paul's exhortation to be of "one mind" is thoroughly countercultural. The crucial question then is: What is this one mind-set? In the next verse (2:3), Paul explains the one attitude through a contrast. This disposition is characterized by humility, which precludes selfishness and conceit. Humility is further defined as the outlook that considers others better than self. This humility looks to the interests not only of self but also of others (2:4). The Christian frame of mind is a selfless perspective that regards the welfare of others. This attitude is the one Paul recommends not only for the Philippians, but, as we have already seen in the previous section, for believers in Rome and Corinth.

Paul continues to identify this selfless stance as the same in Christ

(2:5): "Think this among you which was also in Christ Jesus."[25] For Paul, Christ demonstrates humility and selflessness in the salvation events. Although Jesus Christ was in the form of God, he did not take advantage of his equality with God (2:6). Jesus Christ exemplifies humility because he does not see equality with God as the platform for self-promotion but an opportunity for service. Rather, he empties himself, takes the form of a slave (2:7), and refuses to show off his divinity. Serving others is his primary concern, which goes hand in hand with his humility. He continues to link humility and the disposition of a servant with the incarnation: "being born in the likeness of human beings" (2:7). In his incarnation, he humbles himself further by becoming obedient to the point of death, even death on a cross (2:8). Jesus Christ serves as a model for Paul's exhortation to the Philippians to retain the singular disposition of humility and selflessness. Indeed, if Jesus Christ demonstrates humility and selflessness in the incarnation and the cross, then those saved by these very events cannot live in salvation by any other principle. It is precisely so that we can live in humility and selflessness before God and others that Jesus Christ hung on the cross. How different the church would be if all its members lived according to this one maxim!

The Paradigm of Footwashing: John 13:1–20

The character of selflessness expressed through humility and service to others is found as a command in the Gospel of John (13:14–15) when Jesus washes the feet of the disciples (13:1–20). The foot-washing scene is set within the context of the coming event of the cross: "[Jesus] knowing that the Father had given all things into his hands and that he came out from God and he is returning to God" (13:3). The reference "returning to God" is to the ascension after Jesus' death on the cross. Further, the claim "The one who has bathed does not need to wash, except for his feet, but is completely

---

25. Phil. 2:5 is notoriously difficult to translate and has received much scholarly attention for various positions. The main difficulty lies in the fact that the verb "was" is missing in the Greek. Yet the best option is to account for the parallel between believers and Christ: "Think this among you, which also [was] in Christ Jesus."

clean" (13:10) is most likely a reference to the cleansing work of the cross.[26]

In view of his death and departure, Jesus washes the feet of his disciples. The depiction of a slave is conveyed by the description: "wraps a towel around himself." Thus, Jesus assumes the role of a slave as he washes the disciples' feet.[27] Jesus instructs the disciples to imitate his actions:

> If I then, the Lord and the Teacher, have washed your feet, you also ought to wash one another's feet. For I have given you an example, that you also should do just as I have done to you (13:14–15).

It is possible for a slave to endure and execute humble tasks such as foot washing but be devoid of selflessness. In this situation, however, Jesus willingly takes on the role of a slave and similarly commands his disciples to *willingly* imitate his model. Note also that the command is directed to all of the disciples; no one is precluded from serving others selflessly. The servant disposition is tied to salvation (redemption of sin) and the ensuing discipleship of those redeemed. This story provides a convicting portrait of how those in the community of the redeemed should relate to each other—through mutual and selfless service.

Conclusion

The ethical norm of the redeemed community is selfless service to each other expressed through humility, gentleness, patience, and enduring one another in love. If there is to be unity in the church, these attributes must be demonstrated. The required point of view for living together in a multiethnic setting is not different from the posture required in any church. Indeed, the ethnically diverse congregation presents different issues from that of a congregation comprised of single ethnicity or race. Nevertheless, the issues particular to a

---

26. D. A. Carson, *The Gospel According to John* (Grand Rapids: Eerdmans, 1991), 465.
27. See G. R. Beasley-Murray, *John* (Waco: Word, 1987), 233.

multiethnic congregation are not wholly different from an undiversified congregation. The core disposition that resolves any conflict is the mind-set of Christ: it concedes to the other, sacrifices personal preferences, and ultimately seeks to serve the other. Regardless of the difficulties of becoming a church that welcomes ethnic diversity, this mind-set, above all others, produces unity and demonstrates the reconciliation effected in the cross.

Is the story of Jesus' foot washing, as well as Paul's description of the mind-set of Christ (Phil. 2:6–8), *too* countercultural and counterintuitive? The practical implications of both passages are highly offensive to all racial groups. Is it possible for Japanese and Koreans to lay aside historical enmity and mutually serve one another in the form of a slave as modeled by Christ? Is mutual, self-sacrificing love of Christ possible for ethnic groups scarred by historical oppression and violence? Given the prominence of slavery in North America and the practice of segregation until the Civil Rights Act of 1968, these questions of mutual submission raise the level of discomfort to a new height. Yet these questions are critical and necessary if genuine reconciliation is to be present in the church. Can white Christians adopt the mind-set of a "slave" as demonstrated by Jesus Christ toward a black Christian? Or does the notion of racial superiority still have a residual effect in the church? While it might be easy enough for white Christians to receive black Christians into their fellowship, Jesus' model of humility as a "slave" calls for a removal of even small traces of racial bias. The offense also runs in the opposite direction. How easily can a black Christian serve a white Christian in the form of a "slave" as Christ commands? Humility as demonstrated by Jesus (Phil. 2:6) mandates that equality is not a platform for self-promotion. Can black Christians, in spite of past horrors, perceive equality as an occasion to "serve" white Christians? Or are they relegated to reject the virtue of humility due to painful history and memory? Everyone must ask, What precisely has been put to death on the cross?

If the primary character of the church is self-sacrificing love of Christ, would it be difficult to overcome obstacles to common worship and table fellowship for diverse races? Living under the reconciliation of the cross, can black and white Christians exercise mutual submission? Can white Christians enjoy the fellowship of black Christians without defensive self-justification or guilt for previous sins? Can the black Christians receive white Christians without accusation or suspicion? Does Christ's love have the power to draw both groups into a mutually vulnerable and transparent fellowship? The portrait of Christ on the cross is the depiction of love at the height of vulnerability: the Son of God hung on the cross, rejected, despised, and ridiculed. This love necessarily involves risk of rejection and hurt. But it is precisely through this poignant vulnerability of the Son of God that we are saved. Are Christians able to risk such love?

Racial tension and enmity are found not only in black-white relations. The Los Angeles riots of 1992 started a chain reaction exposing the reality of racial tension and discrimination not only between blacks and whites but also Hispanics and Koreans with side-effects long after the initial incident. As time passed, the tension intensified. In particular, the Koreans were criticized by the blacks for "raping" the black community. Koreans had established many liquor stores throughout the Crenshaw district in southwest Los Angeles. While the Koreans were happy to sell liquor to the blacks, they did not build up the community through finances or civic responsibilities. With the financial gain from liquor sales, they bought fine houses in the suburbs. It was reported that many Korean businesses treated blacks with discrimination and disdain. Although I did not live on the West Coast during these years, I felt the ripple effect even in Chicago. Anytime I encountered a black person in stores, restaurants, or public transportation, I felt a heightened level of tension I had not experienced before.

In the 1990s, when I was in Pasadena, California, finishing my degree at Fuller Theological Seminary, the racial tension between Koreans and blacks was still an issue that I encountered frequently in Los Angeles. In one of the classes at the seminary, the discussion turned to the issue of racial reconciliation, especially in light of the Los Angeles riots. The question on the table was "How can the church be salt and light to the city of Los Angeles?" I took the opportunity to share my experience and to confess that some Koreans, just like the rest of humanity, practiced racism. I also confessed that some Koreans were highly driven and ambitious even at the expense of injuring others. I was ashamed that so many Koreans who professed the Christian faith could simultaneously treat the black community with ethics foreign to the love of Christ. In view of the fact that some Koreans were guilty as charged, I did not mind enduring occasional mistreatment. In response, a fellow black student stood up and asked for my forgiveness on behalf of the black people. Although it sounds typical and trite, both of us wept for the injuries each of us endured and for the sins of our respective "people." It was a unique healing experience possible only within the community of Christ. If we are saved, it is possible for former enemies to live in love and mutual submission.

In recent history, several denominations have actively pursued racial reconciliation in various ways. The United Methodist Church formed a Commission on Religion and Race in 1968 to oversee racial integration on all levels (including leadership) of church life.[28] The Episcopal Church formalized several resolutions to address racial reconciliation in its General Convention in 2006.[29] These formal declarations are critical for the church as a witness to the world that all races have truly been reconciled by the cross. But perhaps the most significant public declaration is that of the Southern Baptists. Given the historical association of Southern Baptist churches and racism, the resolution formalized in June 1995 by the Southern Baptist Convention is highly symbolic and provides hope for change in racial relations. Indeed, the observations that we (Park and Mathews) have made throughout this volume are echoes of sentiments already expressed in this resolution. The two resolutions that appear at the end are applicable to all races and worthy of citation:

> Be it further RESOLVED, That we hereby commit ourselves to eradicate racism in all its forms from Southern Baptist life and ministry; and

---

28. For more information see the Web site of The General Commission on Religion and Race of The United Methodist Church. http://www.gcorr.org/site/c.mwKWJ9NTJtF/b.4279561/k.AF94/Our_History.htm.
29. Daphne Mack, "Toward Columbus: Actions on slavery, racial reconciliation, reparations proposed for General Convention," April 21, 2006. http://www.episcopalchurch.org/75383_73860_ENG_HTM.htm.

Be it further RESOLVED, That we commit ourselves to be doers of the Word (James 1:22) by pursuing racial reconciliation in all our relationships, especially with our brothers and sisters in Christ (1 John 2:6), to the end that our light would so shine before others, that they may see (our) good works and glorify (our) Father in heaven (Matthew 5:16).[30]

Has the local church pursued these resolutions for racial reconciliation? Official resolutions or a one-time ceremony on racial reconciliation, while significant, have no profound meaning if reconciliation does not permeate the daily life of the church. It is insufficient if only proxies are reconciled to one another and the rest of the body of Christ remains unreconciled. This sentiment was echoed by the president of Southeastern Baptist Theological Seminary, Daniel Akin: "We must pursue a vision for our churches that looks like heaven. . . . Yes, we must go around the world to reach Asians and Europeans, the Africans and the South Americans. But we must also go across the street, down the road, and into every corner of our local mission field where God, in grace, has brought the nations to us."[31]

In spite of these bold words, it's not difficult to figure out why the local church does not pursue ethnic diversity. It is an entirely different matter to live together than hold a single symbolic ceremony or make noble proclamations. The three passages concerning the mindset of Christ as the operative norm within the church indicate that while living together is no easy matter, it is how the church experiences the profound love of Christ that bridges all gaps and heals all wounds. The only question that remains is this: Is it possible for all races, as members of Christ's body, to live in self-sacrificing love and mutual submission to one another?

---

30. Resolution on Racial Reconciliation on the 150th Anniversary of the Southern Baptist Convention, June 1995. http://www.sbc.net/resolutions/amResolution.asp?ID=899.
31. Urban Onramps, "Racial Reconciliation in Every Southern Baptist Church," April 17, 2009. http://www.urbanonramps.com/?p=455.

THOUGHT PROVOKERS

1. Based on the model of the early church (Acts 10 and 15), what traditions require revision in light of Christ?

2. Are the contemporary road-blocks to table fellowship or common worship formulated on Scripture's teaching?

3. How will Paul's advice to "walk in love" and concede to the "other" affect the efforts to hold common worship and table fellowship for all races?

4. If Christ's self-sacrificing love is the model for love within the church, how does this modify individual believer's attitudes and behaviors?

5. What racial prejudice or bias do we still retain that hinders us from adopting Christ's example of a "slave" toward other races? What are some practical ways we can wash the feet of others? Do you or your church understand the notion of equality to mean a platform to promote self-advantage and privilege or does it mean self-sacrifice as described in Philippians 2:6–8?

6. How important is the notion of unity as described in Ephesians 4–5 for you or your church?

7. If love as demonstrated by Christ on the cross is necessarily risky business, what are the risks we undertake in adopting the mindset of humility and self-sacrifice?

From Here to Eternity

"**FROM HERE TO ETERNITY**" was a popular 1950s movie based on the novel of the same title by James Jones. The book title is borrowed from a line in Rudyard Kipling's poem "Gentlemen-Rankers." A gentleman ranker was an enlisted soldier who was qualified to be an officer but declined the responsibility and remained a common solider. The plight of these men was believed to be determined by fate, their destiny was fixed and beyond their control. Kipling's poem describes gentlemen rankers as pitiable men, adrift and "damned from here to eternity."

Unlike gentlemen rankers, believers are not "damned from here to eternity." We are not anchored to a doomed fate due to our sinful character or a series of events marred by sin. Rather, Christians are able to choose the path of righteousness because Jesus Christ brought an end to the reign of sin and death (Rom. 5:12-19). We are new creations in Christ (2 Cor. 5:17). This new life in Jesus Christ means that we no longer live according to a worldly mind-set of sin but according to righteousness. We are able to hear exhortations and obey; and obedience leads not to damnation but eternal life (Rom. 6:20-23).

THE PAST, THE PRESENT, AND THE FUTURE

Our use of the phrase "from here to eternity" also refers to the question that all Christians need to address: "Given that God's plan of salvation throughout Scripture is for all people groups, how then should we live from here to eternity?" Our book, on the one hand, focuses on the singular issue of racial reconciliation. On the other hand, it does not dismiss or relegate as secondary the salvation story central throughout both Testaments. In truth, the proper understanding of racial reconciliation is possible only in light of God's saving activity throughout human history. If racial reconciliation is intricately woven into God's saving acts throughout both Old and New Testaments, the question of how we should live needs to be answered. This question deals with what we must do in the present and simultaneously recognizes the future goal. For those who profess the name of Christ, how we live now is determined by the future coming of Jesus Christ and the destination of the New Jerusalem. Our existence is not simply a matter of being "in the moment"; it is always directed toward the future. At the same time, it is the past that determines our current reality. What does all of this talk about past, present, and future have to do with racial reconciliation?

The primary task of this book was to provide a description of God's saving activity for all of humanity. But the purpose of the book is not simply descriptive; it's also *prescriptive*. Just as the Christian's present life is determined by God's historical saving activity for his people in both Old and New Testaments, our immediate life with respect to racial reconciliation is also informed by God's saving activity in the past.

All life forms and humanity have their beginning in God's identity as Creator. Human beings are created in God's image and designed for blessings from God and for worship of God. Knowing God as Creator of all humans also means understanding that each person has value and dignity as God's creation. Recognition of each individual as God's handiwork is the foundation for living in unity with one another in the midst of diversity. God's creative act as the beginning of all human life affects how we relate to one another today. People of all ethnic groups have but one origin, God's creative activity. To treat any human being in hatred and violence, regardless of ethnicity, challenges God's assessment of his own creative work as "good" (Gen. 1:31). Myths such as the "mark of Cain" or the "curse of Ham" are misinterpretations of Scripture that have spawned racism for generations and stand in contradiction to the teaching that all human beings are created by God for blessing. In spite of human sin, God's consistent desire is to bless humanity by calling them to an appropriate relationship with him as his creation. In order to worship

God as Creator, we must recognize in one another the dignity and value God has deemed to his creation. Looking ahead to the future, we see that God judges all oppressive and unrighteous acts against humanity (Rev. 6:1-11; 18:1-24). Our treatment of one another as God's creation is informed by God's past creative act and God's future judgment of all unrighteousness.

But how we should live in the now is not based simply on God's identity as Creator. God is also Redeemer. In spite of humanity's descent into sin, God continues to pursue a covenant relationship with humanity through various individuals such as Noah, Abraham, Moses, and David. The election of these individuals and Israel as God's people has often engendered the false belief that God's salvation is exclusively for the Hebrew people. God's covenant with the patriarchs and Israel was never intended for exclusion of all other people groups. God's promise to Abraham, "I have made you the father of many nations" (Gen. 17:5), indicates that God's election reaches far and wide to all nations. This is how Paul understands God's promise to Abraham (Rom. 4:16-17): Abraham is the father not only of Israelites but also Gentiles. God's election of Israel as his people through Moses also looks beyond Israel; the purpose of Israel's covenant with God is for Israel to be a testimony to the nations (Isa. 42:6). Both promises, along with God's oath to David that his "throne will be established forever" (1 Chron. 22:10), are fulfilled through Jesus Christ.

In Jesus Christ, God's promises to the patriarchs and Israel are fully realized; God's blessing of salvation, the answer to the plight of sin, is offered to all nations (Matt. 28:19). The early church recognized this fundamental truth at the Jerusalem Council: "and he [God] made no distinction between us and them, having cleansed their hearts by faith" (Acts 15:9). The unique role of Abraham as the father of one nation and simultaneously the father of many nations is also found in Jesus Christ. Jesus Christ is the Savior descended from the Jews, and at the same time he is the Savior not only for Jews but also for all nations. Through Jesus Christ, God's desire for Israel to be "a light for the nations" (Isa. 49:6) is fulfilled. As the parable of the prodigal son communicates (Luke 15:11-32), God desires the return of all those who live separated from him. In Jesus Christ, all humanity is reconciled to God and to each other through the cross (Eph. 2:14–18). God's desire for all peoples to worship him shapes our perspective on racial diversity.

There is no justification for racial supremacy—God desires all nations to receive his blessing, and he calls them to worship him. Election should not elicit conceit and elitism, for its purpose is testimony of God's goodness to all peoples. In view of this, we must not practice ethnic exclusion or be indifferent to hatred and violence based on discrimination. Racial purity, elitism, or superiority founded on election of Israel as God's people dismisses that Israel was composed of many peoples. Its identity as the people of God was not anchored on racial purity but covenant relationship with God. Instead of practicing exclusion, we must ask ourselves how we can be a "light for the nations," not only abroad but also in North America. The apostle Paul conveys this thought:

> To me, the least of all saints, this grace was given, to preach to the Gentiles the unsearchable riches of Christ and to bring to light for everyone the plan of the mystery hidden for ages in God who created all things, so that the manifold wisdom of God might be made known now through the church to the rulers and authorities in heaven. (Eph. 3:8–10)

As we practice multiethnic inclusion in our worship of God, we point to and look forward to standing before the throne of God with all nations (Rev. 7:9–17). We can eagerly anticipate the fullness of fellowship and unity among all nations that comes only from the collective worship of God.

FOUR WINDOWS OF OPPORTUNITY

With this brief summary, we turn to issues broached in preceding chapters that require further attention: immigration, interracial marriage, multiethnic worship and evangelism/missions. Since these four issues have contemporary relevance, the church needs to carefully re-evaluate its position on each topic based on the teachings of Scripture.

Immigration

Immigration is a hot issue in North America. Our purpose is not to advocate policy or civil action but to focus on how the church should respond. Immigration is a concern not only in major cities but throughout the United States. The church needs to shape its response through biblically based knowledge of God's perspective on immigrants. In chapter 3, we learned that God's directive to Israel to receive the Egyptians into their midst (Deut. 23:7) was based on the rationale that Israel had been a sojourner in Egypt. Israel's identity as sojourner in her past forms her response to sojourners (Deut. 10:19). Stipulations (Lev. 19:22-23) lay out the guidelines for Israel to treat aliens among them with the same neighborly love necessary within the covenant community (Lev. 19:9-18). The laws that regulate Israel's internal relations also apply to Israel's external relations. Israel's identity as a sojourner recalls Joseph's life in Egypt (Gen. 37:36; 39:1-41:57) and Moses' life in Egypt (Exod. 2:1-14) and Midian (Exod. 2:15-22).

This identity of the people of God as sojourners continues in the New Testament, where Christians are called "sojourners" or "exiles" (1 Peter 1:1). The same word is later repeated and coupled with "resident aliens" (2:11). Together, "sojourner" and "resident alien" suggest that our Christian life is similar to that of an immigrant—living in a land that is not our home. Jesus specifies that he goes ahead of us to prepare a place for us in his Father's house (John 14:2). Paul accentuates our alien status by referring to our "citizenship in heaven" (Phil. 3:20) and exhorting the Philippians to "live worthily as citizens of the gospel of Jesus Christ" (1:27). And the author of Hebrews not only describes the faithful of the Old Testament as "strangers" and "exiles" (Heb. 11:13) but also exhorts his readers to show hospitality to strangers: "Do not overlook hospitality, for through this some have entertained angels unaware" (13:2).

How does our own identity as "sojourners" and "alien residents" frame our response to immigrants in our cities? The church's response to immigrants should not mirror secular xenophobia but should reflect God's heart for displaced peoples. Although the world may reject the aliens and treat them with contempt and disdain, Christians extend grace and love. Love and grace can be creatively demonstrated through partnership with various ethnic churches in any given city. Courses such as English as Second Language (ESL), for example, are always received well within immigrant communities. But before these steps of action can be taken, the church needs to be motivated by reasons provided in Scripture.[1]

Interracial Marriage

The United States is "a nation of immigrants."[2] As the original immigrants lived together, interracial marriage was the natural consequence. Nearly everyone in the United States claims two if not more ethnic heritages. Traditionally, racial problems haven't involved the multiethnicity of whites (e.g. English, Scottish, Irish, Italian, German), but marriage unions of different *colors*. The taboo against interracial marriages is not as strong today as in the 1950s. Yet if traces of this social convention against interracial marriages still remain, perhaps Scripture can aid us. In chapter 3, we learned that Israelites by no means could champion racial purity. Abraham descends from the Amorites, who can be traced back to the Shemites (Gen. 10:21-31; 11:10-26; 24:10; Acts 7:2). Joseph marries an Egyptian (Gen. 41:50), and Moses marries a Midianite (Exod. 2:21). As already noted, Israel's identity as the people of God is not characterized by racial purity but by covenant faithfulness and exclusive worship of Yahweh.

Interracial heritage is true not only of the patriarchs but also of Jesus himself. Matthew prominently features several Gentile women in the genealogy of Jesus Christ. Included in the list are Rahab, a Canaanite (Matt. 1:5; Josh. 6:25), Ruth, a Moabite (Matt. 1:5; Ruth 1:4), and Bathsheba, a Hittite by marriage (Matt. 1:6; 2 Sam. 11:3). As was true of the Israelites, Christians are not defined by

---

1. See Matthew Soerens and Jenny Hwang, "Mother of Exiles" in *Prism: America's Alternative Evangelical Voice* (July-August, 2009), 9-14; and M. Daniel Carroll R., "The Immigration Debate: Can the Bible Help?" in *Prism: America's Alternative Evangelical Voice* (July-August, 2009), 15-17.
2. John F. Kennedy, *A Nation of Immigrants* (New York: Harper & Row, 1964). See also the Web site of the Anti-Defamation League, http://www.adl.org/immigrants/.

racial purity; their identity comes from their belief in Jesus Christ as Lord and Savior. The inclusion of Gentiles in Jesus Christ's lineage foreshadows the universal significance of the salvation Jesus Christ provides to all humanity. The explicit description of interracial heritage in both Israel and the early church shows that Christians are not united by ethnic blood but by the blood of Christ. Although some Christians still struggle with interracial marriage, Scripture directs us to re-evaluate the factors that define "kinship"— is it culture, ethnicity, or Christ?[3]

Multicultural Worship

If a church follows biblical guidelines on receiving the "foreigner" into its midst, interracial marriage is not the only natural outcome. Multiethnic worship is inevitable for believers who receive "sojourners" as one of their own. Here we direct our attention to practical issues of multiethnic worship. A definition of multiethnic worship is a good place to start. Multiethnic worship can mean a worship style (praise and hymns) that reflects diverse ethnicity. Multiethnic worship can also refer to the ethnic composition of the congregation. Both Testaments indicate that God desires worship from all ethnic groups. In Christ, all nations are forged together as one body and one temple (Eph. 2:14-22). As we look ahead toward the Second Coming, multiethnic worship is normative before the throne of God (Rev. 5:9-10; 7:9-17). So then, how shall we live here and now? Should each church pursue racial integration?

Passages such as Ephesians 2:11-22 and Revelation 7:9-17 provide a portrait of the church as an *integrated* assembly. Should the church in the suburbs composed primarily of whites close its doors and move to the inner city to practice multiethnic worship? In such a case, how many would retain their membership? Perhaps such a

---

3. The issue of interracial marriage and other concerns of multiethnic worship are not peculiar to white or black churches. These issues are relevant for all churches, including Asian American Churches. See Peter Cha, S. Steven Kang, and Helen Lee, eds., *Growing Healthy Asian American Churches* (Downers Grove: InterVarsity, 2006) for insight on the struggles of culture clash between Asian and American culture as well as Asian and Christ culture.

radical move is counterproductive. Rather, such a church can adopt the model of the Jerusalem church and begin with the affirmation that God shows partiality to no one and all races are equally saved. Along with this affirmation, perhaps the church can resolve to be open to receiving the "other." And perhaps this openness will lead to evangelistic efforts in multiethnic communities. We do not feel the need to press every church to be integrated, but we do strongly encourage each church to be ready to receive those of diverse ethnicity, and, where possible, to seek out peoples of different ethnic backgrounds.

This raises another question. Which culture is dominant in multiethnic worship? Is the diversity cosmetic, or is there a genuine celebration of cultural differences? What does it mean to recognize God as the creator of diversity (cf. chapter 1)? How do we celebrate ethnic diversity and simultaneously stand united? Does the culture of Christ erase or highlight ethnic diversity? There are no easy answers to these questions, and our objective is not to offer glib solutions. Each ethnic culture has virtues and flaws, and the centrality of "Christ culture" as revealed in Scripture should guide the church to celebrate and not denigrate ethnic diversity.

Evangelism/Missions

In broad terms, the church has been receptive to foreign missions and active in gathering resources (people as well as money) to fulfill the Great Commission (Matt. 28:16–20; Mark 16:14–15; Acts 1:8). This is not to state, however, that we can be satisfied with our testimony to the nations. The phrase "10/40 Window" refers to "the rectangular area of North Africa, the Middle East and Asia approximately between 10 degrees north and 40 degrees north latitude."[4] Two-thirds of the world's population live in the 10/40 Window. These countries are the most resistant to the gospel message, and their governments actively prohibit Christian missionary activity. The commitment to fulfill the Great Commission in these countries requires not only money and

---

4. For more information about the 10/40 Window, see the Joshua Project Web site. http://www.joshuaproject.net/10-40-window.php.

people but also firm resolve to endure possible persecution. Missionary activity in the 10/40 Window mandates a fresh approach to Christian witness; the testimony that Jesus Christ is Lord must be accompanied by a genuine concern for the socio-economic needs in these countries. Given that engineers, physicians, lawyers, and teachers will gain easier access than preachers and pastors, the call to missions must be directed to tentmakers (Acts 18:3).

However, fulfilling the Great Commission refers not only to international missions but also to local missions. As already mentioned, the presence of ethnic diversity in every state provides ample opportunity for evangelism and missions within the borders of the United States. Both international and local missions need to be pursued actively by the church. The mandate to make disciples of all nations does not come with a caveat "if you are called to missions." All are commanded to give testimony to the goodness of God and to call all peoples to worship the one true living God. The burden to serve as a witness to God's grace is consistent in both Old and New Testaments; indeed, it is the purpose of our election as the people of God. The question remains: How can we effectively evangelize all those around us?

Perhaps we can begin with practical points. Which districts or sections in your city lack Christian testimony? Which districts provide opportunities for building relationships of trust as foundations for evangelism? Is it possible to provide sustained support in lower-income communities? Finding partners with local churches in these areas can supply not only venues for good works within the community but also testimony of the Good Samaritan to members of these churches, both leaders and laity. Evangelism through good works can be more creative than working in the local soup kitchen for the homeless. Lower-income communities require support on various levels. Schools in these communities often are unable to offer the attention and care children require. They also need tutors. These opportunities are windows for evangelism and discipleship. Parents in these communities also benefit from emotional support to deal with a wide range of issues (e.g., drug abuse, gang activity). Pro bono medical or legal services might also be welcomed. Reaching out to various communities in our cities might not change the ethnic composition of our churches, but it does put our faith to work (James 2:17). And it will provide opportunities for evangelism to the unreached in our cities.

A TESTIMONY OF CONVERSION AND HOPE

Racism Begets Racism

I (Park) was not always a Christian. Although I grew up in a Christian home, attending church every Sunday (Presbyterian), I proclaimed myself an atheist in college and came to faith in January of 1987, a year and a half after college graduation. My conversion was different from many "coming to faith" stories I've heard through the years. I came to confess Jesus Christ as my Savior after thinking about the process of photosynthesis and ecology, which ultimately led to a reconsideration of creation and evolution. The entire process took approximately four hours on one cold January afternoon in my apartment in Evanston, Illinois. But this story is not simply about my conversion from atheism to Christianity. It is a story of how the Christian faith eventually affected my perspective on people outside of my own racial heritage, Korean. In 1971, when I was eight years old, I immigrated to the United States with my family. While attending public schools in Chicago, I quickly learned that I was a "Chink." The school playground, not always a setting for innocent play, was often a platform for cruelty and malice. Racial slurs such as "flat-face," "moon-face," and "slanty-eyes" were droned into my ears on a daily basis. Name calling and demeaning gestures (drawing out the eyelids to make slants, the repeating of "ah-so," etc.) led to physical jostling and sometimes blows. I learned that in order to cope with the daily onslaught of racial prejudice, I needed to develop my own arsenal of racial insults.

After a couple of years in inner-city Chicago, we moved to the western suburbs. My parents were convinced that the move to the suburbs would diminish playground disasters and improve my language. They were right to assume that suburbia would offer a more genteel class of people, but they were entirely wrong about less racism being a by-product of higher economic status. Yes, the playground brawls ceased, but racism was practiced on a whole new level. When I was a high school freshman in the 1970s, there were four Asian families, three black families, and one Indian family in our school district. And the minorities were subtly but firmly rejected from the popular cliques. Without any physical violence or even verbal insults, racism enveloped me from every direction—hushed whispers every time I approached, the burst of laughter and giggles each time I passed by, unsmiling stares that made me feel not just different but *alien,* silent stares from the grocery store clerk who greeted the white customer before me with ease and friendliness. I knew that I was different and an object of ridicule in the city; in the suburbs, I learned that I would never be accepted as an equal. Living in the suburbs convinced me, a teenage girl going through adolescent identity issues, that unless I looked "white" I would never be pretty.

But college changed everything. I was surrounded not only by numerous Asians but also Jews. I found friends who understood racism through personal experience. This solidarity as victims of racism gave strength and courage to our reverse racism against the whites. After all, the whites were the primary source of my experience with racism. As I had learned in high school and college history courses, they were also the oppressors of Jews and blacks. Why shouldn't I treat them with equal hatred and racism? But as I progressed in college, I experienced racism from an entirely different group—African Americans. The university was located next to a neighborhood classified as the "ghetto," populated predominantly by blacks. Anytime I walked through these neighborhoods, I was greeted with racial slurs and all-too-familiar gestures. I was the object of ridicule not only from whites but also from blacks. I began to develop a deep-seated anger and resentment toward all races apart from my own. I was suspicious of all races, expected racism everywhere, and in my mind racial profiling was on auto-pilot. I did not seek ways to get along; life was about the Hobbesian ethos, "survival of the fittest."

"One of Us?"

I wish I could say that after I became a Christian my encounter with racism vanished; it didn't. When I was attending Southwestern Baptist Theological Seminary in Fort Worth, Texas, I was a "foreigner" to the Southerners (yes, the school is more accurately in the

Southwest, but it attracted students from many Southern states). I was not only a Yankee but also an "oriental." What made things more interesting was that I developed a southern drawl during my stay in Texas. A student once confessed to my white friend: "She dresses like us, she talks like us, but she doesn't look like us! I'm so confused!" Even when I had removed the differences as much as possible, I was still "not the same" simply because of my ethnicity. Of course, the accent didn't help—it just confused people even more. Once, when I was driving from Houston to Fort Worth, I lost my sense of direction and couldn't find Interstate 45, so I stopped to ask a man for directions. The man scratched his head and said, "Honey, is your daddy white?" No matter how "American" I became, people would always ask: "Where are you from?" meaning, "Where are your people from?" But racism or discomfort with ethnic difference was not particular to the South or even North America. When I was in Aberdeen, Scotland, I encountered the forms of mockery (giggling, the gesture with the eyes, and blatant racial slurs) I experienced in high school and college.

The Cross: The Healing Balm for Racism

If I continued to be the victim of racism in various degrees after I became a Christian, then what is the "conversion" story? It is not the world that changed, nor how the world views me or treats me, but how *I* changed through the process of knowing Christ. As significant as my conversion from atheism to Christianity was, my conversion was thorough on several levels. Although it took time, through the years of being a disciple of Christ I discovered I no longer had reason to practice racism. My initial reason for racism may have been simply retaliation, but the deeper motive went beyond "getting back at them." The effects of racism filtered down to the deepest level of my psyche and made me feel less than human. I was never "good enough," and I never would be. I was perpetually second class in the eyes of the majority—always the "foreigner" even though I became a naturalized U.S. citizen in 1977 and spoke perfect English. The incentive for lashing out against other races was the impact racism had on my self-esteem. The profound need for worth was met through Jesus Christ.

That the Son of God hung on the cross to save me from inveterate sin supplied me with all the self-esteem I needed. There is no greater statement on the worthiness of human life than the cross. God the Creator made me fully human, and God the Redeemer made me fully reconciled.

In one small group session students shared what served as an encouragement and motivation for them on any given day. Some said that kind words from people were encouraging, others confessed that love of their family (wives, children, parents) supplied the needed strength, and still others pointed to the simple beauty of God's creation reflected in nature as uplifting elements in their lives. I realized then that there was only one thing that truly gave me hope and encouragement with respect to my self-esteem. It was not the kind words of friends, for I was sure that my friends sought to see me in the best possible light and that they did not truly "know me" in all my sin. It was not even the love of my family, for I could not imagine my parents ceasing to love me despite my flaws. In the Asian culture, the chance that parents would not love their children is about as good as an orange tree bearing apples. "*Of course*, my parents love me! Isn't it obligatory?" The only thing that truly encouraged me was Jesus Christ on the cross. Given God's holiness and righteousness, he is not obligated to love me, yet he does. Given God's omniscience, he sees my sins more clearly than I can admit them to myself, yet instead of turning away he hangs on the cross. God sees me as I am in my frailty and failure. He sees me in my desperation to be loved, and he provides his profound love willingly and eternally. Beauty of the world will pass, friends will come and go, and even my family may reject me, but God's love as seen in the cross endures forever.

With respect to other races, there is no more enmity, there is no more striving for approval, there is now peace (Eph. 2:11–16). I have no more reason to approach other races with suspicion, anger, and resentment, and I have no need to accuse. Whatever race I encounter is an occasion for testimony to the goodness of God through his son Jesus Christ (1 Cor. 9:19–23). Regardless of race, all Christians are my "kin," and I call people not of my own race "my brothers and sisters." The most genuine and penetrating relationships I have are with people who have the same abiding love for Christ, regardless of race or ethnicity. My world has most certainly changed from anger and resentment to peace. It has also been transformed from one ethnicity to multiethnic diversity. Even more, it is not only the North Americans but also the Scottish and the English that comprise my new family in Christ. Is the gospel message as conveyed in Scripture really a message of truth? Is it true that sin has been put to death on the cross? Is it true that peace is possible between races? Unless the gospel of Jesus Christ is true, we all profess Christ in vain and there is no hope for us individually or corporately. If I genuinely believe that I am saved by the cross, then I must also believe I am saved from my former life of sin for a life marked by God's righteousness. My prejudices against all those who mocked me and made me feel inferior through verbal and physical abuse and silent disdain come to an end at the cross.

THOUGHT PROVOKER

1. In this Thought Provoker we offer a real case that challenges us to think through practical implications of our study.

Two church congregations, one predominantly black and the other predominantly white, are separated by a mere seven miles, but they are culturally and ethnically separated by "many miles" of tradition and suspicion. The black congregation suffers growing pains, expressed by its pastor as a "challenge" whose "ministries and membership [were] larger than what our facilities could properly accommodate." The white congregation is shrinking, and its one hundred people cannot regularly manage to raise the annual budget necessary to maintain its imposing facilities. Moreover, the demographics are changing in the neighborhood, estimated to be 30 percent African American in a year's time. But the population of 300,000 people within the five-mile radius of the church places it in one of the most populated areas of the state. The pastors and leaders of the two churches see the advantages of merging the two congregations. Discussions within and between the two churches consider a merger.

A number of issues must be addressed. Is a merger truly advantageous to both groups? Should the smaller, white congregation yield its facilities and move its membership to other white churches in the city? Can white members accept black leaders and, in turn, can black members accept white preferences for leadership in financial decisions although the white church members are fewer? If a merger were undertaken, what steps should be taken to achieve it in an ethical and effective way? Should other factors beside the financial consideration be worked out in advance, such as worship style, ethnic leadership, and the target audience for future expansion in evangelism and missions? How should disaffected members of each congregation who resist a merger, should one take place, be acknowledged? Treated? Should they still have a role in the newly formed church?

After working through the issues, learn how the two congregations faced their financial and social challenges by accessing the Baptist Press report by David Winfrey, September 2, 2009, at http://www.bpnews.net/BPnews.asp?ID=31185.

Person and Subject Index

A

ABEL   48, 52, 53, 59

ABRAHAM   60, 69, 72, 76, 79, 82, 83, 85, 87, 88, 89, 90, 97, 102, 107, 120, 125, 126, 130, 215, 259, 262

covenant   31, 53, 60, 77, 81, 82, 83, 84, 86, 89, 95, 98, 101, 102, 104, 107, 110, 114, 116, 119, 140, 142, 143, 149, 151, 152, 160, 161, 166, 167, 168, 170, 179, 181, 237, 239, 242, 244, 259, 260, 261, 262

father   86, 89, 90

ADAM   31, 48, 55, 58, 59, 68, 90

AFFIRMATIVE ACTION   175

AFRICANS   37, 55, 60, 61, 62, 63, 174, 187

ALSO PEOPLES   96, 97

AMERICA

ethnicity   18, 33, 34, 112

post-racial   18, 81

public policy   18, 19, 111, 112, 117

race relations   16, 17, 18, 19, 26, 32, 68, 187, 216, 261

segregation   19, 20, 21

slavery   19, 20, 67, 187, 223, 225, 252

AMMONITES   105, 107, 108

ASIANS   19, 27, 187

ASSIMILATION   101, 103, 104, 105

ATHEISM   28

B

BLESSING   41, 42, 43, 47, 51, 55, 56, 60, 61, 64, 69, 70, 71, 77, 79, 82, 83, 85, 95, 118, 120, 127, 140, 149, 179, 190, 258, 259, 260

C

CAIN   48, 52, 53, 54, 55, 59, 62, 63, 72, 258

CANAAN   38, 54, 58, 59, 61, 62, 63, 74, 75, 76, 78, 88, 89, 91, 99, 101, 107, 113, 114, 142

CANAANITES   59, 60, 62, 78, 79, 88, 91, 92, 101, 105, 109, 120, 126, 133, 147, 239, 262

CHRISTIANITY   11, 12, 19, 21,

22, 23, 24, 25, 26, 28, 45, 48, 61, 63, 102, 105, 113, 116, 121, 128, 133, 136, 169, 173, 179, 185, 188, 201, 209, 210, 211, 212, 216, 217, 220, 224, 225, 231, 244, 246, 249, 261, 262

CHURCH   7, 24, 27, 61, 64, 86, 129, 130, 133, 143, 173, 186, 219, 225

early church   16, 22, 26, 61, 80, 105, 138, 232, 234, 243, 244, 245, 246, 259, 263, 264

evangelism and mission   19, 29, 86, 130, 145, 210, 230, 232, 233, 234, 235, 260, 265

force for integration   15, 16, 20, 21, 22, 27, 29, 39, 112, 130, 146, 170, 174, 201, 212, 214, 219, 225, 230, 231, 232, 245, 247, 253, 254, 261, 263

force for reconciliation   213

multiethnic   15, 20, 25, 26, 29, 33, 41, 47, 49, 67, 80, 150, 151, 156, 170, 174, 182, 186, 187, 188, 192, 197, 211, 212, 213, 251, 255, 263, 264

CIRCUMCISION   82, 89, 98, 102, 103, 105, 116, 120, 151, 162, 233, 242, 243

CIVIL RIGHTS   17, 19, 20, 21, 187

COLSON, CHUCK   113

COMMUNITY   24, 25, 27, 31, 34, 47, 53, 56, 80, 101, 107, 109, 115, 121, 127, 128, 132, 133, 134, 135, 137, 142, 143, 160, 161, 170, 184, 185, 203, 247, 248, 251, 254, 261, 265

CONVERSION OF CORNELIUS   233, 235, 236, 238

COOPERATION   15, 16, 41

CREATION   15, 38, 39, 40, 41, 42, 43, 44, 45, 46, 48, 49, 50, 52, 53, 63, 64, 68, 69, 70, 77, 80, 95, 118, 127, 141, 142, 189, 191, 213, 225, 258

created order   38, 44, 50, 58

God's created order   38, 39, 40

theology   48

CROSS   176, 179, 180, 181, 182, 183, 186, 188, 201, 202, 204, 208, 211, 212, 225, 243, 247, 249, 250, 252, 260, 269, 270

CURSE   52, 53, 64, 77, 82, 107

D

DAVID   31, 59, 85, 99, 126, 138, 238, 259

DETERMINISM   32, 118

DISCIPLESHIP   160, 162, 163, 164, 165, 167, 170, 194, 214, 215, 226, 251, 265

DISCRIMINATION   181

DIVERSITY   15, 33, 40, 41, 42, 46, 47, 69, 80, 97, 98,

106, 129, 137, 160, 174, 187, 197, 198, 213, 231, 252, 255, 258, 260, 264, 265, 270

E

ECONOMIC DISCRIMINATION 230
EDOMITES 84, 105, 108
EGYPTIANS 61, 70, 88, 89, 97, 104, 108, 140, 261
ENDOGAMY 90, 96, 117, 118, 119, 120
ENLIGHTENMENT 23, 24
EQUALITY 23, 43, 44, 45
ESAU 84, 90, 99, 108, 120
ETHIOPIAN EUNUCH 233, 234
ETHNICITY 30, 69, 86, 92, 97, 102
    stereotypes 37
EVANGELICALS 19, 20, 25, 26, 33, 112
EVE 48, 52
EXOGAMY 91, 118

F

FELLOWSHIP 130, 135, 136
FOOTWASHING 250
FRANCE
    race relations 17
FREEDOM 29, 49, 50, 64, 243

G

GARDEN OF EDEN 46, 47, 49, 50, 51, 52, 56, 59, 68, 72, 77

GENEALOGIES 31, 67, 68, 75, 76, 83, 84, 85
GENOCIDE 17, 28, 39, 50, 57, 59, 60, 71, 174
GENTILES 80, 82, 96, 102, 105, 109, 111, 143, 146, 147, 148, 149, 151, 153, 160, 161, 173, 176, 179, 180, 181, 182, 183, 184, 185, 205, 206, 207, 208, 209, 210, 212, 213, 231, 232, 233, 234, 235, 237, 238, 242, 243, 245, 259, 262
GER 110, 113, 115, 133, 142
GLOBALIZATION 16, 19, 47, 69
GOD 7, 15, 22, 30, 31, 47, 48, 53, 55, 69, 71, 72, 77, 82, 97, 102, 107, 126, 130, 135, 137, 160, 202, 203, 239, 240, 243, 259, 262
    as Creator 38, 39, 40, 41, 42, 45, 46, 47, 48, 49, 53, 64, 68, 69, 70, 105, 129, 174, 189, 194, 211, 213, 214, 258, 264, 269
    as Redeemer 48, 49, 51, 52, 68, 69, 78, 79, 80, 83, 84, 85, 119, 127, 129, 140, 141, 156, 157, 171, 178, 191, 194, 196, 206, 214, 244, 257, 258, 259
    image of God 37, 39, 41, 42, 43, 46, 48, 49, 50, 52, 56, 62, 63, 64, 69, 258
    judgment against oppression 217, 218, 224, 226
    plan for reconciliation 38, 39,

52, 58, 61, 63, 64, 74, 79,
83, 85, 86, 87, 89, 95, 113,
141, 149, 151, 154, 156,
157, 162, 182, 188, 190,
201, 202, 203, 204, 206,
210, 213, 258
relationship with humans
24, 42, 43, 44, 47, 52, 53,
56, 63, 78, 116, 151, 159,
160, 182
sovereignty   73, 79, 188, 189,
195, 197, 212, 217,
219, 223
GOSPEL   19, 20, 22, 61,
64, 80, 86, 126, 128, 136,
143, 145, 161, 183, 192,
204, 205, 207, 208, 209,
210, 214, 215, 225, 230,
232, 234, 238, 244, 247,
261, 264, 270
GRACE   50, 51, 80, 82,
85, 141, 143, 178, 179, 205,
206, 208, 210, 211, 238,
242, 244, 255, 262, 265
GRAHAM, BILLY   19, 20
GREAT COMMISSION   145,
146, 231, 232, 264, 265

H

HAM   54, 58, 59, 60, 61, 62, 72,
75, 77, 78
curse of   58, 59, 60, 61,
62, 63, 69, 78, 258
HATE CRIMES   19
HEBREW   31, 53, 54, 62,
73, 78, 84, 85, 86, 87, 88,
89, 90, 91, 95, 96, 97, 98,

99, 104, 107, 108, 109, 110,
113, 115, 118, 120,
126, 259
HENRY, CARL F. H.   19
HISPANICS   19, 27, 34,
187, 230
HOSPITALITY   108, 114, 127,
128, 133, 234, 237, 261
ancient   127, 129, 130,
131, 132, 134, 137
Christian   128, 129, 130,
131, 134, 135, 136, 137,
138, 139, 143
modern   128, 133,
134, 137
worship   135, 137
HUMAN DIGNITY   22, 23, 24, 28,
39, 40, 42, 43, 46, 47, 64
distorted   38, 39
HUMAN FAMILY   15, 31, 41, 42,
43, 44, 45, 46, 47, 48, 51,
53, 55, 59, 64, 68, 69,
70, 90

I

IDOLATRY   238, 239, 240,
241, 242, 243
IMMIGRANTS   96, 97, 102, 104,
105, 106, 109, 111, 112,
113, 114, 115, 133, 137
IMMIGRATION   29, 97, 103, 106,
111, 112, 113, 216,
260, 261
INDIVIDUALISM   24
INTEGRATION   15, 16, 17, 18,
29, 40, 51, 55, 67, 77, 146,
185, 208, 209, 210, 211,

212, 214, 215, 216, 245, 254, 263

Isaac 84, 86, 89, 90, 96, 120, 215

Israel 60, 61, 70, 75, 76, 77, 78, 81, 82, 83, 87, 88, 89, 90, 96, 109, 112, 113, 114, 115, 125, 127, 130, 137, 138, 140, 141, 149, 151, 152, 181, 186, 206, 214, 236, 259, 261

Israelites 31, 59, 60, 68, 69, 74, 75, 76, 77, 79, 88, 91, 92, 96, 97, 98, 99, 100, 101, 102, 104, 106, 107, 108, 109, 110, 111, 113, 114, 115, 118, 119, 120, 129, 236, 237, 259, 262

J

Jacob 76, 84, 87, 89, 90, 91, 96, 98, 100, 106, 108, 120, 140, 209

Japheth 58, 72, 75, 77, 78

Jesus 7, 64, 80, 86, 96, 102, 126, 130, 138, 143, 179, 186, 244, 259, 262, 263
and the Gentiles 146, 147, 148, 149, 150, 161, 170
and the Pharisees 148, 156, 158, 230
as healer 82, 146, 149, 150
as peace 180, 183, 186
as Savior of all people 39, 51, 63, 80, 86, 145, 146, 154, 162, 173, 176, 178, 179,

180, 182, 183, 186, 188, 190, 191, 192, 193, 205, 209, 213, 229, 232, 242, 248, 249, 250, 257, 259, 269
as Son of God 79, 85, 145, 163, 164, 180, 253
as teacher 53, 148, 149, 151, 156, 162, 165, 168, 169, 171, 245
unity in 24, 41, 69, 105, 182, 183, 184, 186, 190, 197, 198, 201, 204, 208, 210, 211, 212, 213, 215, 229, 230, 231, 236, 247, 254, 255, 263

Jews 12, 13, 28, 63, 80, 81, 82, 86, 87, 88, 95, 98, 102, 103, 104, 105, 109, 120, 138, 141, 143, 146, 151, 152, 153, 154, 167, 174, 176, 180, 181, 182, 183, 184, 185, 202, 207, 209, 213, 231, 233, 235, 236, 237, 238, 243, 245, 259

Job 111, 126, 132

Joseph 57, 88, 91, 104, 106, 108, 154, 261, 262

K

Kaleidoscope 7, 15

King Jr, Martin Luther 20, 21, 51, 175

L

Lot 132

Love 248

LUKE 136

M

MELCHIZEDEK 126
MOABITES 107, 108, 109
MOSES 47, 76, 98, 100, 101, 102, 106, 109, 113, 114, 116, 127, 259, 261, 262
MUSLIMS 17, 19, 63

N

NEIGHBOR 165, 166, 167, 168, 169, 170
NEW BABEL 79
NEW JERUSALEM 193, 194
NOAH 46, 55, 56, 58, 59, 61, 68, 71, 72, 74, 77, 78, 83, 126, 259

O

OBAMA, BARACK 17, 187
OBAMA, MICHELLE 17
OPPRESSION 222

P

PARABLES 129, 150, 151, 155, 156, 157, 158, 160
  Good Samaritan 150, 162, 165, 166, 167, 169, 170
  lost coin 155
  lost sheep 155
  prodigal son 150, 151, 155, 156, 162, 259
PAUL 47, 64, 69, 79, 82, 86, 105, 116, 118, 121, 145, 146, 151, 173, 176, 178, 179, 183, 202, 204, 205, 206, 207, 208, 209, 210, 211, 212, 213, 215, 226, 238, 243, 244, 247, 248, 249, 252, 259, 260, 261
PEOPLE 31, 44
PERSECUTION 16, 112, 174, 196, 225, 232, 233, 265
PETER 16, 22, 80, 81, 96, 101, 102, 113, 161, 181, 206, 232, 234, 235, 236, 237, 238, 261
PHARISEES 143, 148, 149, 156, 157, 230
PHILIP 16, 232, 234
PREJUDICE 31, 32, 33, 39, 64, 143, 175
PROMISE KEEPERS 15

R

RACE 30, 31, 102
  interracial marriage 16, 17, 18, 29, 30, 32, 37, 91, 117, 121, 260, 262, 263
  race relations 18, 19, 20, 23, 25, 81, 113, 151, 169, 180
  racial discrimination 17, 23, 28, 31, 32, 33, 54, 62, 69, 70, 73, 79, 81, 145, 147, 148, 149, 150, 170, 174, 175, 176, 181, 216, 223, 224, 225, 230, 253, 254, 258, 266, 267, 268
  racial groups 15, 27, 28, 47, 192, 252
  racial lines 15
  racial profiling 80
  racial reconciliation 25, 105,

146, 150, 151, 156, 157,
169, 170, 175, 176, 182,
183, 185, 186, 187, 188,
198, 201, 203, 207, 209,
210, 211, 212, 213, 214,
215, 216, 225, 232, 247,
253, 254, 257, 258

racial tensions 19, 253
segregation 25
stereotypes 37, 60, 176
RECONCILIATION 180, 202, 203,
208, 252
REPENTANCE 155, 156, 206
REVELATION 142, 173, 174,
187, 188, 189, 190, 191,
192, 193, 195, 196, 197,
216, 217, 218, 219, 220
Great Prostitute 220, 221,
223, 224

S
SABBATH 48, 49, 102, 105,
116, 127, 149, 151
SALVATION
post-salvation 176, 179
pre-salvation 176, 179
SAMARITANS 82, 151, 153,
154, 233
SECULARISM 22, 23, 28
SERVANT ETHICS 245, 247, 248,
249, 250, 251, 252
SHEM 58, 69, 71, 72, 75, 77, 78,
82, 83, 85
SIN 41, 49, 50, 51, 52, 53, 55,
56, 59, 68, 73, 77, 79, 86,
132, 155, 156, 178, 186,
257, 258, 259, 269, 270

SINNERS 160, 161
SLAVERY 21, 28, 29, 39,
43, 44, 49, 54, 55, 62, 63,
67, 69, 71, 110, 111, 114,
174, 222, 223, 251, 252

T
TABLE FELLOWSHIP 156,
160, 161, 162, 207, 230,
231, 234, 235, 236, 237,
243, 244, 252
TABLE OF NATIONS 68, 70,
71, 74, 76, 77, 78, 79, 80,
82, 87, 90, 100, 106, 118
THEOLOGICAL HISTORY 77
THEOLOGY OF GEOGRAPHY 74, 75
TIMOTHY 13, 16
TOLERATION 16, 22, 89, 186
TORAH 101, 102, 104,
151, 181
TOWER OF BABEL 71, 72, 73, 74,
79, 80, 83, 85, 87

U
UNITED NATIONS 16, 70
UNITY 15, 22, 40, 41,
42, 45, 46, 47, 64, 69, 71,
72, 73, 79, 80, 179, 184,
185, 187, 198, 208, 209,
210, 211, 212, 213, 214, 215,
216, 231, 247, 248, 249,
251, 252, 258, 260

W
WILBERFORCE, WILLIAM 21
WOODS, TIGER 18
WORSHIP 15, 48, 49, 80,

96, 100, 101, 107, 109, 116,
125, 126, 127, 129, 130,
135, 140, 141, 152, 170, 174,
185, 186, 187, 188, 189,
190, 209, 258, 260, 262
God's welcome   129, 139, 143,
145, 229

multiethnic   15, 26, 27, 29,
33, 41, 49, 126, 128, 129,
140, 141, 142, 143, 174,
182, 188, 190, 191, 192,
194, 195, 197, 198, 204,
231, 245, 252, 260,
263, 265